BREW
better
BEER

BREW
better
BEER

LEARN (AND BREAK) THE RULES FOR MAKING IPAS,
SOURS, PILSNERS, STOUTS, AND MORE

EMMA CHRISTENSEN

Photography by Katie Newburn

TEN SPEED PRESS
Berkeley

Introduction 1

CHAPTER 1: **Know Your Ingredients** 5
Malts **6**
Water **10**
Hops **10**
Yeast **14**
Other Fun Ingredients **16**

SAY HELLO TO THE BEER FAMILY! 19

CHAPTER 2: **Assemble Your Beer Kit** 23
General Equipment **24**
Brewing Equipment **27**
Fermenting Equipment **28**
Bottling Equipment **29**

WHAT TO EXPECT ON YOUR FIRST VISIT
TO A HOMEBREW STORE **34**

CHAPTER 3: **Brew Your First Beer** 37
Bird's-Eye View of How to Brew Beer **38**
How to Brew an All-Extract Beer **40**
All-Extract Amber Ale **49**
How to Brew a Partial-Extract Beer **50**
Partial-Extract Amber Ale **53**
How to Brew an All-Grain Beer **54**
All-Grain Amber Ale **62**
A Photographic Guide to Brewing Beer **60**

SHOULD YOU BREW A 1-GALLON OR
A 5-GALLON BATCH? **64**

CHAPTER 4: **Pale Ales** 69
A Very Good American Pale Ale **71**
Bitter Brit English-Style Pale Ale **72**
Bitter Monk Belgian-Style Pale Ale **73**
Pine Woods Pale Ale **74**
Amarillo SMASH Pale Ale **77**

WHAT TO WORRY ABOUT,
WHAT NOT TO WORRY ABOUT **78**

CHAPTER 5: **India Pale Ales (IPAs)** 81
A Very Good IPA **83**
Centennial Dry-Hopped Double IPA **84**
Double-Take Black IPA **86**
Two-Left-Feet American Barleywine **87**
Campari IPA **89**

HOW TO POUR AND TASTE BEER 90

CHAPTER 6: **Brown Ales** 93
A Very Good American Brown Ale **95**
Pecan Pie Brown Ale **96**
Brown Bear Seeks Honey Braggot **98**
The Great Pumpkin Ale **99**
Chai-Spiced Winter Warmer **101**

GET GEEKY WITH THE MASH 102

CHAPTER 7: **Porters and Stouts** 105
A Very Good Porter **107**
A Very Good Stout **109**
Smoky Chipotle Porter **111**
All-Day Dry Irish Stout **112**
Affogato Milk Stout **113**
Boss-Level Barrel-Aged Imperial Stout **114**

PLAY WITH YOUR HOPS 116

CHAPTER 8: **British Ales** 119
A Very Good British Mild **121**
Tea Time Extra-Special Bitter (ESB) **122**
High Seas British IPA **124**
Sugar and Spice Strong Ale **125**
Figgy Pudding British Barleywine **127**

BREWING IN WARM WEATHER,
BREWING IN COLD WEATHER 128

CHAPTER 9: Belgian Ales 131
A Very Good Abbey Ale 133
Maple Cider Dubbel 134
Tropical Island Tripel 136
Fuzzy Nose Sour Ale 137
Peach Melba Sour Lambic 139

GET FUNKY WITH SOUR BEERS 140

CHAPTER 10: Scottish and Irish Red Ales 143
A Very Good Scottish Ale 145
A Very Good Irish Red Ale 147
Day Hiker Irish Red 148
Caramel-Coconut Wee Heavy 151
Smoke & Scotch Ale 152

TEN SMALL HABITS THAT WILL MAKE
YOU A BETTER BREWER 154

CHAPTER 11: Wheat Beers 157
A Very Good Wheat Beer (Hefeweizen) 159
Sweet-Tart Berliner Weisse 160
Salty Dog Gose 161
American Summer Wheat Ale 162
Lavender-Orange Witbier 165

ADDING FRUITS, SPICES, AND OTHER
FUN THINGS TO BEER 166

CHAPTER 12: Rye Ales 171
A Very Good Rye Pale Ale 173
Dark Pumpernickel Roggenbier 174
Finnish Juniper Rye Sahti Ale 177
No Apologies Imperial Rye Ale 178
Red Eye Chicory Rye Porter 179

FIVE EASY WAYS TO LEVEL-UP
YOUR BREW GAME 180

CHAPTER 13: Session Ales 183
A Very Good Session Ale 185
Riding Lawn Mower Pale Ale 186
Watermelon Saison 188
Lemonade Stand Shandy 189
Farmers' Market Gruit 191

HOW TO DESIGN YOUR OWN
HOMEBREW 192

CHAPTER 14: Gluten-Free Beers 197
A Very Good Gluten-Free Pale Ale 199
Gluten-Free Saison 200
Gluten-Free Chocolate Porter 202
Jasmine Honey Sparkler 203
Hoppy Hard Cider 205

THE REAL DEAL WITH LAGERS 206

CHAPTER 15: Lagers 209
A Very Good Pilsner 211
Spring Blossom Maibock 212
McNally's Oktoberfest 214
Chocolate Doppelbock 215
Ode to San Francisco Steam Beer 217

COMMON PROBLEMS, EASY SOLUTIONS 218

Glossary: Homebrewer's Lingo 222

Recommended Resources 226

Acknowledgments 227

About the Author 228

Index 229

INTRODUCTION

My relationship with homebrewing did not get off to the best of starts. I was plenty eager and I had a lot of shiny new equipment, but an hour after returning from my first trip to the homebrew store, I felt completely and utterly baffled. I was also not in the kitchen; I was sitting on the couch in my living room with three different, slightly contradictory sets of brewing instructions laid out on the coffee table before me. My husband was tackling this new hobby with me, and neither of us had any idea where to begin or which instructions to follow or even how to move off the couch.

Once we formed a plan of action, the situation (unfortunately) did not improve. The liquid malt extract we'd purchased was roughly the consistency of tar and wouldn't come out of the container. Our beer juice (which some, though not all, instructions mysteriously referred to as "wort") took forever to come to a boil. And once it did, it continued to boil right over the side of the pot, extinguishing the burner's pilot light and making a gigantic mess. My husband and I argued about whether the batch was ruined or if we could just add some more water and carry on—the first of many such stressed-out and frustration-fueled fights to follow. To date, some of our most ferocious battles as a married couple have happened while brewing beer.

Sound familiar? Maybe your first brew day (and possibly many others) went along similar lines. Maybe you've never brewed before and are reading this in horror, wondering what possessed you to ever think homebrewing might be "fun to try."

Don't worry. I've got your back. What you're holding in your hands right now is the result of many years of learning and tinkering with how to brew beer at home—without the tears or cursing. My number one goal is to guide you through those first few brews—the ones where everything is brand-new, you have no idea what's going on, and the potential for frustration is high—and into a place where you feel confident stepping into the kitchen with nothing but a bag of grains and a desire for beer. The title for this book is also a promise: I want to help you brew better beer.

Why homebrew in the first place? Because it's seriously fun. Because it tickles your inner science geek. Because your first batch is instant membership into a fellowship of homebrewers that stretches back for eons. Because there is no finer feeling than flicking the cap off a bottle of beer, hearing that hiss of carbonation, and taking the first sip of a beer you brewed yourself.

NEW HOMEBREWERS, START HERE

Here's what I didn't know when I started brewing and what took me many years to realize: there is no "one right way" to brew beer. When it comes to homebrewing, there are many ways to arrive at the same end—which is to say, beer. The basic method is the same (we'll talk about that in chapter 3), but when you peer a little closer, you'll find a million different variations and tweaks that you can make at almost every step of the process.

This is both reassuring and potentially confusing. It's reassuring because any way you go about it, you'll make beer. Hooray! Don't sweat the details; pick a path and be confident that you'll have beer at the other end. But it's also confusing because, *Which path do you choose?* It's like trying to navigate through a new city—three different people give you three different sets of directions. One is the most direct but has the most traffic; another takes you on a scenic route but takes an extra hour; another is a shortcut but might get you lost. Beer brewing is like this. If you have three slightly different sets of instructions telling you how to brew beer, where do you start? How do you even get off the couch?

I might be a little biased, but I think you should start here, with this book. The methods I describe in the first few chapters give you a solid foundation for brewing your own beer. They give you the tools and the know-how to navigate this wily world and to make better decisions when you encounter new ideas and opinions later on. I promise you this: stick with me and you *will* make beer!

And once you have a handle on how home-brewing works, it's just a small jump into brewing all sorts of different beers. All the recipes in this book follow the same master method described in chapter 3. **Keep an eye on the boldfaced text within each recipe—this indicates a variable that changes from brew to brew.** Chapters 4 through 7 cover some basic styles: pale ales, IPAs, brown ales, porters, and stouts. In chapters 8 through 10, we get into styles that are specific to different parts of the world: British ales, Belgian abbey ales, Scottish ales, and Irish ales. Next up, we play with

grains in chapters 11 and 12: wheat beers and rye ales. Chapters 13 and 14 cover session ales, which are low alcohol by design, and gluten-free beers, for all our gluten-free beer-loving friends. Last but not least, in chapter 15 we take a swing at brewing lagers—yes, lagers! (Looking for your favorite German beer? You'll probably find it here or in chapter 11.)

One last note: You might be under the impression that you need a man-cave or a huge garage or some other such area in order to brew beer at home. Nope. If my experience for the past six years is anything to go by, an 800-square-foot apartment works just fine—and I know people who brew fantastic beer in even smaller spaces. You can tailor your homebrew habit to match your space, your budget, your free time, and any other constraints you may have. I'll show you how.

VETERAN HOMEBREWERS, NOW HEAR THIS!

You've been brewing beer for a while and you've already got a system that works for you—I respect that. Here's what I want for you: I want to help you brew the beer of your dreams. Your beer is already good; let's make it even better.

I want to give you the keys to the brewery. Figuratively speaking, of course. I want to show you exactly when and where and how you can tweak a recipe to make it your own. You'll find a lot of great information in the essays between each chapter—like what happens when you change the mash temperature, how to turn any brew into a sour beer, and habits that will make you a better homebrewer. You can also see these ideas put into practice as we move through the recipes in each chapter, going from the basic "Very Good" beers to the variations that follow.

I give you full permission to take these methods and use them however you see fit. If you can imagine it, you can brew it. Be adventurous. Brew the beer you want to drink.

IS HOMEBREWING LEGAL?

Yes, homebrewing beer is totally, completely legal. In the United States, you are limited to 100 gallons of homebrew per adult or 200 gallons per household, which should really be quite enough to keep anyone happy, don't you think? Drink your homebrew yourself, share it with friends, or even trade it with other homebrewers—it's yours to do with as you will.

The only thing that's illegal is selling your homebrew without a license. If you want to start brewing beer to sell, dig into the rules and regulations for the sale of alcoholic beverages in your area.

IS HOMEBREWING SAFE?

Beer has been brewed and consumed for centuries as a way of making sure water is safe to drink. Homebrew might make you loopy or tipsy or sleepy, but it won't do you serious harm when consumed responsibly. Even if you make a few mistakes here and there, anything that might be truly harmful will be eliminated though the brewing process itself, and by the acidity and alcohol in the finished beer.

This said, use your best judgment. Beers can still pick up infections from poor sanitation or errant bacteria, and while these aren't likely to harm you, they are still mighty unpleasant to drink. If anything looks, smells, or tastes especially nasty, best to play it safe and start over with a new batch. Check out "Common Problems, Easy Solutions," page 218, to troubleshoot what might have gone wrong. As with all alcoholic beverages, homebrew should be consumed responsibly and in moderation.

GO FORTH AND BREW

Your first batch of beer might not be perfect. You might spill some on the floor or forget to add the yeast. You might wonder if something is right or if you made a horrible, beer-destroying mistake. You might wish your beer had turned out just a little better. Yes, all of this is possible. Or, despite some spills and scary moments, you might end up with something truly fabulous. This is the best. The. Best. Beers like these keep us homebrewers coming back for more, die-hard devotees of grains and hops and yeast to the end.

Brewing isn't a "nail it on the first time" kind of endeavor, but rather a "get more awesome as you do it" affair. Be patient with yourself. Read through the recipe before you begin. Crack open a beer and enjoy it while you brew. Whatever you do, keep brewing. You'll be brewing great beer faster than you think.

Malts, water, hops, and yeast: These four ingredients are all you need to brew a good batch of beer. That's it. Various combinations of these ingredients make any beer you could ever want to brew, from a pale gold hefeweizen to a pitch-black stout.

KNOW YOUR INGREDIENTS

[chapter 1]

MALTS

It all starts with malted grains. Packed within each tiny grain are the starches and enzymes that we need to make beer. It's our job as brewers to transform those starches into easy-to-eat sugars, feed them to the yeast, and down the line a bit, make some beer.

But let's back up a second. Where do malted grains come from in the first place? The short answer would be the homebrew store. (Wakka wakka!) The longer answer would be . . . well, a bit more complicated. Grains straight from the field cannot be made into beer—first they have to be malted. This involves soaking the grains until they start to sprout, a process that frees up the starches in the grains and develops their potential to become beer. The maltmaker locks in that potential by toasting the half-sprouted grains in a kiln to stop the germination process.

Once we have these freshly malted grains, we can do a few things. As they are, the grains are bursting with sugar potential but don't have a lot of flavor. If we roast them for a little while, their starches start to break down (losing their sugar potential), but they pick up lots of interesting flavors that we can add to our beer. Here's a quick run-down of the general types of malts; the Common Malts and Grains chart on opposite page has descriptions of specific malts.

- **Base malts:** Unroasted or very lightly toasted malts with lots of sugar potential but little flavor. In a recipe, the base malts (called "base" because they form the base of your beer) make up the majority of the grains. Examples are pale malts, 2-row malts, wheat malts, and pilsner malts.

- **Specialty malts:** Malts that have been roasted to varying degrees and contain less sugar potential but lots of flavor. They also give our beers darker colors, ranging from light amber to black. They are called "specialty" because they give the beer special flavors and colors. You don't need a lot of specialty malts to get the job done. They usually form a smaller proportion of the grains in a recipe. Examples are crystal malts, brown malts, chocolate malts, and black patent malts.

- **Adjunct grains:** Any unmalted grains. Some adjuncts contribute sugars, but they are also used to do things like give the beer creaminess, add a particular color, or enhance the foam. Examples are unmalted barley, corn, rice, oats, and sorghum.

When it comes to actually brewing a batch of beer, we typically use one base malt or a combination of base malts to make up the majority of the beer recipe and then a smaller percentage of specialty malts and adjuncts. This ensures that the yeast has plenty of sugars to eat and that we get decent alcohol content in our beer (from the base malts), but that we also get good flavors, aromas, and color (from the specialty grains and adjuncts).

The malting and roasting of the grains is usually done by professional maltsters before you or I enter the picture. All we homebrewers need to do is pick out the malts we need for our beer at a homebrewing store and have them packaged up to take home. If you're in the mood for a project, it can be fun to either sprout and malt your own grains or buy one of the base malts and roast them at home to make your personal "house specialty" grain.

Barley is the Number One Grain that we use in brewing. This is due to the simple fact that barley contains the most sugar potential, more than any other grain. Barley also has a natural hull that makes it easy to work with. Other kinds of grain do come into the picture, like malted wheat and malted rye, but barley is king.

As homebrewers, we can use malts in two different forms: whole grain malts and malt extracts. Let's take a look at both.

Whole Grain Malts

Whole grain malts are exactly what we've been talking about so far: grains like barley and wheat that are malted to develop their sugar potential and then kilned to preserve that potential. They look like little seeds—which they are!—and smell toasted and sweet. Crunch a few grains between your teeth and you'll get a sense of what they will add to your beer. Smelling and chewing different grains is a great way to familiarize yourself with the differences among them.

COMMON MALTS AND GRAINS

MALT	TYPE	COLOR	FLAVOR AND AROMA
Pilsner Malt	Base Malt	Very lightly toasted	Mild sweetness
2-Row Malt	Base Malt	Very lightly toasted	Mild sweetness
Pale Ale Malt	Base Malt	Lightly toasted	Mild sweetness
Maris Otter	Base Malt	Lightly toasted	Slightly sweeter and roastier than Pale Ale malts
Rye Malt	Base Malt/Specialty Malt	Lightly toasted	Crisp and slightly spicy flavor; can make up to 50% of the malt bill
Wheat Malt	Base Malt/Specialty Malt	Lightly toasted	Soft and smooth flavor; can make up to 75% of malt bill
Vienna Malt	Base Malt/ Specialty Malt	Mid-light roasted	Smooth caramel flavor; can make up to 50% of grain bill
Cara-Vienna Malt	Specialty Malt	Medium-roasted	One step up from Vienna malts
Munich Malt	Base Malt/Specialty Malt	Mid-light roasted	Freshly-toasted bread; can make up to 50% of grain bill
Cara-Munich Malt	Specialty Malt	Medium-roasted malt	One step up from Munich malt
Crystal/Caramel 20° to 120°	Specialty Malt	Mid-light roasted to very dark roasted	As the degree of roasting darkens, the flavor goes from quite lightly sweet to nutty and caramelized.
Smoked Malt	Specialty Malt	Light to medium roasted	Smoky!
Aromatic Malt	Specialty Malt	Medium toasted	Adds malty aroma and flavor
Honey Malt	Specialty Malt	Medium toasted	Warm honeylike flavors and aromas
Biscuit Malt	Specialty Malt	Medium toasted	Baked bread flavors and aromas
Special B Malt	Specialty Malt	Dark roasted	Dark caramel along with lots of dried fruit flavors (raisins, figs, dates)
Brown Malt	Specialty Malt	Dark roasted	Very dark nutty, roasted flavors, also gives beers a fair amount of bitterness
Chocolate Malt	Specialty Malt	Dark roasted	Imparts a bittersweet chocolate (rather than milk chocolate) flavor
Carafa Malt	Specialty Malt	Very dark roasted	Mellow roasted flavor with less bitterness and tannins than other dark malts
Black Patent Malt	Specialty Malt	Extremely dark roasted	Sharply bitter flavor, very assertive; use in moderation
Roasted Barley	Specialty Malt	Extremely dark roasted	Extremely bitter and dry; use in moderation
Rice Hulls	Adjunct	N/A	Adds no flavor or character to the beer; lightens the mash and makes it easier to sparge (see Glossary, page 222)
Flaked Corn	Adjunct	N/A	Lightens the body of beer; adds a grainy flavor
Flaked Rice	Adjunct	N/A	Lightens the body of beer; adds crispness and some very light fruit notes
Flaked Wheat	Adjunct	N/A	Helps foam retention and adds body
Flaked Barley	Adjunct	N/A	Helps foam retention and adds creaminess
Flaked Oats	Adjunct	N/A	Adds a rich body and creaminess, too much hurts foam retention (the old-fashioned rolled oats in your cupboard are fine for this ingredient!)

To transform the complex starches inside the grains into simple, easy-to-eat sugars for the yeast, we need to soak the grains in warm water—a process called "mashing." During the mash, the carbohydrates inside the grains dissolve into the water, and two enzymes (called alpha-amylase and beta-amylase) go to work chomping them into smaller, simpler sugars. At the end of the mash, the grains get discarded or composted; the sugary liquid left behind (called "wort") is what will become beer.

Always mill your grains before using them to brew beer. This cracks the grains open and makes it easy to extract the starches inside; without milling, they stay trapped. Most brewing stores will mill your grains for you on their professional equipment, but if you have a grain mill, you can mill your own grains at home. Don't grind your grains so finely that they become flour—you'll get fantastic sugar extraction, but separating the sugary water from the mass of sticky, gummy flour will give you a migraine. Simply cracking the grains to expose their insides does the job just fine.

Malt Extract

Malt extract is our second option for making beer. In this case, someone else has done all the work for us of mashing the grains and transforming the starches into simple sugars—we don't have to deal with the actual grains at all. You can think of malt extract as concentrated, unfermented beer juice. It has all the sugars, nutrients, and flavor compounds we need for a tasty batch of beer, and all we have to do is mix it with water.

Extract comes in two forms: liquid malt extract (LME) and dried malt extract (DME). There are no real advantages or disadvantages to using either, so use whichever you can find. You can even use both liquid and dried extracts in the same recipe! To convert between liquid and dry malt extracts, use the formula in "Converting Between Malted Grains and Malt Extract," at right.

Converting Between Malted Grains and Malt Extract

There are many instances when you may find the need to convert between grains and extract in a recipe. Most likely, you've found an all-grain recipe that you want to try, but you'd rather stick to doing an extract or partial-extract brew. You might also find an extract recipe that you'd like to try with grains.

Here are the ratios for converting between grains and extracts:

1 pound malted grain
=
.75 pounds liquid malt extract (LME)
=
.60 pounds dried malt extract (DME)

To convert an all-grain recipe to malt extract, use these formulas:

DME = Grains x .6
LME = Grains x .75

To convert a recipe with extract to all-grain, use these formulas:

Grains = DME x 1.67
Grains = LME x 1.33

And to convert between dried and liquid extract, use these equations:

DME = LME x .8
LME = DME x 1.25

NOTE: ALL EQUATIONS ARE CALCULATED IN OUNCES AND POUNDS.

Extracts are usually identified by their color—extra-light or pilsner, light, amber, or dark—but you can also find extract in specific styles, like Munich, rye, or wheat. By combining different colors and styles of extracts, you can customize recipes to your liking.

Extract is a boon for new brewers because it takes some of the guesswork out of the process: you already have your wort, so all you really have to do is add yeast. This super-simple brew is called an all-extract beer. To make things one step more exciting, you can use extract for your beer's base malts (the source for the sugar, remember) but then add some specialty whole grains to give your beer more interesting flavors and aromas—this is called a partial-mash (or partial-extract) beer. To convert grains into extract (or vice versa), use the formulas in "Converting Between Malted Grains and Malt Extract," page 9.

Even after you get adventurous and tackle all-grain brewing (i.e., brewing a beer using only whole grains), extract is still a useful ingredient. If you want to brew a big batch of beer but don't have a big enough brew pot, you can use extract to replace some or all of your base malts and reduce the total amount of grain. You can also add malt extract to any beer to increase its sugars (and thus its final alcohol content) without changing the base recipe.

Buy extract in bulk and measure what you need by weight. Liquid extract can be very sticky; to make it easier to use, place the cans or pouches of extract in hot water to help loosen it up before you pour it. Keep the remaining extract tightly sealed and at room temperature; it keeps for several months and can be used for other brews. *Do not buy prehopped malt extract.* This is extract that already has hops added. Besides throwing off a recipe, this kind of extract is often of subpar quality.

WATER

Water is both the most important and the least important part of the beer recipe. We can't make beer without water, after all. But as long as the water from your tap is safe to drink and tastes good to you, it's totally fine to use for homebrewing. There's no need to filter it, purify it, or add anything to it. In fact, if you live in a city and are connected to the city's water supply, water from the tap is safe enough that you can add it directly to beer wort without much fear of bacterial contamination.

This said, it's certainly possible to get geeky with your brewing water. By adding certain minerals and other additives, you can imitate the exact water from famous brewing areas and therefore come closer to imitating their beer—like the very soft water used to brew German pilsners or the minerals in the water around Burton-on-Trent used in making English-style pale ales.

If you find that the specific gravity readings or final ABV (see Glossary, page 222) of your homebrews is consistently lower than you expect, the pH of your water might be to blame. If your water is slightly above neutral, higher than 7 on the pH scale, it becomes more difficult for enzymes to convert starches into fermentable sugars. You can test your water with pH strips and find additives at homebrew stores that will help improve your water and therefore your beer.

HOPS

Hops are a relative newcomer to the beer brewing party. While beer has been brewed with malts, water, and yeast for centuries, it was usually flavored with herbs and spices. When hops came on the scene in the early 1800s, brewers recognized immediately that they had stumbled on a good thing: a seemingly magical ingredient that could tame the cloying sweetness of the malts, help filter out impurities, and also preserve the beer so it would stay fresher longer. Plus it made beer taste amazing, elevating it from herbal remedy and pedestrian brew into something much more refined and elegant.

Hops look a lot like miniature pinecones, but they are in fact the flowers of the hop vine. Hidden within their many paper-thin layers, hops hold two things that are of particular interest to brewers: resins and oils.

Hop resins are responsible for making beer bitter. If you've ever sipped an IPA and felt your tongue curl at the walloping bitterness, you can thank (or blame) the resins from the hops. Resins are measured in terms of alpha acids; hops with a high alpha acid content contribute much more bitterness to a beer than hops with a lower alpha acid. When substituting hops during brewing or when creating your own recipes, it's a good habit to check the alpha acid of the hops you're using so you can adjust your recipe as needed. The alpha acid is always printed on the outside of the package; to calculate substitutions, use the equation at the end of the Common Hops chart on page 12.

Hop oils, on the other hand, have nothing to do with bitterness and everything to do with flavor and aroma. Depending on the variety, you might taste apricot, grapefruit, damp forest floor, tobacco, or even tropical fruits like pineapples and guava. You might also smell aromas wafting from your glass that range from wildflowers to winter baking spices. New hop varieties are being developed all the time, and perusing the hop selection at a homebrew store is becoming a bit like walking into Willy Wonka's Chocolate Factory.

When it comes to getting the resins and oils into our beers, the hop flower presents us with a bit of a conundrum. To properly dissolve (or, technically, "isomerize") the hop resins into beer wort, the wort needs to be kept at a rapid boil for at least an hour. However, this same long boil completely destroys the more delicate hop oils. The solution is simple: add hops at multiple points throughout the boil. In a typical brew, a small amount of hops is added at the beginning of the boil for bittering purposes, followed by another dose of hops midway through for flavor, and a final addition at the end for aroma. Hops added at other points in the brewing process contribute other characteristics; read more about this in "Play with Your Hops" on page 116.

You can use just one variety of hop to make your beer (as in our Amarillo SMASH Pale Ale on page 77), but more often, you'll use two or three different kinds to give your beer a layered, balanced flavor. Some hops are great at bittering (called "bittering" hops), some are great at flavoring and adding aroma (called "aroma" hops), and some are pretty darn good at doing both (called "dual" or "hybrid" hops). Personally, I tend to stick to one or two kinds of hop in a beer; I find that adding more starts to muddy the flavors and aromas. But that's just me! Many craft breweries routinely use three, four, five, or even more varieties of hop in one batch of beer. As you brew more batches

and learn your own style, you'll find your hoppy happy place. Check out the Common Hops chart on page 12 to get started.

While we've been talking about whole hop flowers, as homebrewers we're more likely to find hops in the form of pellets. Fresh hop flowers are incredibly delicate and prone to spoilage, so the majority of every hop harvest is quickly dried and compressed into more shelf-stable pellets. They look like rabbit food and dissolve into a green sludge in your beer. It may not look appealing or feel very romantic to add pellets to your beer, but they will flavor your beer just as well as the flowers.

By the way, you'll quickly start collecting a stash of half-used packets of hops once you start brewing. They stay quite fresh and usable for about six months but gradually lose their awesome hopping power. Using them past their prime will make your beer taste stale and vegetal. To avoid this predicament, just put them in a sealed bag, write the date you opened the hops on the outside of the package, squeeze out as much air as possible, and stash them in the freezer. Discard any packages that are more than six months old.

If you're interested in experimenting with fresh (or "wet") hop flowers, your best bet is to either grow your own or keep an eye out for them at homebrew stores in the late fall and winter after the hop harvest has come in. Since pellets are so compressed, you usually need to use a larger amount of flowers to pellets in your recipe.

Noble Hops

History lesson! German brewers were among the first to catch on to the potential of hops and start using them to flavor their famous pilsners and bocks. These hop varieties were, and still are, referred to as the "noble" hops: Saaz, Tettnanger, Spalt, and Hallertau. These hops are usually lower in alpha acid and are typified by mild bitterness with spicy flavors and aromas.

COMMON HOPS

HOP	ALPHA ACID %	TYPICAL USE	DESCRIPTION
Ahtanum	5%–8%	Flavor and aroma	Ruby red grapefruit with floral aromas
Amarillo	7%–10%	Flavor and aroma	Freshly squeezed orange juice
Apollo	16%–19%	Bittering	Orange zest and pith; a bit spicy
Bravo	14%–17%	Bittering	Earthy and spicy with a fruity aroma
Calypso	12%–16%	Dual use	Fruity with hints of pear and apple
Cascade	4%–7%	Dual use	Grapefruit, citrus pith, juicy
Centennial	9%–12%	Dual use	Huge citrus flavor
Challenger	6%–9%	Dual use	Spicy, clean bitterness
Chinook	10%–12%	Dual use	Herbal, earthy, pine woods
Citra	11%–13%	Flavor and aroma	Crazy tropical fruit flavors, mostly pineapple and mango
Cluster	5%–8%	Dual use	Gentle bitterness with a spicy and floral aroma
Crystal	3%–6%	Flavor and aroma	Spicy like cinnamon
Delta	4%–7%	Flavor and aroma	Earthy and herbal with a splash of citrus
Fuggles	4%–6%	Dual use	Gentle bitterness, earthy flavor
Galaxy	12%–14%	Flavor and aroma	Tropical fruits, especially passion fruit and citrus
Hallertauer	3%–5%	Flavor and aroma	Floral perfume and earthy with a touch of spice
Hersbrucker	2%–5%	Flavor and aroma	Grassy and haylike
Kent Goldings or East Kent Goldings	5%–8%	Dual use	Smooth, mellow bitterness; almost sweet
Liberty	3%–5%	Flavor and aroma	Mild, earthy, and herbal
Magnum	11%–14%	Bittering	Warm and spicy, like nutmeg
Mosaic	10%–13%	Flavor and aroma	Tropical fruit flavors, plus citrus
Mt. Hood	4%–7%	Flavor and aroma	Earthy and slightly spicy
Northern Brewer	8%–10%	Dual use	Earthy and woodsy, minty notes
Nugget	9%–12%	Bittering	Bitter floral perfume
Palisade	5%–9%	Flavor and aroma	Grassy and floral, like fruit blossoms
Perle	7%–9%	Dual use	Spicy and floral
Saaz	2%–4%	Flavor and aroma	Spicy like cinnamon, soft bitterness
Santium	5%–7%	Flavor and aroma	Floral and spicy
Simcoe	11%–14%	Dual use	Pine and wood
Sorachi Ace	10%–16%	Flavor and aroma	Lemon candy, white pepper
Spalt	2%–5%	Flavor and aroma	Very delicate, slightly spicy
Sterling	6%–9%	Dual use	Softly spicy, herbal aroma
Styrian Goldings	3%–5%	Dual use	Spicy and delicate, smooth bitterness
Tettnanger	3%–5%	Flavor and aroma	Floral and herbal; a bit spicy
Warrior	14%–16%	Dual use	Clean, robust bitterness
Willamette	4%–6%	Flavor and aroma	Earthy and woodsy

When substituting hops, use this equation to keep bitterness consistent:
GRAMS NEW HOP = AA% ORIGINAL HOP (GRAMS ORIGINAL HOP) / AA% NEW HOP

pellet hops

white leaf hops

milled malts

whole malts

YEAST

Really, it all comes down to yeast. If the yeast isn't happy, you won't have beer. Luckily, yeast is fairly easy to please.

Yeast eats the sugar in your beer wort, producing alcohol and carbon dioxide as a by-product. Yeast eats the easily fermentable sugar within a few days—this is why you see a lot of frothing and activity in the beer the week after brewing. Once those sugars are gone, the yeast calms down and goes on to the more difficult task of breaking down the complex sugars left in the brew. Think of it like eating candy and then eating a turkey dinner. Fast, then slow. As brewers, we aim for a lot of fermentable "candy" sugars in our beer, but having some of the other kind is okay, too.

There are two kinds of yeast used for brewing beer: ale yeast and lager yeast, which are used to make (no surprise here) ales and lager beers. Ale yeast prefers living on the top of the beer while lager yeast likes hiding out on the bottom, but of more importance to us is the temperature at which each kind of yeast is most comfortable.

Ale yeast is happiest in a relatively warm environment—65°F is ideal, but it's usually just fine within 65°F to 75°F. Some yeast strains, particularly Belgian strains, are also happy up into the 80s; if your house gets hot during the summer, that's a great time to brew a saison or an abbey ale! Ale yeasts tend to give beers fuller flavors and produce fruity esters and spicy phenols (chemical compounds that add flavor), particularly at temperatures above 75°F.

Lagers, on the other hand, prefer cooler environments—50°F for the first few days of active fermentation and then around 40°F for the weeks of conditioning (aka lagering) that follow. The cool fermentation temperatures make a very crisp and clean-tasting beer with very little of the fruity flavors found in ale beers. To make a really good lager, you need a temperature-controlled fridge; read more about this in "The Real Deal with Lagers" on page 206.

Any variety of yeast can be used to ferment any kind of beer, but many yeast strains have been developed to go with specific styles of beer. For instance, hefeweizen yeast produces the banana and clove flavors desired in a good hefeweizen, while a Belgian ale yeast produces the fruity flavors beloved in saisons and abbey ales. When you're starting off, just use the type of yeast specified in the recipe or that matches the style you're brewing. When you start feeling adventurous, you can mix and match yeasts and styles to bring out desired flavors and characters in your finished beer. The Common Yeasts chart on the opposite page shows the characteristics for the most common kinds of yeast used for homebrewing.

You can find beer yeast in either dried or liquid form. Packages of dry yeast can be stored nearly indefinitely, are easy to use (just sprinkle the yeast over the top of the wort), and are very reliable when it comes to fermenting beer. The downside is the lack of variety of dry yeasts, though I suspect we'll see more varieties being added in the years to come as homebrewing becomes increasingly popular.

Liquid yeast comes in a huge variety of yeast strains but has a refrigerated shelf life of about 6 months. In the past, liquid yeast has been a little less reliable for fermenting beer, but with better production and storage technology, I haven't had problems with liquid yeast in years. Be aware that some varieties of liquid yeast, specifically the Wyeast brand, need to be activated several hours before being used; other varieties merely need to be warmed. Check the instructions on the package before your brew day so you are familiar with any additional requirements.

One package of either dry or liquid yeast is typically sufficient to ferment 5 gallons of beer. For 1-gallon batches, I use half a package of yeast—this is slightly more yeast than is strictly necessary, but it makes measuring easier and the extra fermentation insurance doesn't hurt! Tightly wrap any leftover dry yeast in plastic and store in the freezer for up to 6 months. Transfer any leftover liquid yeast to a sanitized jam jar or other small container and store in the fridge up to the expiration date on the packaging. With both

COMMON YEASTS

YEAST	DESCRIPTION*	BEST FOR
California Ale and American Ale	Clean fermentation with low esters; well balanced; usually accentuates hop flavor	American-style ales, including pale ales, IPAs, rye ales, and ambers
Saison Ale	Finishes crisp with mild fruity flavors; some earthy and spicy notes	Belgian-style saisons, Belgian pale ales
Abbey Ale	Produces distinctly fruity beers	Belgian-style ales, including pale ales, saisons, dubbels, tripels, and quadrupels
Belgian Strong Ale	Very balanced, produces beers with fruity, spicy flavors	High ABV Belgian-style ales, including dubbels, tripels, and quadrupels
Belgian Wit Ale	Finishes crisp with mild spicy, earthy, phenolic flavors	Belgian-style wit beers, pale ales, and saisons
English Ale and British Ale	Finishes with clean malty flavors; often leaves some residual sweetness; some mild fruit flavors	English-style ales, including pale ales, ESBs, IPAs, milds, browns, porters, and stouts.
Edinburgh Ale and Scottish Ale	Produces malty, complex ales; sometimes with a woodsy, oaky character	Scottish ales, Scotch ales, and wee heavies
Irish Ale	Makes a crisp, full-bodied beer; some diacetyl and fruity flavors	Irish reds and Irish stouts
Hefeweizen Ale	Finishes crisp with flavors of banana and clove; also makes beers cloudy	German-style wheat beers
German Lager	Finishes clean and malty	German lagers, including pilsners and Oktoberfests
German Bock Lager	Produces balanced beers with crisp, malty flavors	High ABV lagers, including bocks, doppelbocks, Oktoberfests, and maibocks
San Francisco Lager and California Lager	Can handle slightly warmer fermentation temperatures than other lagers; produces a fairly crisp and malty beer	California common and steam beers, American lagers
Brettanomyces (bruxellensis and lambicus)	Very slow fermenting; produces funky, barnyard flavors in beer	Sour ales, gueuze, lambics
Lactobacillus	Lactic acid–producing bacteria; gives beer tart, sour flavors	Sour ales, gueuze, lambics, Berliner weisse, gose

These are general descriptions of yeast varieties; for in-depth descriptions of specific yeast strains, refer to the manufacturer.

1-gallon and 5-gallon batches, there are certain brews where the yeast needs to be extra active before using it; in these cases, you need to make a yeast starter. See "How to Make a Yeast Starter," page 16, for more details on this.

I've brewed with both dry and liquid yeast, and ultimately, I prefer liquid. I find that the flavors of beers brewed with liquid yeast seem more nuanced and refined, plus I like the wide variety of strains available. I suggest two different varieties of yeast in the recipes in this book, White Labs and Wyeast; they are both good, so use whichever you can find. If neither is available, substitute the closest strain of yeast you can find.

How to Make a Yeast Starter

The yeast available to homebrewers these days is of extremely good quality and can normally be pitched directly into your wort. Occasionally, however, we need to give the yeast some help. This is especially true for high-alcohol beers and lagers. The increased sugar levels in the former and cold fermentation temperatures in the latter make for some rough conditions. To make sure the yeast is strong and ready to get down to business, we need to make a yeast starter.

In the recipes in this book, I indicate if a starter is needed. However, you can always make a starter if you'd like a little extra fermentation insurance or if you're working with yeast near its expiration date.

Get the starter going 12 to 18 hours before you plan to brew. If you're using liquid yeast, remove it from the refrigerator, and if necessary, activate according to package instructions. Place the package on the coun-ter to warm.

Bring 1 cup of water to a boil for a 1-gallon batch (or 4 cups for a 5-gallon batch). Stir in 2 heaping tablespoons (or ½ cup for a 5-gallon batch) of light dried malt extract until dissolved. Let cool to room temperature.

Sanitize a 1-quart (or 2-quart for a 5-gallon batch) glass canning jar or similar-sized container. Combine the cooled liquid with ½ package of yeast for a 1-gallon batch and the whole package for a 5-gallon batch in the jar. Whisk thoroughly with a sanitized whisk to aerate. Cover the jar with foil or plastic wrap secured with a rubber band and leave on the counter and out of direct sunlight for 12 to 18 hours. You may see some bubbles, indicating active yeast fermentation, but it's fine if you don't see much activity. You'll also see a layer of sediment on the bottom. Shake the jar occasionally to aerate.

When it's time to pitch the yeast (see Glossary, page 222), shake or whisk the starter again, then pour it into your cooled wort. Proceed with fermentation as usual.

OTHER FUN INGREDIENTS

While all you really need to brew beer is malts, water, hops, and yeast, there are a few other ingredients that we use on a regular basis.

Irish Moss

Irish moss is actually a seaweed, not a moss at all. Its role is to help clarify your beer. It smells awful but won't affect the flavor or aroma of your beer. It helps suspended proteins clump together and fall to the bottom of your beer so that the finished product isn't hazy. Use ⅛ teaspoon for 1-gallon batches and 1 teaspoon for 5-gallon batches, and add the Irish moss in the last 20 minutes of the boil.

Sugar

Besides the sugar from malted grains, we can also add other sugars to our brews. Granulated sugar, brown sugar, turbinado sugar, rice syrup, molasses, corn syrup, corn sugar—any sugar that you use in baking can be used to add flavors and increase the alcohol in your beer. These sugars are also highly fermentable; using a lot lightens the body of your beer and makes it very dry (i.e., unsweet). Some complex sugars that aren't fermentable by yeast, like maltodextrin and lactose, add body and mouthfeel to beers (and some sweetness) without changing the alcohol content.

Fruit, Spices, Herbs, and Other Flavorings

Here's where the fun starts! Just about anything, from fresh summer strawberries to shredded coconut, can be added to beer to change its flavor. In general, start with adding a little bit of your extra ingredient, taste the beer after a few days using a wine thief (see page 29), and add more if needed. You can always add more, but you can't take it out once it's there. Read more about when, why, and how to add these extra ingredients on page 166.

SAY HELLO TO THE BEER FAMILY!

As is polite at the beginning of any great relationship, you need to get to know the family. There are literally hundreds of specific beer styles, all fabulous in their own way, but for our "getting to know you" purposes, let's just focus on the main styles we cover in this book.

First things first, all beer is . . . beer. The term "beer" refers to any fermented malt beverage, no matter what color it is, what hops are added, what yeast is used, or any of the other details that distinguish specific beer styles. Beer is king and all styles great and small fall beneath its mighty rule.

Beer is then divided into two major beer families: ales and lagers. In the ale family are beers like English ales, Scottish and Irish ales, American ales, Belgian ales, and German ales, each of which has their own subset of styles. In the lager family, there are beers like pilsners, oktoberfests and marzens, bocks, and Califorina common beers, which also have their own subsets. To get a better understanding of the relationship between all these beers, take a look at the illustration on pages 20–21.

Some beer styles also belong to their own special clubs that are separate from the families. There's the wheat beer club, which includes hefeweizens, witbiers, American wheat beers, and a few others. These beers are usually made with up to 50% wheat and have a unique crispness and creamy quality that ties them together. There's also the session ale club, which all clock in under 5% ABV (see Glossary, page 222). Some members of the session ale club are grandfathered in, like English milds and dry stouts, which are low ABV by style. The rye ale club includes German roggenbiers and Finnish sahti ales, along with some new rye ales brewed in the United States. These are all brewed with some percentage of rye malts, making them a bit rough around the edges and spicy.

As homebrewers, it's good to have an awareness of how these different styles relate to each other, because the styles in each family or club tend to share similar characteristics. Many styles also emerged linearly, the way porters evolved into stouts and American IPAs evolved into double and imperial IPAs. Once you know these characteristics and relationships, it's easier to play with them, either by leaning into the style or pulling away from it.

Brewing "true to style" is a term that gets bandied about quite a bit in the homebrewing world. I say how "true to style" you want to be depends on you as a homebrewer. Personally, I think it's useful to know and brew the true styles at least once so you have some basis for spinning off later—the way you might learn a basic recipe for lasagna, but then make it your own by using chorizo instead of hamburger or adding mushrooms along with the tomatoes. In this book, I've kept the "Very Good" beers that start each chapter fairly close to style, but then show you ways to spin off from the base style in the recipes that follow.

In short: Know the styles, but don't be confined by them. Learn to brew them, then make them yours.

ALES

Ales are top-fermenting beers, meaning the yeast used to make them likes to party at the top of the fermenting beer. These yeasts also favor warmer climes, so ales are typically brewed at an average room temperature of 65°F to 75°F—though some ale yeasts can tolerate even warmer temperatures. The combination of ale yeast and warmer fermentation temperatures produces beers that have more sweet and fruity flavors.

ENGLISH ALES

The ales from this clan are typically sweet and malty with very little bitterness. They can also range in color from very pale (pale ales) to opaque black (Russian Imperial Stout). With a few exceptions, English ales also tend to be lower alcohol—the majority are under 5%.

- Pale Ales
- Brown Ales
- Porter
- Stout
- English IPA
- English Strong Ale
- English Barleywine

SCOTTISH AND IRISH ALES

Reddish-hued and very rich, the beers that originate from Scotland and Ireland tend to have a lot of caramelized candy flavors. Irish reds are usually a touch more dry. Both styles can sometimes have smoky flavors. Scottish ales and Irish reds are low alcohol, but things get frisky once you get to the Scotch ales—they're called "wee heavies" for a reason!

- Scottish Ale
- Scotch Ale/Wee Heavy
- Irish Red

AMERICAN ALES

The original American brewers were immigrants who brewed the beers from their native countries, but as younger generations took over, the Old World styles gradually began to shift and evolve into entirely new, and wholly American, kinds of beer. Generally speaking, today's American ales tend to be much more highly hopped than the beers of any other country and are also usually higher in alcohol. In terms of color, they run the gamut from the palest of pales to black.

- Pale Ale
- Amber Ale
- Brown Ale
- American Wheat Beer
- American IPA
- Black IPA
- Double or Imperial IPA
- American Barleywine

BELGIAN ALES

Belgian ales are a unique bunch of brews. They are often fermented at slightly warmer temperatures than the rest of the ale family, so they're typified by a lot of fruity flavors. These flavors range from fresh peaches and citrus to dried figs and berries, with a range of light to dark colors to match. The Belgian clan also includes sour beers fermented with wild yeast, which gives unpredictable funky and tart flavors.

- Abbey Ale
- Belgian Pale Ale
- Dubbel
- Trippel
- Quadrupel
- Gueuze
- Lambics
- Saison
- Witbier

GERMAN ALES

Just because the Germans are famous for their pilsners doesn't mean they don't brew some great ales as well! These ales are often brewed with an extra grain component, like wheat or rye, which give a creamy texture and a frothy head of foam.

- Hefeweizen
- Berliner Weisse
- Gose
- Roggenbier
- Kolsh

LAGERS

Lagers are bottom-fermenting beers. They also prefer cooler temperatures than ale yeasts—typically 50°F or cooler. This slows down fermentation quite a bit, but the upside is a super-crisp, clean-tasting beer with delicate flavors. Most lagers originated in or around Germany.

PILSNER

Pilsners, brewed with pilsner malts, are typically very pale with a soft malt profile and floral or spicy hops.

- Bohemian Pilsner
- Czech Pilsner
- German Pilsner

OKTOBERFEST/MARZEN

Packed with more malts than pilsners, Oktoberfests (also called Marzens) have a sweet caramel flavor and very little (or no) hop aroma. Traditionally, they were brewed in March, cold-conditioned over the summer, and then consumed in September to celebrate Oktoberfest.

BOCKS

Bocks form their own small clan, standing up for the stronger, richer, bolder side of the lager family. They range from tawny gold and sweet as honey (maibocks) to deep, dark brown and rich as bread pudding (doppelbocks).

- Maibock
- Bock
- Doppelbock
- Eisbock

CALIFORNIA COMMON (STEAM BEERS)

This style of beer is a bit of an outlier. It was originally a failed attempt on the part of California immigrants from Germany to brew lagers without refrigeration or the proper cool temperatures, but they discovered the beer was pretty darn good all the same. They continued to brew it and developed a unique strain of lager yeast that works well at slightly warmer temperatures, producing a clean and crisp beer with some light estery ale flavors. California commons are also usually hoppier than other lagers, highlighting American hops.

Beer equipment—much like beer brewing—can be a bit of a rabbit hole. As soon as you settle on one piece of equipment, you'll hear about something bigger or better or shinier that trumps whatever you just got. There are also a million ways that you can upgrade your brew system to make it more efficient, speedy, or easier on your back.

Here's what I recommend: start with a basic kit and make it the best you can justify or afford. In the long run, you'll save yourself money and headaches if you buy what you need to begin with rather than trying to make do with something smaller or cheaper and telling yourself you'll upgrade down the road.

If you're just starting out and are worried about sinking a lot of money into a hobby you're not sure about, start with 1-gallon brews. The equipment for these smaller batches is minimal—it's likely you already have some of the equipment in your kitchen. For more thoughts on this, check out "Should You Brew a 1-Gallon or a 5-Gallon Batch?" on page 64.

ASSEMBLE YOUR BEER KIT

—— [chapter 2] ——

GENERAL EQUIPMENT

This is the basic equipment you'll use again and again, batch after batch, brew after brew. Buy the best that you can, because you'll use it forever.

Electronic Kitchen Scale

You need to buy an electronic kitchen scale. Just do it. Precision is key for all aspects of beer brewing, and the ingredients are no exception. This is particularly true when it comes to hops, where being off by a few grams can make the difference between something pleasant to drink and a gag-inducing bitter brew. Plus, many brewing ingredients aren't the same size, so going by weight instead of volume eliminates the guesswork. Buy a scale that can toggle between ounces and grams, and accurately measures to within 1 gram. Take a look at "Measuring Ingredients," below, for more details.

Measuring Ingredients

The malts and hops in homebrew recipes should always be weighed in ounces or grams on a scale, never scooped in cups or tablespoons. The amounts of these ingredients need to be precise, and weighing is the surest way to go. There's a bit more leeway with some of the "extra" ingredients we use for flavoring, like chopped fruit and shredded coconut. For these, I give weights as well as volume measurements where it makes sense.

Many of the recipes in this book, particularly the 1-gallon recipes, call for very small amounts—sometimes as little as 1½ grams! For small amounts of spices, I give teaspoon equivalents, but I still recommend weighing small amounts of hops on a scale since the exact amount is so important.

To weigh amounts too small for your scale to register, measure double or triple the amount called for and divide the ingredient by hand. For half-gram measurements, measure until the scale begins toggling between two numbers (say, between 4 and 5 when measuring 4½ grams) and call it good. And really, we're talking about half a gram—if the weight is off ever so slightly, it won't adversely affect your brew.

Instant-Read Thermometer

An instant-read thermometer is another thing that will make your brew day much easier. Candy thermometers and meat thermometers will do in a pinch, but they're a headache—slow in the case of the former and imprecise in the case of the latter. An instant-read thermometer is very easy to use and gives you a precise temperature in seconds.

Digital Timer

There are lots of moments in the brew day when you need to do things at certain moments or for specific lengths of time. Don't rely on a clock and your memory: use a digital timer. It doesn't need to be fancy—the timer on your microwave will do—but make sure you have one and use it.

Stovetop

Believe it or not, your stove can make a really big difference in how—and how much—you brew. Electric stovetops are just not powerful enough to properly boil more than a few gallons of liquid. If this is what you have, you're limited to brewing 1-gallon batches or 5-gallon extract and partial-extract batches. Gas stovetops give you more flexibility; 1-gallon batches are no problem and they're powerful enough to brew 5-gallon all-grain batches, though it can take a while to bring liquids to a full boil.

If you get into 5-gallon all-grain batches and really want to speed things up, look into a stand-alone gas burner. These are much more powerful than even a high-end gas stovetop, and using one greatly reduces the time it takes to bring gallons of water or wort to a boil. It also keeps the wort at a good rolling boil during the hop boil stage. These burners are available at any homebrewing store or online and can be used with standard home propane tanks (like for a gas grill). They must be operated outdoors for safety reasons.

racking cane

2-3 gallon stockpot

hydrometer

whisk

2-gallon
bucket

1-gallon jug

airlock

metal strainer

stopper

long-handled
spoon

plastic tubing and clamp

1-gallon tools

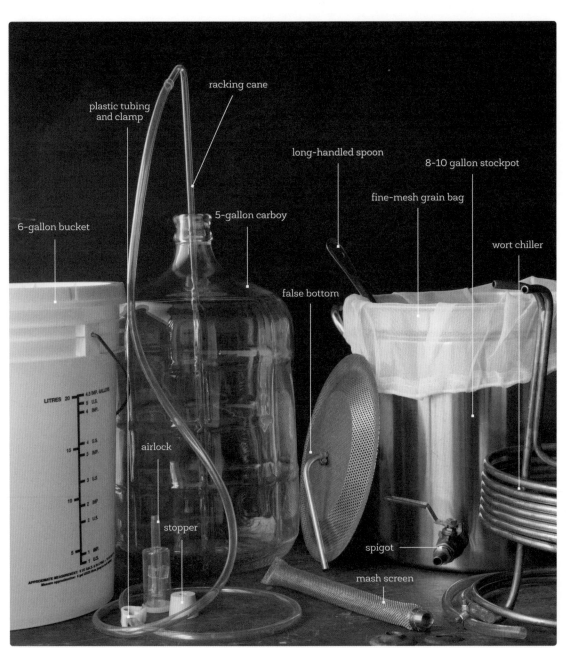

plastic tubing
and clamp

racking cane

long-handled spoon

8-10 gallon stockpot

fine-mesh grain bag

6-gallon bucket

5-gallon carboy

wort chiller

false bottom

airlock

stopper

spigot

mash screen

5-gallon tools

BREWING EQUIPMENT

Time to actually make the beer! This equipment includes everything you need on your brew day to make a batch of beer.

Stockpot

> 2- TO 3-GALLON STOCKPOT (1-GALLON BATCHES)
>
> 8- TO 10-GALLON STOCKPOT WITH A SPIGOT AND A FALSE BOTTOM OR MASH SCREEN (5-GALLON ALL-GRAIN BATCHES)

A stockpot is also your "brew pot," that is, what you use to brew your beer. You use it for both mashing and boiling the beer wort on brew day, and again when it's time to bottle the beer. The stockpot needs to be big enough to hold all the water and the grains during the mash step and the full volume of the beer wort during the boil step (usually ½ to 1 gallon more than your final batch size).

Additionally, for brewing 5-gallon all-grain beers, make sure your stockpot is fitted with a spigot and either a false bottom or a mash screen. The spigot makes it easy to drain the large volume of liquid from the pot and a false bottom or mash screen helps filter the beer wort and keep the spigot from clogging. These are common features available on most stockpots and brew kettles purchased from homebrewing stores.

My advice is to buy the biggest stockpot you think you'll need and the best you can afford. Buy what you think you'll grow into. Making do with something smaller makes your brew day more stressful in the short term (helloooo, boil-overs!), and you'll end up wanting to upgrade after a few batches. A new brew pot is no small pocket change, I know, so if you want to brew 5-gallon batches and are nervous about committing to the brew pot, try a few 1-gallon batches first. (For more on this, see "Should You Brew a 1-Gallon or a 5-Gallon Batch?" on page 64.)

Long-Handled Spoon or Paddle (All Batches)

Make sure your spoon or paddle reaches all the way down to the bottom of your stockpot without putting your hand in danger of a dunking. I like a spoon with a fairly wide, paddle-like head so I can easily move the grains around during the mash step.

10-Inch Metal Strainer or 5-Quart Metal Colander (1-Gallon Batches)

When brewing 1-gallon batches, you need a way to separate the used grains from the sweet wort and then rinse the sugar from the grains (with 5-gallon batches, this all happens right in the pot). A handy, everyday metal kitchen strainer or colander does this job quite nicely. Use one with a diameter of 10 to 12 inches so that it spans your fermentation bucket (see page 28) and comfortably holds all of your used grains. If buying a colander, the more holes the better.

29 by 29-Inch Fine-Mesh Grain Bag (5-Gallon Batches)

Instead of a colander or a strainer, I like to use a big grain bag to hold the mashed grains for 5-gallon batches. Line your brew pot with the grain bag and secure it with a bungee cord around the top or by clamping the bag to the pot with two spring clamps. The bag makes it easier (and safer) to transfer the used grains out of the brew pot and acts as a filter so your wort is clear of excess sediment.

8 by 15-Inch Fine-Mesh Grain Bag (1-Gallon and 5-Gallon Partial-Extract Batches)

When brewing partial-extract beers, you can use this smaller bag to hold the specialty grains. This makes it easy to add and remove the grains from the water during brewing.

Oven Thermometer (Optional; 1-Gallon Batches)

An oven thermometer isn't strictly necessary, but it comes in handy for monitoring the oven temperature when making 1-gallon batches.

Wort Chiller (5-Gallon Batches; Optional for 1-Gallon Batches)

A wort chiller is a long coil of copper tubing sold at most homebrewing supply stores. You put the chiller in the brew pot with the hot wort, then run cool water through the tubing to quickly chill the wort to yeast-pitching temperature (see "Cool the Wort," pages 41-42). Along with the wort chiller, you need two lengths of plastic hosing capable of stretching between your stove and your kitchen sink (or another cold water faucet), two worm gear clamps to attach the hoses to the wort chiller, and a faucet adapter to attach the hose to your kitchen faucet.

Hydrometer and Hydrometer Tube (All Batches)

A hydrometer is used for calculating the alcohol content of your homebrews. With it, you can measure the beer's "specific gravity"—its density as compared to water. Sugar alters the specific gravity of liquids, so by taking one measurement when the beer is first brewed and another after it has finished fermenting, we can calculate how much sugar has been consumed and how much alcohol has been created. For more, see "How to Use a Hydrometer to Calculate Alcohol Content," page 44.

A hydrometer tube is a thin, cylindrical beaker with a base so that it can stand upright. To take a hydrometer reading, you fill the tube with liquid and float the hydrometer inside.

FERMENTING EQUIPMENT

Once the beer wort is made, it's time to let it ferment. You use this equipment to make sure the beer has a safe, protected home while the yeast does its business.

Plastic Bucket and Lid (with a Hole)

> 2-GALLON BUCKET (1-GALLON BATCHES)
>
> 6-GALLON BUCKET (5-GALLON ALL-GRAIN BATCHES)

You'll come to know this simple plastic bucket and its lid as your "fermentation bucket" or "primary fermenter." This is where your beer lives during the first stage of fermentation, just after adding the yeast. This stage is a wild and zany time for the yeast—its frantic feasting on sugars throws lots of bubbles and foam up to the top. Think: Mardi Gras parade. The extra gallon of air space in the bucket allows this to happen without risk that the beer will fizz out the top.

The 6-gallon buckets usually come with measurement markings on the side; the 2-gallon buckets usually do not. Before brewing, mark the sides of your 2-gallon fermentation bucket with 1-gallon and 1½-gallon volume measurements using a permanent marker. Do this by measuring water into the bucket and marking the water line on the outside.

This bucket is useful at other times in the brewing process, too! You can use it for things like sanitizing equipment and when bottling beer.

Air Lock (All Batches)

An air lock lets gases escape from the fermenting beer without letting anything else get in. There are a few different models of air locks; all are fine to use. Before using, you need to fill the air lock with sanitizer, vodka, or water up to the air lock's "fill line"; this liquid is what completes the air lock's seal.

Jug or Carboy and Stopper

> 1-GALLON JUG (1-GALLON BATCHES)
>
> 5-GALLON CARBOY (5-GALLON BATCHES)

The jug or carboy is your "secondary fermenter." It houses your beer during the second stage of fermentation—the period after the yeast activity slows and it's time to let the beer condition. It's a smaller, cozier space for the beer to mellow, which cuts down on storage space and reduces the beer's exposure to air. Carboys can be either glass or plastic; use whichever you prefer.

You'll also need a stopper that fits in the neck of your jug or carboy. Like the lid on the bucket, this is what seals the jug and prevents exposure to air and dust. Make sure your stopper has a hole drilled in the middle so you can insert the air lock.

Racking Cane or Autosiphon

> 13-INCH CANE (1-GALLON BATCHES)
>
> 24-INCH CANE (5-GALLON BATCHES)

The racking cane is used to rack (transfer) the beer from one container to the next. Make sure your cane comes with a removable tip. If you have the option, get an autosiphon over a traditional racking cane; they're much easier to use. For more on this, see "How to Siphon Beer" on page 45.

5/16-Inch Plastic Tubing and Clamp

> 3 FEET LONG (1-GALLON BATCHES)
>
> 5 FEET LONG (5-GALLON BATCHES)

Plastic tubing is needed for siphoning. The tubing attaches to the racking cane or autosiphon on one end and empties into a new container on the other. Tubing comes in various sizes, so make sure you get the size that fits your racking cane and bottle filler. The tubing clamp allows you to close the tubing when needed.

Wine Thief

A wine thief is used to draw out a sample of the beer from the secondary fermenter if you want to taste it or take a hydrometer reading before bottling. It works like a long straw: dip the sanitized wine thief into the beer, cover the top with your thumb, and withdraw the wine thief with the sample held inside.

6 by 8-Inch Mesh Hop Bag

This small mesh bag is useful for dry-hopping beers in the secondary fermenter (see Glossary, page 222) or infusing them with flavoring ingredients, like vanilla beans or cacao nibs. The bag makes it easy to remove the ingredient once the beer is infused to your liking.

BOTTLING EQUIPMENT

Last but not definitely not least, it's time to bottle your finished homebrew. This is the equipment you need to get the job done.

Bottling Bucket

A bottling bucket can be any handy container: the bucket you used for primary fermentation, your brew pot, or any other container big enough to hold your batch of beer. You will transfer your finished beer into this container to mix it with a final dose of sugar before bottling.

bottle

plastic tubing

wine thief

bottling bucket

bottle capper

bottle filler

bottle caps

Bottling tools

Bottle Filler

A bottle filler makes the job of actually getting the beer into the bottles much less messy. The top attaches to the open end of the plastic tubing; the other end has a spring-loaded valve you insert into the bottle. When the valve is pressed to the bottom of the bottle, beer flows into it; when you lift the bottle filler, the flow of beer stops.

Bottle Caps and Capper

Bottle caps are one use only, making them the only piece of equipment you have to buy new every time you brew. Crown bottle caps clamp around the lip of the beer bottle, making an airtight seal. The bottle capper is a butterfly contraption used to crimp the bottle caps in place.

Beer Bottles

10 (12-OUNCE) BEER BOTTLES (1-GALLON BATCH)

48 (12-OUNCE) BEER BOTTLES (5-GALLON BATCH)

You can either buy new beer bottles from a homebrewing store or other supplier, or save all your empties. As long as the lip of the bottle isn't nicked or cracked, beer bottles can be used again and again. Buy (or save!) brown bottles only. Brown glass protects the beer from UV rays, which can cause beer to prematurely stale or develop undesirable flavors.

Homebrewing Checklists

To keep yourself organized throughout the homebrewing process, use these checklists for a quick rundown of the equipment you'll need at each stage for the brewing process.

1-Gallon Kit Checklist

Brew Day

- [ ] 2- to 3-gallon stockpot
- [ ] Long-handled spoon or paddle
- [ ] 10-inch strainer or 5-quart colander
- [ ] Hydrometer and hydrometer tube
- [ ] 2-gallon plastic bucket with lid
- [ ] Air lock

Transfer to Secondary

- [ ] 1-gallon jug
- [ ] Stopper (with a hole)
- [ ] 13-inch racking cane or autosiphon
- [ ] 3 feet of ⁵⁄₁₆-inch plastic tubing
- [ ] Tubing clamp
- [ ] Wine thief

Bottling Day

- [ ] Bottling bucket (your stockpot or primary fermentation bucket)
- [ ] Bottle filler
- [ ] 10 bottle caps
- [ ] 10 (12-ounce) brown bottles
- [ ] Bottle capper

5-Gallon Kit Checklist

Brew Day

- [ ] 3- to 5-gallon stockpot (extract or partial-extract) or 8-to 10-gallon brew pot with false bottom and spigot (all-grain)
- [ ] 29 by 29-inch fine-mesh grain bag
- [ ] Long-handled spoon or paddle
- [ ] Wort chiller (all-grain)
- [ ] Hydrometer and hydrometer tube
- [ ] 6-gallon bucket with lid
- [ ] Air lock

Transfer to Secondary

- [ ] 5-gallon carboy
- [ ] Stopper (with a hole)
- [ ] 24-inch racking cane or autosiphon
- [ ] 5 feet of ⁵⁄₁₆-inch plastic tubing
- [ ] Tubing clamp
- [ ] Wine thief

Bottling Day

- [ ] Bottling bucket (your stockpot or primary fermentation bucket)
- [ ] Bottle filler
- [ ] 48 bottle caps
- [ ] 48 (12-ounce) brown bottles
- [ ] Bottle capper

WHAT TO EXPECT ON YOUR FIRST VISIT TO A HOMEBREW STORE

Walking into a homebrew store can seem a bit like finding yourself in the middle of a mad scientist's laboratory: gleaming pots from floor to ceiling, bins of odd-looking gadgets, jars of sticky syrups, fridges full of pouches and packets, and a dusty haze in the air. When it's your first time, this can feel equal parts thrilling and intimidating.

GET ORIENTED

While every homebrew store is different, they all share some common features. Foremost among these are friendly, eager staff members. People work in homebrewing stores because they love homebrewing, and I have yet to meet any employee who isn't ready and willing to invite a new homebrewer into their world.

So here's the first thing to do: Say hello! Don't be shy! Tell them that you're new to homebrewing and this is your first time. More likely than not, they will immediately take you under their wing and show you around. If you brought a list of equipment or a recipe with you, share it with them and let them help you assemble everything you need.

Another common feature of homebrew stores is what you find there. A big portion of the store is likely devoted to equipment: brew pots of various sizes, hoses, clamps, pumps and filters, cases of bottles, and so on. The whole grains are likely in big bins or barrels with a supply of both liquid and dried malt extracts nearby. Also close at hand are shelves of adjunct ingredients like spices, honey, fruit, and other flavoring extracts, corn sugar for bottling, and various add-ins used during brewing. Keep an eye out for the fridges: that's where the hops and yeasts are kept.

Some homebrew stores are help-yourself affairs, while others prefer that you ask a staff member to assemble supplies and ingredients for you.

The preferred procedure at your store will likely be apparent as soon as you walk in, but asking to make sure is always prudent. Even if you're encouraged to help yourself, ask for assistance if you need it.

BEFORE YOU LEAVE

Before you leave the store, double-check that you have everything you need (and trust me, it's all too easy to forget something crucial):

- [ ] Any new equipment
- [ ] Grains or malt extracts
- [ ] Hops
- [ ] Yeast
- [ ] Bottles for when you eventually bottle your beer
- [ ] Corn sugar for carbonating your beer
- [ ] Bottle caps
- [ ] Sanitizer

Also make sure that you or a staff member grinds the grains for your recipe. Getting home and realizing you forgot to mill your grains can put a serious damper on your brew day.

What should you do if the store is out of, or doesn't carry, an ingredient you're looking for? While not every homebrew store carries exactly the same ingredients, they probably have something close—a different hop with almost the same flavors, a grain roasted to the same color, a variety of yeast that is a near match to the one you want. If you're not confident in your substituting skills, ask for help. If you're dead set on using a specific ingredient or piece of equipment, look for it online: see the Recommended Resources section at the end of the book.

WHEN YOU GET HOME

Unless you're launching into your brew day as soon as you get home, take five minutes to put your new ingredients away properly.

Hops in the freezer. Hops lose many of their best qualities if left at room temperature, even if they're in a sealed package. You can store them in the fridge if you plan to brew within a few days, but keep them in the freezer for longer storage.

Yeast in the fridge. Cool temperatures keep the yeast in a state of hibernation, though freezing can be a little too extreme. Store both dry and liquid yeast in the fridge until it's time to brew.

Grains in an airtight container or plastic bag. Grains can also grow stale if left for too long. If you plan to brew soon, it's fine to keep them in the store packaging. Otherwise, transfer the grains to an airtight container or sealable bag. They can be kept at room temperature.

BEYOND YOUR FIRST VISIT

Homebrew stores are for more than just supplies. The people who work there are great resources for all your brewing questions—I've even seen them field panicked phone calls from brewers in the middle of a brew day! Employees can help you upgrade your equipment or switch from extract brewing to all-grain brewing. They are often happy to taste your homebrew and analyze its flavors. They can also connect you to local homebrewing clubs.

Homebrew stores are the hubs of the home-brewing community; once you're in, you're part of the family.

We're heading into the nitty-gritty details of how to homebrew. In this chapter, we go over everything you need to know to brew your first—or your hundredth—batch of beer. After taking a bird's-eye view of the general brewing process, we jump into the easiest kind of brew: all-extract brewing. From there, we build to partial-extract brewing, and finish with all-grain brewing—the method we use for most of the recipes in this book.

Each one of these brewing methods builds on the one before. As we go from all-extract to all-grain, I spend more time talking about the elements being introduced and less time on the basics. I repeat key steps within each method but assume that you've already mastered the details. If you forget how to do something or need clarification, you can always refer to the prior methods for a refresher.

New to brewing? I recommend brewing your way through this chapter one batch at a time. Already have a few batches of homebrew under your belt? Use this chapter as a reference manual and feel free to dive in wherever you like!

BREW YOUR FIRST BEER

—— [chapter 3] ——

BIRD'S-EYE VIEW OF HOW TO BREW BEER

Before tackling the specifics, let's take a step back and look at the big picture:

> Malted grains + water + hops + yeast = beer

Let's take this one step further:

This is the basic method for every single beer out there, not only homebrewed beers but also those made by your favorite breweries, and every beer since humans first discovered that a drink of fermented grains tastes pretty darn good. Keep this basic big-picture concept in mind as you dive into homebrewing, and it will help keep finer points in context.

> Malted grains steeped in water, flavored with hops, and fermented with yeast make beer.

Brewing beer can be broken down into five basic steps:

- ☐ 1. *Make the wort.*
- ☐ 2. *Boil the wort with hops or other flavorings.*
- ☐ 3. *Add the yeast.*
- ☐ 4. *Ferment the beer.*
- ☐ 5. *Bottle the beer.*

"Wort" (pronounced "wehrt") is a fancy brewing term for "sugary beer juice." Through the process of fermentation, this is what is eventually transformed into real, drinkable beer. As homebrewers, we can get wort by using entirely malted extracts, using some extracts and some grains, or using entirely malted grains. These three wort-making methods are referred to as all-extract, partial-extract, and all-grain; we cover each one in this chapter.

Once we have our wort, the next step is to boil it, called the "hop boil." Depending on the style of beer you're making, wort is typically boiled from 60 to 90 minutes. This concentrates the wort and adds subtle caramelized flavors while also sanitizing it to get rid of unwanted wild yeasts or bacteria. Perhaps most exciting to us as homebrewers, this is also the point at which we start adding hops to our beer. Delicious, lovely hops. (There are a few other ways we can get hop flavors in our beer, too—you can read more about these in "Play with Your Hops" on page 116.)

Okay, we've made the wort and boiled it. Next we quickly cool it down before adding the yeast. From this point onward, it's important to make sure that anything coming into contact with the wort is sanitized, from spoons to the fermentation bucket. This helps reduce the chance of any wild yeast or bacteria coming into contact with the beer and contaminating it.

The wort can be cooled in an ice bath in the kitchen sink (low-tech!), using a wort chiller (medium tech!), or even with a fancy heat exchanger (high tech!), but at the end of the day, we want to cool the wort to around 75°F in about 20 minutes. This can be a tricky step, so we talk about it in much more detail in the next section. Once cooled, we pour the wort into the sanitized fermentation bucket, add the yeast, and seal it with the lid and a water-filled air lock.

Now the fun really starts! Sometime in the next 24 hours, we should see signs that fermentation has started, evidenced by air bubbles popping up through the water in the air lock. This means the yeast is happily eating the sugars in the wort and leaving alcohol and carbon dioxide in its place. The carbon dioxide escapes through the air lock while the alcohol stays in the wort. Only it isn't wort anymore; now it's officially beer.

This super-active fermentation, called the "primary" fermentation, only lasts a few days. Once it slows, we let the beer sit undisturbed for a few more days to give the spent yeast and other sediment time to settle to the bottom. Then it's time to transfer the beer off the sludge and into a smaller jug or carboy for the longer "secondary" fermentation.

The beer hangs out in the "secondary" for another two weeks or up to two months. It might not seem like much is happening from the outside, but there's actually a lot going on in that little jug. Solid particles continue to filter out of the beer and drift to the bottom, leaving the beer free of sediment. The remaining yeast slowly breaks down the more complex sugars and compounds left over from the primary fermentation. Harsh flavor notes soften and the overall taste of the beer starts to come together and mellow, not unlike the way a stew tastes better the day or two after it's made.

Finally, it's time to bottle the beer. To make sure our beer is carbonated and fizzy, we need to give the yeast one last snack of sugar before it goes into the bottle. This sugar is called "priming sugar" and the act of adding it to the beer is called "priming." The priming sugar is a carefully calculated amount—just enough to get the yeast to produce carbon dioxide and make the beer fizzy, but not so much that it changes the overall character of the beer. I usually use corn sugar for this step because it's easy for the yeast to ferment and doesn't leave any residual flavors in the beer.

Once primed, all that's left is to transfer the beer into bottles and cap. Wait another two weeks to give the beers time to carbonate and settle into their new home, and then they're ready to drink. Most homebrew can also be stored for up to a year before you start noticing any objectionable change in flavor.

Not so hard, right? Most of the labor-intensive, hands-on action happens on the first day, and after that, it's a matter of staying out of the way while the yeast does its thing.

Now that you understand the lay of the land, let's get into some of the finer details. We start with the all-extract method.

HOW TO BREW AN ALL-EXTRACT BEER

Think of all-extract brewing as your gateway to homebrewing. It's easy, it makes dependably good and drinkable beer, and it will get you totally and completely hooked after just one batch—if only because you realize that, if all-extract beer is this good, partial-extract and all-grain beers can only be better. All-extract beers are also a fantastic way to learn the ropes and get a feel for the rhythm of a brew day without worrying about things like mashing grains or sugar levels.

A 1-gallon all-extract brew takes approximately 2½ hours from start to cleanup. A 5-gallon brew takes approximately 3 hours. Check out the recipe for All-Extract Amber Ale at the end of this section (page 49) to put your learning into practice.

If you're brewing a 1-gallon batch and haven't already done so, mark the sides of your fermentation bucket with 1-gallon and 1½-gallon volume measurements using a permanent marker. Do this by measuring water into your fermentation bucket and marking the water line on the outside of the bucket.

STEP 1: Dissolve the Extract
Before you begin brewing, remove your liquid yeast from the refrigerator and place it on the counter to warm. If you're using a smack pack, give it a good smack to activate the yeast; when activated properly, the package inflates over a few hours. Dry yeast doesn't need to warm before being used.

Most malt extract is sold in bulk, and you only need a portion of it for a single brew. It's best and easiest to weigh the extract on a scale in a heatproof bowl or measuring cup; the remaining extract can be resealed and kept until your next brew. Liquid extract can be quite thick and difficult to work with. If it's in a pouch, you can squeeze it out like toothpaste; if it's in a metal canister, open the canister and set it in a pot of hot water for a few minutes to make it easier to pour.

Measure 1½ gallons of water into a stockpot for a 1-gallon batch of beer or 5½ gallons for a 5-gallon batch, or as called for in your recipe. Bring to a simmer over high heat, then remove the pot from the heat. Add the extract, stirring gently and occasionally scraping the bottom of the pot to prevent the sugar-rich extract from scorching on the bottom. Once you've added the bulk of the extract, scoop a little of the hot water mixture into the bowl or measuring cup, swirl it around to dissolve any remaining extract, and pour it back into the pot. Continue stirring until the extract is completely dissolved.

Your mix of water and malt extract is now officially wort!

STEP 2: Bring the Wort to a Boil
Place the pot back over high heat and bring the wort to a rolling boil. You can cover the pot with a lid to encourage it to boil faster, but remove the cover once it's boiling. The amount of liquid in most recipes is calculated to allow for evaporation, and there are also some compounds that can leave unsavory flavors in your beer if not allowed to evaporate during the boil.

Foam will start to collect on the surface of the wort as it heats. Keep a close eye as it starts to come to a boil. If your pot is small, the wort can often boil over at this point, which is a big mess and not very fun! If it looks like your wort is in danger of boiling over at any point, quickly reduce the heat, stir the wort continuously, squirt water on the foam with a spray bottle, or remove the pot from the heat until it settles back down.

Watch for the boiling liquid to start breaking through the foam and for the majority of the foam to collapse back into the wort. This is called the "hot break." Once this happens, the danger of boil-overs is past, and it signals that you're ready to start adding the hops.

How to Sanitize Equipment

Keeping things clean and sanitized are two of the more boring parts of homebrewing, but they're also some of the easiest things you can do to ensure good homebrew. Remember that any equipment that comes into contact with the beer once you have finished the hop boil must be sanitized. This means the fermentation buckets and jugs, for sure, but also things like measuring cups, the hydrometer, air locks, and even your hands.

Cleaning and sanitizing are two different things. Cleaning involves removing any physical gunk or dirt from the equipment; sanitizing means killing any errant bacteria or wild yeast still clinging to your stuff.

Clean everything as thoroughly as possible before sanitizing. Use a bristle brush to get inside jugs and bottles. Thoroughly rinse away all soap residue.

To sanitize, fill your fermentation bucket with sanitizer and plop everything in. Run sanitizer through hoses and canes. You can even wedge the lid in there and rotate it to make sure it's completely sanitized. On bottling day, use your bucket to sanitize batches of bottles. For a little extra insurance, dip your hands in the solution before handling equipment. Check the instructions for your sanitizer to figure out how long everything needs to stay in contact with the solution and whether the equipment needs to be rinsed with water afterward.

Lay the sanitized equipment out on clean dish towels. Flip the bucket upside down so that dust and bugs don't fall inside. Keep a small container of sanitizer nearby in case you forgot to sanitize, or need to resanitize, anything. Some sanitizers, like Star San, can be stored and used several times before they lose their potency. Star San also gets quite bubbly; the bubbles are food safe and don't need to be washed away.

STEP 3: Add the Hops

The hop boil for most recipes is between 60 and 90 minutes. Hops can be added at any point during the boil but are typically added at the beginning, in the last 20 minutes, and at the very end. Since hop resins need a lengthy boil in order to be absorbed into the wort, but delicate hop flavors and aromas won't last that long, adding hops in several additions is the best way to make sure you get a rounded bitterness and good hop flavor and aroma in your finished beer.

As soon as the wort comes to a boil, start a timer to remind you of each hop addition. Measure hops by weight and toss them into the boiling wort when directed by the recipe—no need to stir, they will mix in on their own. Keep your wort at a rolling boil with the lid off throughout this step; this is necessary to fully extract all the goodness from the hops.

In the last 20 minutes of the boil, also add the Irish moss, which helps clarify the beer. Other additions, like spices or fruit, are usually added within the last 10 minutes.

STEP 4: Cool the Wort

Starting the second you turn off the heat under the boiling wort, make sure to sanitize every piece of equipment that will come into contact with the beer. Fill your fermentation bucket with sanitizer and use this to sanitize the bucket's lid, the air lock, a strainer, a small measuring cup, the hydrometer, and a whisk. Read through "How to Sanitize Equipment" at left for more details.

Once the boil is finished, cool the wort as quickly as possible before adding the yeast—ideally, to at least 75°F in about 20 minutes. If you wait for the wort to cool off on its own, this increases the risk of uninvited bacteria or wild yeast taking up residence in your freshly brewed wort. Cooling the wort rapidly also helps make a clearer, less hazy beer.

Why the need to cool the wort at all? Why not just pitch the yeast and be done with it? It's really all about creating a happy home for your yeast.

Yeast dies at 110°F and is most comfortable between 65°F and 75°F. Conventional brewing wisdom typically advises cooling the wort all the way to 70°F before adding the yeast. While this might be the ideal, I've found that actually *achieving* this in a home kitchen within that 20-minute window is a daunting and difficult task. Instead, aim for a wort that's between 75°F and 80°F; until you get into homebrewing on a very technical level, this is a good compromise between keeping the yeast happy and keeping you happy. The difference in the finished beer of a wort chilled to 80°F versus one chilled to 70°F is negligible at a beginner homebrewing level. Both beers equalize to room temperature within a few hours anyway. This is one of those points when it's best to quote the godfather of homebrewing, Charlie Papazian: "Relax! Have a homebrew!"

The easiest way to cool a 1-gallon batch of beer is with an ice bath. Just fill your kitchen sink with cold water and ice cubes and set the pot inside. As the water warms, drain the sink and refill it with more cold water and ice. Stir the wort gently every now and again with a sanitized long-handled spoon to help it cool evenly, but avoid splashing; adding oxygen to the wort while it's still warm can give it some oxidized, sherry-like flavors. Check the temperature occasionally until the wort has cooled sufficiently.

You can also use an ice bath to cool down a 5-gallon batch of beer, but be prepared for it to take a little longer and require quite a bit of ice. The easiest and most efficient way to cool a 5-gallon batch is with a wort chiller. For more about setting up a wort chiller and using it to cool your beer, see "How to Use a Wort Chiller" below.

How to Use a Wort Chiller

A wort chiller does exactly what it promises: it chills your wort. Using one is about the only way to get a 5-gallon batch of beer wort cooled down in any reasonable amount of time (short of investing in some other very spendy equipment). It's less essential for a 1-gallon batch but still handy.

Place the wort chiller right in the brew pot in the last 20 minutes of the hop boil, around when you add the flavor hops. This sanitizes it. If you forget, just dunk the coils in sanitizer before you put them in the wort. The coils should be submerged in the wort, with the input and output ends poking out over the top of the pot.

You'll need two lengths of hose: one to run from the faucet to the input opening of the chiller and another to run from the output opening of the chiller to the sink or other runoff receptacle. Attach the hose to the faucet using a faucet adapter, and clamp the hoses tight to the input and output openings of the chiller with worm gear clamps. Arrange the other output hose so that it empties into your kitchen sink. This creates a closed system where cold water runs

from the faucet, through the chiller, and empties out the other end. (The input and output openings on the chiller are interchangeable; just pick one to use as the input and use the other for the output.) Clamps and adapters can be found at homebrewing supply stores or your local hardware store.

Once you have the system set up, slowly turn on the cold water to test for leaks. Water should flow smoothly through the chiller. If you've never done this before, it's smart to do a trial run in advance so you know how everything connects. Adjust clamps as needed, turn off the water, and wait for your wort to finish boiling.

At the end of the boil, turn off the heat and turn on the flow of cold water from your faucet. Be careful—at first, the water coming from the output hose will be extremely hot! Gently stir the wort with the chiller occasionally to make sure it is cooling evenly, and continue running cool water through the chiller until the wort has cooled. Remove the chiller and proceed with pitching the yeast.

Once the wort is chilled, transfer it to the sanitized fermentation bucket, filtering it through a strainer to catch any solid particles. (Pro tip: Before dumping out the sanitizing solution, save a little in a separate container in case of last-minute sanitation needs.) Check the markings on the side of your bucket. If needed, top the wort off with tap water to reach 1 gallon (or 5 gallons). It's okay to use tap water; it's essentially sterile and leaves very little risk of bacterial or wild yeast contamination. Alternatively, you can use store-bought spring water.

If you end up with more than 1 gallon (or 5 gallons), don't worry about it too much. You either started the boil with a little too much liquid or your wort wasn't quite at a full, rolling boil for the whole time. This batch of beer will be a little more diluted than normal (and will wind up with a lower alcohol content, or ABV), but it will still be tasty. Next time, keep an eye on your preboil volume and the strength of your boil.

STEP 5: Check the Original Gravity of the Wort

The "gravity" or "specific gravity" of beer is a measure of its density as compared to water. Since sugar increases density, the specific gravity lets us know how much sugar is in the beer at various points in the brewing process. As beer ferments and sugars are converted into alcohol and carbon dioxide, both the density and the specific gravity of the beer decrease. By taking a specific gravity reading right now before fermentation begins ("original gravity") and another reading at the end before bottling ("final gravity"), we can determine how much sugar was converted into alcohol during fermentation and the alcohol by volume (ABV) of the finished beer.

With your sanitized measuring cup, dip out a little of the wort and pour it into the hydrometer tube. Insert the hydrometer itself and wait for it to stop bobbing. Look at where the surface of the liquid hits the hydrometer and read the specific gravity. Also, check the temperature of the liquid and adjust the gravity reading as needed. Record this number so you can reference it again when you bottle the beer. See "How to Use a Hydrometer to Calculate Alcohol Content," page 44, for more details.

STEP 6: Add the Yeast and Aerate the Wort

Go ahead and add the yeast! In brewing terms, this is called "pitching" the yeast. All you do is open the package and pour the yeast into the wort. If you're using liquid yeast, it should be warm by now; open the package slowly since liquid yeast can be quite fizzy. (If you forgot to warm the liquid yeast, put it in a bowl of warm water for half an hour to warm it up.)

There's one more thing to do before snapping on the lid and stepping away from the brew: give the wort some oxygen. When you add yeast to sugar-rich wort, it spends the first several hours reproducing and growing before it actually starts fermenting the beer. For this to happen, it needs oxygen—all of which has just been boiled out of the water. This is the one and only time in the brewing process when we actually *want* to introduce oxygen into the beer. At any other time—while cooling the wort, while transferring it, or when bottling the beer—adding too much oxygen can oxidize the beer and give it stale, "off" flavors.

My favorite way to aerate the wort is to whisk it like mad with a standard balloon whisk. Be sure to sanitize it first and then *whisk whisk whisk!* Once you see a good amount of foam build up on the top of the wort, you're good. You can also pour the wort back and forth a few times between the fermentation bucket and the brew pot. (If you didn't clean your brew pot, it is still technically sanitized from the boil. If you did clean your brew pot, be sure to sanitize it again before aerating the wort.)

After aerating, snap the lid on your fermentation bucket, fill the air lock partway with water, and insert the air lock into the lid. Set the bucket somewhere out of direct sunlight and at a moderate room temperature.

STEP 7: Ferment for 1 Week

The first few days of primary fermentation are the most active. You should see signs of active fermentation, as evidenced by bubbles in the air lock, within 24 hours. (If not, see "Common Problems, Easy Solutions," page 218.) At first, you'll see bubbles in the air lock almost constantly, then they become occasional, and then infrequent as the days pass.

Once the bubbles seem to stop, let the wort—now officially beer!—sit for a few more days to give the spent yeast and other sediment a chance to settle to the bottom. In total from the time you pitch your yeast, this should take about a week. If you need to go to the next step a day or two early, that's fine. It's also fine if you aren't able to go to the next step for more than a week. Don't wait longer than a month since the beer can start to pick up weird flavors from the sludge at the bottom of the bucket.

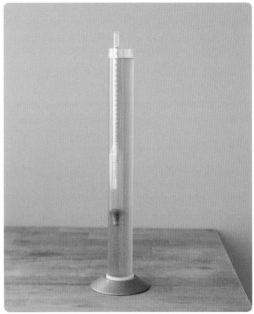

Hydrometer

How to Use a Hydrometer to Calculate Alcohol Content

Scoop a little wort into the sanitized hydrometer tube, filling it to about 2 inches from the top. Insert the sanitized hydrometer and let it float in the liquid (add more liquid if necessary to make it float). Give the hydrometer a gentle spin to shake off any bubbles and let it come to a complete stop.

Look to where the surface of the liquid hits the hydrometer and record the number. Most hydrometers have multiple units of measurement—you're looking for the gravity reading, which is expressed as a 1 followed by three decimals. A typical gravity reading at the start of brewing will be around 1.050; at the end of brewing, it will be around 1.015.

Remove the hydrometer and check the temperature of the liquid with a sanitized thermometer. Adjust your gravity reading as necessary; hydrometers are usually calculated to be accurate at 60°F and include instructions for adjusting the reading based on the temperature of the liquid.

Take a gravity reading just before you pitch your yeast to get its original gravity (OG) and again just before you bottle your beer to get its final gravity (FG). The difference of the two readings tells you how much sugar has been converted to alcohol during fermentation. Use this formula to calculate the final alcohol by volume (ABV):

$$(FG - OG) \times 131.25 = ABV\%$$

The original gravity and final gravity of your beer can be affected by many factors. The gravity and ABV% for any recipe is a target: aim for it, but don't fret too much if you don't hit the bull's eye. You'll get better at hitting it as you go.

STEP 8: Transfer the Beer to a Smaller Jug or Carboy

Transferring the beer to a smaller container gets it off the sediment and reduces the risk of exposing the beer to oxygen during the longer "secondary fermentation."

Sanitize a 1-gallon jug (or a 5-gallon carboy), its stopper, the racking cane or autosiphon, its tip, the siphon hose, and the hose clamp. Place the bucket of beer on a counter with the jug on a chair or the floor a few feet below. Siphon all of the beer into the jug, leaving behind just the last half-inch or so of heavy sludge. It's fine if some of the lighter sediment is transferred toward the end; this will settle out in the next phase of fermentation. Seal the jug with its stopper. Sanitize the air lock, fill it with water, and insert it into the stopper. (See "How to Siphon Beer," below, for more information.)

How to Siphon Beer

Unless you're in the habit of stealing gas from the neighbor's gas tank, chances are good that you've never used a siphon before. Conceptually, it sounds daunting; in reality, if gas thieves can do it, so can you. Try it a few times with water to get the hang of things before you try it with your homebrew.

Starting a Siphon

You need an autosiphon or racking cane, a length of plastic tubing, a container of liquid (i.e., the liquid you're about to transfer), and an empty container. Make sure all your equipment is sanitized.

Place the container of liquid on the counter and the empty container on a chair or the floor a few feet below it. Attach one end of the plastic tubing to the crooked end of the autosiphon or racking cane. Slip a hose clamp over the open end of the hose.

There is also a detachable tip that fits over the tip of the autosiphon or racking cane; make sure it's on there.

If you're using a racking cane, run tap water through the hose until it runs out the end of the cane, then clamp the hose shut, trapping the water inside. This primes your racking cane so that it will start siphoning right away. Place the racking cane inside the container of liquid so that the tip touches the bottom and the crooked part hangs over the side.

Place the open end of the hose in the empty container. Then open the hose clamp to start siphoning. (You can direct the water into a cup until the beer gets pulled into the siphon if you'd like to avoid mixing water into your homebrew.)

If you're using an autosiphon, be very careful to hold the open end of the hose in your hand or be sure it's clamped to the side of the empty container before you begin siphoning; if unsecured, it will spray homebrew all over your kitchen. Once the hose is secure, pump the autosiphon a few times to start the flow of liquid. You may need to recruit a helper if you don't have enough hands to do everything at once.

Once siphoning has begun, you just need to make sure everything proceeds properly. Keep the open end of the hose slightly submerged beneath the surface of the liquid to prevent splashing as the container fills. You may also want to tilt the original container when it's nearly empty to siphon as much liquid as possible.

If you have trouble getting the siphon started or if it stalls after a few seconds, try moving the two containers further apart. Your plastic tubing might also be too long. You only need enough to stretch between the two containers; trim it down as needed.

Continued on page 46

Siphoning from the Primary to the Secondary

The main reason to transfer beer from the primary to a smaller secondary is to get the beer off the thick sludge produced during the first few days of fermentation. The sludge is fairly compacted, but it can get stirred up (and go back into your beer) if you jostle the bucket or constantly move the racking cane as you siphon.

Place the primary container on the counter an hour or two before you plan to siphon so that the sludge has time to settle. When you start siphoning, slip the racking cane along the side of the bucket nearest to you and hold it there (or use a clamp to secure it).

You have two choices: you can siphon until the bucket is empty and transfer a bit of sediment into the secondary, or you can stop siphoning as soon as you see sediment in the hose and lose a few cups of beer. When brewing 1-gallon batches where those cups are precious, I usually opt for the first option and figure the transferred sediment will settle into a thin layer in the secondary, which is then easy to avoid when bottling.

Siphoning from the Secondary into the Bottling Bucket

When transferring from the secondary into the bottling bucket, siphon the same as before. Try not to disturb the sediment and stop siphoning once you get close to the bottom and see sediment in the hose. Since this beer is about to go into bottles, we want to avoid transferring any sediment.

Avoid splashing or overly agitating the beer at this point; the oxygen can give your beer off flavors. If you add your priming sugar to the bottling bucket before siphoning, the siphoning action thoroughly mixes the beer and the sugar. If you add the priming sugar afterward, use a sanitized long-handled spoon to gently stir the two together.

Siphoning from the Bottling Bucket into the Bottles

Clean and sanitize your siphon before continuing with bottling. If you're using a racking cane, fill it with water as before, clamp the hose shut, and attach the bottle filler to the open end of the hose. Siphon as usual to fill all the bottles.

If you're using an autosiphon, begin with the open end of the hose inside one of the bottles. Once the siphon has started, clamp the hose shut, remove the hose from the bottle, and attach the bottle filler. Continue siphoning as usual to fill all the bottles.

Syphoning beer process

STEP 9: Ferment for 2 Weeks

Put the jug somewhere cool and dark and leave it for at least 2 weeks or up to 2 months (unless otherwise specified by your recipe). During this time, more yeast and sediment settle out of the beer, leaving your finished beer much clearer. The yeast continues to break down some of the more complex sugars and other compounds in the beer. Aging also gives the beer time to mellow—the flavors even out, the alcohol flavor becomes less pronounced, and harsher notes soften.

STEP 10: Bottle the Beer

Right now the beer is completely flat. In order to give it some carbonation, we need to mix in a little sugar just before bottling, called "priming" the beer. I like to use corn sugar for this step because it has a clean flavor and dissolves easily, but refer to "Priming Sugar Substitutions," page 48, for other kinds of sugar. The amount of priming sugar used depends on the level of carbonation you want in your finished beer. For most 1-gallon batches, use .80 ounces (22 grams) of corn sugar dissolved in 1/4 cup of boiling water; for most 5-gallon batches, use 4 ounces (113 grams) of corn sugar dissolved in 1 cup of boiling water. Let this solution cool completely before mixing it into the beer.

If you lost more than a few cups of beer over the course of brewing, adjust the amount of sugar you add here. Read "How (and When) to Adjust the Amount of Priming Sugar," page 48, for more details on how to do this.

When you're ready to bottle the beer, sanitize your bottling bucket, a hydrometer, 10 (12-ounce) beer bottles for a 1-gallon batch or 48 (12-ounce) bottles for a 5-gallon batch, their caps, the siphon hose, the racking cane or autosiphon, its tip, and the bottle filler. The bottling bucket can be your empty fermentation bucket, your stockpot, or another container big enough to hold all of your beer.

Pour the cooled sugar solution into your bottling bucket. Siphon about ½ cup of beer into the hydrometer tube to determine the final gravity, then siphon the rest of the beer into the bottling bucket with the sugar, splashing as little as possible. After determining the final gravity, record your findings and either drink the beer or pour it into the bucket.

Attach the bottle filler to your siphon and siphon the beer into bottles (see "How to Siphon Beer," page 45, for more info on starting the siphon for this step). To fill the bottles, insert the bottle filler into each bottle and press the tip against the bottom. This starts the flow of beer. Keep the tip pressed against the bottom until the bottle is completely full, with the beer just reaching the lip of the bottle. Lift the bottle filler to stop the flow of liquid and withdraw it from the bottle. This leaves exactly the right amount of head room.

To cap the bottles, place a sanitized bottle cap over the mouth of the bottle and position the butterfly capper on top. Press down on either side of the capper (the "wings") to clamp the bottle cap and crimp it down over the lip of the bottle. This doesn't take much force; once the wings are horizontal, the cap is crimped. If you've never done this before, try it with a few empty bottles first so you get the hang of it.

Once the bottles are capped, label them with the beer and the date. I use labels made of masking tape, but you can use chalk markers to write on the bottles themselves, permanent markers to write on the caps, or print your own labels. Last but not least, calculate the alcohol content using the original and final gravity readings from the hydrometer.

STEP 11: Wait 2 Weeks Before Drinking

Let the bottles sit at room temperature out of direct sunlight for at least 2 weeks to fully carbonate, or store for up to a year. For safekeeping, I recommend storing homebrews in a cupboard, cardboard box, or other closed container. Even the most careful brewer occasionally gets bottles that shatter under the pressure of carbonation, and trust me, the whole experience is much safer and easier to clean up if the bottles have been kept somewhere enclosed!

STEP 12: Refrigerate and Serve

Refrigerate your beers for a few hours before drinking them. Open bottles of homebrew very slowly over a sink and have a pint glass handy. The amount of priming sugar is calculated to avoid overcarbonating the beer, but the occasional gusher still happens. Better safe than sorry. Sit back, relax, and enjoy your homebrew.

How (and When) to Adjust the Amount of Priming Sugar

The amount of priming sugar for the recipes in this book is based on the assumption that you will end up with around 3½ quarts (10 bottles) of beer from a 1-gallon batch and around 4½ gallons (48 bottles) from a 5-gallon batch. Some beer is always lost in the brewing process (poetically called "the angel's share").

But what if you end up with less than the expected amount of beer on bottling day? Adding the whole amount of sugar to a smaller batch can be trouble since you'll be overcarbonating your beer and risking some bursting bottles. This is more of an issue with 1-gallon than 5-gallon batches since the surplus sugar gets distributed over fewer bottles.

You can adjust the amount of priming sugar using this ratio: 2 grams of corn sugar for every 12 fluid ounces (1½ cups) of beer. Normally, it's easiest to mix the priming sugar with the beer when you transfer it to the bottling bucket, but if you're unsure how much sugar you'll need, wait until after you've siphoned it into the bottling bucket. Then use the measurements on the side of the bucket to calculate your batch size, and use that to calculate how much priming sugar to add. Dissolve the sugar with hot water as usual, and stir it into the beer **very gently**. Avoid splashing or adding too much air to the beer.

One final note: A few of the beers in the book use less priming sugar than calculated here. The 2 grams of corn sugar per bottle gives the beer an average level of carbonation, but some styles (like stouts) are better with less carbonation. To adjust the sugar used in these recipes based on your batch size—or to give yourself an extra guarantee against gushers—scale down the amount of sugar per bottle.

Priming Sugar Substitutions

Corn sugar is just one of many sugars you can use to carbonate your beers. If you want to experiment with other sugars, the chart below will give you the rough ratios to use. Keep in mind that flavorful sugars, like honey and molasses, will add a noticeable flavor to your beer.

SUGAR	1-GALLON BATCH	5-GALLON BATCH
Corn Sugar	.80 ounce (22 grams)	4 ounces (113 grams)
Cane Sugar	.75 ounce (21 grams)	3.7 ounces (104 grams)
Brown Sugar	.80 ounce (22 grams)	4 ounces (113 grams)
Honey	.95 ounce (27 grams)	4.7 ounces (133 grams)
Maple Syrup	1.09 ounces (31 grams)	5.5 ounces (155 grams)
Molasses	1.55 ounces (44 grams)	7.8 ounces (222 grams)
Dry Malt Extract	1.06 ounces (30 grams)	5.4 ounces (152 grams)

AMOUNTS GIVEN ARE FOR AN AVERAGE LEVEL OF CARBONATION.

All-Extract Amber Ale

Ready to put your newfound knowledge to the test? This amber ale is a great place to start. It's an easy-to-make and easy-drinking beer that will both teach you the ropes and give you something tasty to enjoy at the end.

Brew Notes A 1-gallon brew takes approximately 2½ hours from start to cleanup. A 5-gallon brew takes approximately 3 hours.

Follow the detailed master method for brewing 1-gallon or 5-gallon all-extract batches as described on pages 40–48 (5-gallon measurements in parentheses).

• Remove liquid yeast from the refrigerator and, if necessary, activate according to package instructions. Place on the counter to warm.

• In a large stockpot over high heat, warm **1½ (or 5½) gallons of water to simmering**; then add the pale extract followed by the amber extract and stir to dissolve.

• Bring to a boil over high heat. Add the hops for bittering and boil vigorously for 40 minutes. Add the hops for flavoring and the Irish moss and continue boiling for another 20 minutes. Add the hops for aroma and remove from the heat. (Total boil time: 60 minutes.)

• Cool to at least 75°F and transfer to the sanitized primary fermentation bucket. Add the yeast and aerate the wort.

• Let ferment for at least **1 week or up to 4 weeks at 70°F**; then transfer to a sanitized jug or carboy for secondary fermentation. Continue to ferment for another **2 weeks or up to 2 months at 70°F**.

• Dissolve the sugar in ¼ (or 1) cup of boiling water and let cool. Mix with the beer, bottle, and store for **2 weeks or up to a year**. Refrigerate before drinking.

INGREDIENTS	1-GALLON	5-GALLON
White Labs California Ale yeast, Wyeast American Ale yeast, or equivalent	½ package	1 package
Pale liquid malt extract	12 oz (340 g)	3¾ lbs (1.70 kg)
OR Pale dried malt extract	9.60 oz (272 g)	3 lbs (1.36 kg)
Amber liquid malt extract	12 oz (340 g)	3¾ lbs (1.70 kg)
OR Amber dried malt extract	9.60 oz (272 g)	3 lbs (1.36 kg)
Cluster pellet hops (6.8% AA), for bittering	.15 oz (4 g)	.75 oz (21 g)
Cluster pellet hops (6.8% AA), for flavoring	.15 oz (4 g)	.75 oz (21 g)
Irish moss	¼ tsp	1 tsp
Cluster pellet hops (6.8% AA), for aroma	.15 oz (4 g)	.75 oz (21 g)
Corn sugar, for bottling	.80 oz (22 g)	4 oz (113 g)

TARGET ORIGINAL/FINAL GRAVITY: 1.054/1.013
TARGET ABV: 5.4%

HOW TO BREW A PARTIAL-EXTRACT BEER

Time to level-up! The next step in your beer-brewing education is to give partial-extract brews a try. For this, we're going to keep malt extract for the base of the recipe but add in some specialty grains. As we discussed in chapter 1, these specialty grains won't add much sugar (i.e., yeast food), but they do add some interesting flavors to your beer and give it a better color. Where all-extract beer can taste a little one-note, partial-extract beer is getting much closer to the kind of layered, complex flavors and rich color of all-grain brews.

Just in case you're feeling a little nervous, let me lay your mind at ease: all we're doing here is adding one extra step at the beginning. Everything from the hop boil on is exactly the same as with the all-extract brewing. Also, because everything after the boil is the same, I'm assuming you've already got the hang of these basic steps. If you need to brush up on anything, refer to "How to Brew an All-Extract Beer" on pages 40–48.

A 1-gallon brew takes approximately 3 hours from start to cleanup. A 5-gallon brew takes approximately 3½ hours. Check out the recipe for Partial-Extract Amber Ale at the end of this section (page 53) to put your learning into practice.

If you're brewing a 1-gallon batch and haven't already done so, mark the sides of your 2-gallon fermentation bucket with 1-gallon and 1½-gallon volume measurements using a permanent marker. Do this by measuring water into your fermentation bucket and marking the water line on the outside of the bucket.

STEP 1: Steep the Specialty Grains

First off, make sure your specialty grains have been milled—this is to say, crushed, ground, or cracked so the insides of the grains are exposed. Most of the time, you can ask for your grains to be milled when you buy them. If not, you can pulse them in a food processor or put them in a plastic bag and roll over them with a rolling pin. Either way, the goal is to crack the grains, not pulverize them; grind them too finely and you'll end up with oatmeal when you brew, which is a pain to work with.

Note: Flaked barley, flaked oats, flaked wheat, and any other flaked grain do not need to be milled; add them to the rest of the grains after milling.

Combine all of your milled specialty grains inside a fine-mesh bag and knot it closed. This makes it easier to separate the grains from the water once we're done steeping them—like a giant tea bag.

Pour the amount of water specified in your recipe into a stockpot and heat it to the specified temperature. (Usually, this is around 2 quarts of water for a 1-gallon batch and 2½ gallons for a 5-gallon batch, heated to 160°F.) Turn off the heat and add the specialty grains in their bag. Swish the grains around a bit to make sure they are fully hydrated, then hang the knotted part of the bag over the side of the pot and cover with a lid.

Let the grains steep for ½ hour. Ideally, we want to keep the water between 148°F and 152°F, but don't worry too much about this (temperature is something that becomes more important with all-grain brewing; for now, it's just practice). If you notice the temperature dropping below 148°F, turn on the heat for a minute while swishing the bag of grains through the water. Turn off the heat as soon as the liquid gets back to the temperature range.

While the grains are steeping, remove liquid yeast from the refrigerator and place it on the counter to warm. If you're using a smack pack, give it a good smack to activate the yeast. Dry yeast doesn't need to warm before being used.

STEP 2: Separate the Grains and the Liquid

After a half hour, you've extracted all the goodness from the specialty grains and it's time to pull them out of the water. Grab the knotted end of the bag, bob the grains up and down a few times in the liquid, then lift the bag out. Hold it above the pot and let drain for a few seconds to get as much steeped liquid as possible. Don't squeeze the bag, though—squeezing can add bitter tannins to your beer.

Set the bag of grains aside. Once they're cool, you can compost or discard them. Clean and dry the grain bag for your next batch of beer.

STEP 3: Dissolve the Extract

If you're making a 1-gallon batch, add enough water to your brew pot to make 1½ gallons. For a 5-gallon batch, add enough water to make 5½ gallons. Begin heating the liquid (now called wort!) over high heat.

When the wort comes to a simmer, slowly pour in the malt extract called for in your recipe. Stir gently and occasionally scrape the bottom of the pot. This prevents the sugar-rich extract from scorching on the bottom of the pan. Once you've added the bulk of the extract, scoop a little of the hot water mixture, into the bowl or measuring cup, swirl it around to dissolve any remaining extract, and pour it back into the pot. Continue stirring until the extract is completely dissolved.

STEP 4: Bring the Wort to a Boil and Add the Hops

Bring the wort to a full, rolling boil over high heat. Watch for foam to collect in a thick layer on the top and for boiling wort to start breaking through (the hot break). Be careful that the wort doesn't boil over, especially if your pot is on the small side. Stir or lower the heat as needed.

Add the hops according to the schedule in your recipe—typically, bittering hops are added at the beginning of the boil, flavoring hops and Irish moss in the last 20 minutes, and aroma hops at the end.

If you're cooling your wort with a wort chiller, place it in the wort in the last 20 minutes of the boil to sterilize it.

STEP 5: Cool the Wort

Prepare an ice bath in your sink and set your pot inside, or use a wort chiller to cool your wort. If using an ice bath, change out the water as it warms. If using a wort chiller, occasionally swirl the chiller inside the pot to make sure the wort is cooling evenly. Cool to 75°F–80°F.

STEP 6: Transfer the Wort to the Fermentation Bucket

From this point on, it's important for everything coming into contact with the wort to be sterilized. Sanitize your fermentation bucket and lid, the air lock, a strainer, small measuring cup, hydrometer, and a whisk.

Once the wort is chilled, transfer it to the sanitized fermentation bucket, filtering it through a strainer to catch any solid particles. Check against the markings on the side of the bucket to make sure you have around a gallon of wort for a 1-gallon batch or 5 gallons for a 5-gallon batch. Add more water if needed.

Scoop out a little wort and transfer to the hydrometer; take a reading to determine the original gravity and pour the wort back into the bucket.

STEP 7: Add the Yeast and Aerate the Wort

Pour the yeast into the wort and whisk the wort vigorously until very foamy to aerate. Alternatively, pour the wort back and forth between the fermentation bucket and the brew pot a few times. (If you didn't clean your brew pot, it is still technically sanitized from the boil. If you did clean your brew pot, sanitize it again before aerating the wort.)

After aerating, snap the lid on your fermentation bucket, fill the air lock partway with water, and insert the air lock into the lid. Set the bucket out of direct sunlight and at a moderate room temperature.

STEP 8: Ferment for 1 Week

You should see bubbles in the air lock within 24 hours. Let the beer ferment undisturbed for at least 1 week or up to 4 weeks, until fermentation has slowed and the sediment has had a chance to settle.

STEP 9: Transfer the Beer to a Smaller Jug or Carboy

Sanitize a 1-gallon jug or 5-gallon carboy, its stopper, the racking cane or autosiphon, its tip, the siphon hose, and the hose clamp. Siphon all of the beer into the jug, leaving the last half-inch or so of sludge. Check your recipe for any extra ingredients that need to be added at this point.

STEP 10: Ferment for 2 Weeks

Seal the jug with its stopper. Sanitize the air lock, fill it with water, and insert it into the stopper. Let sit somewhere cool and dark for at least 2 weeks or up to 2 months. Check your recipe for any late additions or other instructions for the secondary fermentation.

STEP 11: Bottle the Beer

Make your priming sugar solution and let cool. Sanitize your bottling bucket, a hydrometer, 10 (12-ounce) beer bottles for a 1-gallon batch or 48 (12-ounce) bottles for a 5-gallon batch, their caps, the siphon hose, the racking cane or autosiphon, its tip, and the bottle filler.

Pour the cooled sugar solution into your bottling bucket. Siphon the beer into the bucket, splashing as little as possible. Also, siphon ½ cup of beer to the hydrometer and use that to determine final gravity. Once a measurement is obtained, drink the beer or pour it back into the bucket.

Attach the bottle filler to your siphon and siphon the beer into bottles. Cap and label. Calculate the alcohol content using the original and final gravity readings.

STEP 12: Wait 2 Weeks Before Drinking

Let the bottles sit at room temperature out of direct sunlight for at least 2 weeks to fully carbonate, or store for up to a year. Refrigerate before serving.

Partial-Extract Amber Ale

This is the same recipe as the All-Extract Amber Ale (page 49), but now we're replacing the amber malt extract with specialty grains. You'll notice a darker color and a richer flavor in this version. If you made the all-extract recipe first, be sure to hang on to a bottle or two until this one is done so you can see how they compare!

Brew Notes A 1-gallon partial-extract brew takes approximately 3 hours from start to cleanup. A 5-gallon brew takes approximately 3½ hours.

Follow the detailed master method for brewing 1-gallon or 5-gallon partial-extract batches as described on pages 50–52 (5-gallon measurements in parentheses).

• Remove liquid yeast from the refrigerator and, if necessary, activate according to package instructions. Place on the counter to warm.

• In a large stockpot over high heat, warm ½ gallon (or 2½ gallons) of water to 160°F, then turn off the heat. Combine the grains in a mesh bag and knot closed. Place the bag in the water and swish to fully hydrate the grains. Hang the knotted end of the bag over the edge of the pot and cover loosely with a lid. Steep for ½ hour.

• Lift the bag of grains and hold it over the pot, letting the excess liquid drip back in. Do not squeeze the bag—this releases bitter tannins into the liquid. Discard the used grains.

• Add enough water to make 1½ (or 5½) gallons and bring to a simmer. Stir the malt extract into the wort until completely dissolved.

• Bring to a boil over high heat. Add the hops for bittering and boil vigorously for 40 minutes. Add the hops for flavoring and the Irish moss and continue boiling for another 20 minutes. Add the hops for aroma and remove from the heat. (Total boil time: 60 minutes.)

• Cool to at least 75°F and transfer to the sanitized primary fermentation bucket. Add the yeast and aerate the wort.

INGREDIENTS	1-GALLON	5-GALLON
White Labs California yeast, Wyeast American Ale yeast, or equivalent	½ package	1 package
Crystal/Caramel 20 malt, milled	12 oz (340 g)	3¾ lbs (1.70 kg)
Caramunich malt, milled	4 oz (113 g)	1¼ lbs (567 g)
Pale liquid malt extract	12 oz (340 g)	3¾ lbs (1.70 kg)
OR Pale dried malt extract	9.60 oz (272 g)	3 lbs (1.36 kg)
Cluster pellet hops (6.8% AA), for bittering	.15 oz (4 g)	.75 oz (21 g)
Cluster pellet hops (6.8% AA), for flavoring	.15 oz (4 g)	.75 oz (21 g)
Irish moss	¼ tsp	1 tsp
Cluster pellet hops (6.8% AA), for aroma	.15 oz (4 g)	.75 oz (21 g)
Corn sugar, for bottling	.80 oz (22 g)	4 oz (113 g)

TARGET ORIGINAL/FINAL GRAVITY: 1.051/1.011
TARGET ABV: 5.2%

• Let ferment for at least **1 week or up to 4 weeks at 70°F**; then transfer to a sanitized jug or carboy for secondary fermentation. Continue to ferment for another **2 weeks or up to 2 months at 70°F**.

• Dissolve the sugar in ¼ (or 1) cup of boiling water and let cool. Mix with the beer, bottle, and store for **2 weeks or up to a year**. Refrigerate before drinking.

HOW TO BREW AN ALL-GRAIN BEER

Without further ado, I bring you all-grain beer. Cue the trumpets and start the parade! This is the top of the ladder when it comes to brewing—and we got here in just three batches!

As the name "all-grain" implies, we're stepping away from malt extracts altogether and relying entirely on malted grains. This means that we're getting all the sugars, all the flavors, all the colors, all the *everything* from different combinations of grains. This can be a little tricky—we're about to get nerdy about how we make the wort and add a technique called sparging—but once you get to the boiling step, everything is exactly the same as for all-extract and partial-extract brewing.

If you've been putting off getting a larger brew pot or thinking you can get by without a digital thermometer, this is the moment to think about upgrading. All-grain brewing isn't that hard, but trying to make do with less-than-ideal equipment gets tricky. I follow the Boy Scout motto when it comes to brewing: be prepared. Take a look back through the "Brewing Equipment" section on page 27 to see if there's any equipment you still need.

Also, if you're feeling a little gun-shy about buying the equipment needed for 5-gallon all-grain brews, consider doing a few 1-gallon batches first. The equipment for a 1-gallon batch is much less of a commitment in terms of both money and space; I also find 1-gallon all-grain batches to be less stressful and intimidating. For more pros and cons to fuel your inner debate on this issue, check out "Should You Brew a 1-Gallon or a 5-Gallon Batch?" on page 64.

I'm assuming that by now you've got the basic techniques like cooling the wort and bottling the finished beer down pat. I mention these steps as we go along, but if you need a more in-depth refresher, skim back through "How to Brew an All-Extract Beer," pages 40–48.

A 1-gallon all-grain brew takes approximately 4 hours from start to cleanup. A 5-gallon brew takes 5 to 6 hours. See "Average Timeline for All-Grain Batches," page 55, for a detailed timeline of the all-grain brewing process, and check out the recipe for All-Grain Amber Ale at the end of this section to put your learning into practice.

If you're brewing a 1-gallon batch and haven't already done so, mark the sides of your fermentation bucket with measurements, as described on page 28 in "Fermenting Equipment."

STEP 1: Mash the Grains

Before you start the mash, remove liquid yeast from the refrigerator and place it on the counter to warm. If you're using a smack pack, give it a good smack to activate the yeast. Dry yeast doesn't need to warm before being used.

Also, be sure to mill or crush all of your grains before brewing. Flaked barley, flaked oats, flaked wheat, and any other flaked grain do not need to be milled; add them to the rest of the grains after they've been milled. Some recipes also call for rice hulls, which don't add anything to the beer itself but make it easier to separate the sugary wort from the heavy, wet grains. Rice hulls also should not be milled; combine them with the milled grains after milling.

The mash process differs slightly for 1-gallon and 5-gallon batches, but the principle is the same: soak the grains in water at a specific temperature for a set amount of time. While the grains are soaking, the starches stored inside the grains dissolve into the water, and enzymatic reactions take place that convert them into easily fermentable sugars for the yeast to eat later on. The amount of water to grain, the water temperature, and the soaking time are all factors here.

This is one of the places in the brewing process where it's possible to get incredibly geeky. Change one factor here or nudge something there, and it can change your finished beer in any number of ways. When you're new to brewing, just trust your recipe and try to follow its instructions as closely as you can. For the recipes I've given you in this book, I've already made decisions about the mashing process for you—as long as you stick pretty close to the recipe, your beer will be awesome. If you want to know more about what's going on in the mash and how to tweak it once you get more confident with your homebrews, read "Get Geeky with the Mash," page 102.

The mashing process is a little different for 1-gallon and 5-gallon batches, but the basic concept is the same.

MASHING A 1-GALLON BEER

In a large stockpot over high heat, warm the amount of water called for in your recipe to the specified temperature—in brewing terms, this is your "strike water"; the temperature to which you warm it is called the "strike temperature." At the same time, preheat your oven to 150°F to 155°F to create a nice, comfy environment for mashing the grains. If you don't have an oven setting this low or don't own an oven thermometer, warm your

Average Timeline for All-Grain Batches

If this is your first batch, tack on an extra hour or so to the total brew day time estimate—everything is new and unfamiliar, and each step will probably take you a bit longer. As you learn and become more confident, you will start getting faster and your brew day will get shorter.

Don't skimp on the time it takes to ferment the beer and to let it sit in bottles before drinking. You can make something fizzy and alcoholic in less time, but you'll be happier with the flavor and overall character of your beer if you stick to the time frame outlined here.

STEP	TIME
Warming strike water	15–30 minutes, depending on batch size
Mashing grains	60 minutes
Mash-out	15–30 minutes, depending on batch size
Sparging	30–60 minutes, depending on batch size
Bringing wort to a boil	15–30 minutes, depending on batch size
Hop boil	60 minutes
Cooling wort	20–30 minutes
Cleanup	15–30 minutes
TOTAL BREW DAY (1 GALLON): 4–4½ HOURS	
TOTAL BREW DAY (5 GALLONS): 5–6 HOURS	
Primary fermentation	1 week–1 month (2 weeks minimum for lagers)
Secondary fermentation	2 weeks–3 months (1 month minimum for lagers)
Time in bottles	2 weeks–1 year
TOTAL TIME FROM BREW DAY TO DRINKING: 5 WEEKS MINIMUM	

oven for about 5 minutes on the lowest setting. Turn off the oven once it has warmed.

Pour all of the grains (including flaked grains and rice hulls) into the heated water off the heat and stir. This is now your mash. Check the temperature with an instant-read thermometer and stir until it falls within the range specified in your recipe.

Cover the pot and put it in the oven. Set a timer for the mash time in your recipe (usually 1 hour). Every 15 minutes, pull the pot out, stir the grains, and check the temperature. If it starts to drop below your temperature range, set the pot on a burner for a minute or two to warm it up again—stir frequently and check the temperature as it warms. If the mash is too warm, stir off the heat for a few minutes to bring the temperature down.

If you have trouble with high or low temperatures during your mash, give the grains an extra 15 minutes in the oven to be sure you've extracted all of the sugar. The liquid—now called wort—should taste very sweet.

MASHING A 5-GALLON BEER

Attach a false bottom or mash screen to the inside of your brew pot; make sure the outside spigot is closed. Line the pot with a 29 by 29-inch grain bag and let the excess hang over the sides of the pot. Secure the bag by wrapping a bungee cord around the top of the pot or clamping it with two spring clamps.

Place the pot on the stove and fill it with the amount of water called for in your recipe. Warm over high heat to the specified temperature, then turn off the heat. In brewing terms, this is your "strike water"; the temperature to which you warm it is called the "strike temperature." Pour all of the grains (including flaked grains and rice hulls) into the water and stir with a long-handled spoon or paddle. This is now your mash. Check the temperature with an instant-read thermometer and stir until it falls within the specified temperature range.

Cover the pot and set a timer for the mash time in your recipe (usually 1 hour). Every 15 minutes,

stir the grains and check the temperature. If it starts to drop out of your temperature range, turn on the burner for 2 to 3 minutes and stir to warm it up again. If the mash is too warm, stir for a few minutes to bring the temperature down.

If you have trouble with high or low temperatures, give the mash an extra 15 minutes to make sure you've extracted all the sugar. At this point, the wort should taste very sweet.

STEP 2: Mash Out

Now we need to raise the temperature of the mash both to stop the enzymatic reactions taking place inside the pot and to loosen up the sugars and make them easier to rinse from the grains. This is called the "mash-out."

For a 1-gallon batch, remove the pot from the oven and place it on the stovetop over medium heat. For a 5-gallon batch, turn to high heat. (I recommend a lower heat for the 1-gallon batch because it heats so quickly that it's easy to overshoot your temperature mark.)

Stirring occasionally, warm the mash to 170°F. Try not to overshoot this temperature; if the mash gets much warmer, bitter tannins and other undesirables can be released from the grains.

In a separate pot, begin warming the amount of sparge water called for in your recipe. Heat to 170°F and hold it there until the mash is ready. If you are sparging with more than 2 gallons of water, you may want to start heating the sparge water a little sooner so that it's fully heated by the time the mash-out is finished.

STEP 3: Sparge the Grains to Separate the Wort

Now we separate the sugary wort—our future beer—from the grains, which can then be discarded. Just draining out the wort isn't quite sufficient since a lot of sugar gets left behind on the grains. To make sure we collect every last bit of sugar, we need to rinse the grains with fresh water—a process called sparging—and add that to the wort. The bed of spent grains also acts as a filter to clear grist and other solid particles out of the mash.

The sparging process is a little different for 1-gallon and 5-gallon batches, but again, the basic concept is the same.

SPARGING A 1-GALLON BATCH

Set a 10-inch-wide strainer or 5-quart colander over your fermentation bucket and place this in your kitchen sink. Pour the mashed grains into the strainer. The wort collects in the bucket beneath. Slowly pour the warmed sparge water over the grains, rinsing them evenly, until you have collected 1½ gallons of wort (as measured against the marks on the outside of your bucket). The amount of water needed varies depending on how much liquid the grains absorbed during mashing.

Clean the stockpot used for making the mash and transfer the strainer with the used grains to this pot. Slowly pour the wort over the grains again. Be careful, as the wort can sometimes overflow the strainer when the grain bed becomes more compacted. Repeat this step twice more, ending with the wort back in your stockpot.

After the last round of sparging, transfer the grains back to the bucket once the runoff from the grains has slowed to a few drips. Another cup or two of wort will continue to drain from the grains as you proceed to the next step; you can add this extra to the wort at any time. Discard the grains.

SPARGING A 5-GALLON BATCH

Set your empty fermentation bucket on a stool or chair just below the brew pot. Open the spigot on the brew pot partway, allowing the wort to flow from the pot into the bucket. At first, the wort will be cloudy and filled with bits of grain and husk. Once you see this begin to clear—usually after you've collected a few quarts of wort—close the spigot to stop the flow of liquid. Pour the wort you've collected back into the brew pot over the top of the grains. This recirculation helps filter out sediment.

Begin draining the wort into the bucket again. As it drains, the grains will begin to settle and form a bed. When the level of the wort falls to within a few inches above the grains, gently begin pouring the heated sparge water over top in small batches. Try to pour evenly, disturbing the grains as little as possible. Keep 1 to 3 inches of liquid above the grain bed at all times.

The hot sparge water helps rinse all of the sugars from the mashed grains into your wort. Going slowly and keeping just a few inches of liquid above the grain bed prevents the grains from compacting so much that liquid can no longer easily flow through, a situation appropriately called a "stuck mash." Check the temperature of your sparge water during this step to make sure it stays around 170°F; reheat if necessary. (If you do get a stuck mash, see "Common Problems, Easy Solutions" on page 218 for help.)

When you've collected 5½ gallons of wort in your bucket, close the spigot and stop sparging. You should have used most or all of the sparge water. It's fine if there is some liquid remaining with the grains in the brew pot; by this point, most of the sugars will have been rinsed from the grains. This whole step takes anywhere from half an hour for basic recipes to an hour or longer for recipes with a lot of grains.

Remove the grains from the brew pot by knotting the grain bag closed and either lifting, sliding, or dumping the bag of grains into a separate container. The grains will be very heavy and hot, so I recommend having a helper nearby. Once the grains have cooled, empty them from the bag and discard or compost them. Clean the grain bag for another brew day.

There should be little or no grain residue left in the brew pot; if there is, rinse the pot before continuing with the hop boil. Pour the wort from the bucket back into your cleaned brew pot. The wort will be heavy and hot, so enlist help if needed.

STEP 4: Bring the Wort to a Boil and Add the Hops

From this point on, brewing the beer is exactly the same as for all-extract and partial-extract beers. Congrats, the hard part is done! If you need a more detailed review of what comes next, look back to "How to Brew an All-Extract Beer" on pages 40–48.

After sparging, place the stockpot with the wort over high heat and bring to a rolling boil. Watch for foam to collect in a thick layer on the top and for boiling wort to start breaking through. Be careful that the wort doesn't boil over. Stir or lower the heat as needed.

As soon as the wort comes to a full boil, begin adding the hops according to the schedule in your recipe—typically, bittering hops are added at the beginning, flavoring hops and Irish moss in the last 20 minutes, and aroma hops at the end.

If you will be cooling your wort with a wort chiller, place it in the wort in the last 20 minutes of the boil to sterilize it.

STEP 5: Cool the Wort

Prepare an ice bath in your sink and set your pot inside, or use a wort chiller to cool your wort. If using an ice bath, change out the water as it warms. If using a wort chiller, occasionally swirl the chiller inside the pot to make sure the wort is cooling evenly. Cool to 75°F to 80°F.

STEP 6: Transfer the Wort to the Fermentation Bucket

From this point on, everything coming in contact with the wort should be sterilized. Sanitize your fermentation bucket and lid, the air lock, a strainer, small measuring cup, hydrometer, and a whisk.

Once the wort is chilled, transfer it to the sanitized fermentation bucket, filtering it through a strainer to catch any solid particles. Check the markings on the side of the bucket to make sure you have around a gallon of wort for a 1-gallon batch or 5 gallons for a 5-gallon batch. Add more water if needed.

Scoop a little of the wort and transfer to the hydrometer; take a hydrometer reading to determine the original gravity and pour the wort back into the bucket.

STEP 7: Add the Yeast and Aerate the Wort

Pour the yeast into the wort and whisk vigorously until very foamy to aerate. Alternatively, pour the wort back and forth between the fermentation bucket and the brew pot a few times. (If you didn't clean your brew pot, it is still technically sanitized from the boil. If you did clean your brewpot, sanitize it again before aerating the wort.)

After aerating, snap the lid on your fermentation bucket, fill the air lock partway with water, and insert the air lock into the lid. Set the bucket out of direct sunlight and at a moderate room temperature.

STEP 8: Ferment for 1 Week

You should see bubbles in the air lock within 24 hours. Let the beer ferment undisturbed for at least 1 week or up to 4 weeks, until fermentation has slowed and the sediment has had a chance to settle.

STEP 9: Transfer the Beer to a Smaller Jug or Carboy

Sanitize a 1-gallon jug or 5-gallon carboy, its stopper, the racking cane or autosiphon, its tip, the siphon hose, and the hose clamp. Siphon all of the beer into the jug, leaving the last half-inch or so of sludge. Check your recipe for any ingredients that need to be added.

STEP 10: Ferment for 2 Weeks

Seal the jug with its stopper. Sanitize the air lock, fill it with water, and insert it into the stopper. Let sit somewhere cool and dark for at least 2 weeks or up to 2 months.

Check your recipe for any late additions or other instructions for the secondary fermentation.

STEP 11: Bottle the Beer

Make your priming sugar solution and let cool. Sanitize your bottling bucket, a hydrometer, 10 (12-ounce) beer bottles for a 1-gallon batch or 48 (12-ounce) bottles for a 5-gallon batch, their caps, the siphon hose, the racking cane or autosiphon, its tip, and the bottle filler.

Pour the cooled sugar solution into your bottling bucket. Siphon the beer into the bucket, splashing as little as possible. Also, siphon ½ cup of beer to the hydrometer and use that to determine final gravity. Once a measurement is obtained, drink the beer or pour it back into the bucket.

Attach the bottle filler to your siphon and siphon the beer into bottles. Cap and label. Calculate the alcohol content using the original and final gravity readings.

STEP 12: Wait 2 Weeks Before Drinking

Let the bottles sit at room temperature out of direct sunlight for at least 2 weeks to fully carbonate, or store for up to a year. Refrigerate before serving.

One-Stage Fermentation: Another Option

While I generally like to use a two-stage fermentation (where the beer goes through primary and a secondary fermentation in two separate containers), there is another option: one-stage fermentation. For this, you leave the beer in one container from the time you pitch the yeast until the time you bottle it. The total fermentation time is the same, but there's no fussing around with transferring it between containers. There is a little risk with this—the beer can start to pick up weird flavors from the yeast sludge on the bottom of the container if left for more than a month or so, and there's a greater chance you'll transfer sediment into your beer when you bottle. If you container is small (say, a jug or a carboy) there is also some risk that the beer will foam out the air lock in the first few days of active fermentation.

If you're doing a quick-fermenting beer, like a simple pale ale or saison, and you're sure you'll have time to bottle it within a month, then you can try the one-stage approach. A two-stage fermentation is still best for more involved or longer-fermenting beers and, I feel, as an overall best practice when homebrewing.

A PHOTOGRAPHIC GUIDE TO BREWING BEER

1

Pour grains into
heated water

2

Mash grains

3

Sparge grains
1 gallon

5 gallons

7

Cool wort
1 gallon

5 gallons

8

Sanitize tools

9

Transfer to
fermentation bucket

14

Transfer beer for
secondary fermentation

15

Add sugar and bottle beer

16

Check final gravity

17

Cap

4

emove grains
gallon

5 gallons

5

Boil wort until hot break

6

Add hops

10

easure original
avity

11

Add yeast

12

Aerate the wort

13

Primary fermentation

18

ait

19

Enjoy!

All-Grain Amber Ale

This is once again the same amber ale we brewed as an all-extract and as a partial-extract. Here, we're going all-grain! You'll notice that this beer has a richer, more complex flavor than even the partial-extract version. It's also one of my personal favorites for everyday drinking. Not too sweet and not too bitter, this one is just right.

Brew Notes A 1-gallon brew takes approximately 4 hours from start to cleanup. A 5-gallon brew takes 5 to 6 hours.

Follow the detailed master method for brewing 1-gallon or 5-gallon all-grain batches as described on pages 54–59 (5-gallon measurements in parentheses).

• Remove liquid yeast from the refrigerator and, if necessary, activate according to package instructions. Place the yeast on the counter to warm.

• Heat **1 gallon (or 3½ gallons) of water to 160°F**, then stir in the grains. Maintain a mash temperature of **148°F to 152°F** for 60 minutes. Raise the temperature of the mash to 170°F, then sparge using **1 gallon (or 3 gallons)** of 170°F water to make 1½ (or 5½) gallons wort.

• Bring to a boil over high heat. Add the hops for bittering and boil vigorously for 40 minutes. Add the hops for flavoring and the Irish moss and continue boiling for another 20 minutes. Add the hops for aroma and remove from the heat. (Total boil time: 60 minutes.)

• Cool to at least 75°F and transfer to the sanitized primary fermentation bucket. Add the yeast and aerate the wort.

INGREDIENTS	1-GALLON	5-GALLON
White Labs California yeast, Wyeast American Ale yeast, or equivalent	½ package	1 package
Pale ale malt, milled	1 lb (454 g)	5 lbs (2.27 kg)
Crystal/Caramel 20 malt, milled	12 oz (340 g)	3¾ lbs (1.70 kg)
Caramunich malt, milled	4 oz (113 g)	1¼ lbs (567 g)
Cluster pellet hops (6.8% AA), for bittering	.15 oz (4 g)	.75 oz (21 g)
Cluster pellet hops (6.8% AA), for flavoring	.15 oz (4 g)	.75 oz (21 g)
Irish moss	¼ tsp	1 tsp
Cluster pellet hops (6.8% AA), for aroma	.15 oz (4 g)	.75 oz (21 g)
Corn sugar, for bottling	.80 oz (22 g)	4 oz (113 g)

TARGET ORIGINAL/FINAL GRAVITY: 1.051/1.011
TARGET ABV: 5.2%

• Let ferment for at least **1 week or up to 4 weeks at 70°F**; then transfer to a sanitized jug or carboy for secondary fermentation. Continue to ferment for **2 weeks or up to 2 months at 70°F**.

• Dissolve the sugar in ¼ (or 1) cup of boiling water and let cool. Mix with the beer, bottle, and store for **2 weeks or up to a year**. Refrigerate before drinking.

SHOULD YOU BREW A 1-GALLON OR A 5-GALLON BATCH?

There was a time not so long ago when all homebrewers were making 5-gallon batches. All the equipment was built for 5 gallons and all the recipes were written for 5 gallons, so that's just what we did. And then someone somewhere realized you could brew darn good beer on a smaller scale. Imagine that! Suddenly, we homebrewers had a choice.

PROS AND CONS OF A 1-GALLON BATCH

With a 1-gallon batch, everything about brewing becomes easier. The equipment is smaller, so people living in tiny apartments and brewing in tiny kitchens don't have to find so much storage space. The equipment is less expensive, so it's less of a commitment if you're not sure brewing is your thing. It's easier to control the temperature and cool down the wort, not to mention lift pots of hot wort and move buckets of fermenting beer. The brew day goes more quickly—once you have the hang of it, you can go from heating the mash water to tapping down the lid on the fermentation bucket in about 4 hours, easy.

A 1-gallon batch also opens the door to creativity and experimentation. You're only brewing 10 bottles, so you're not stuck drinking your way through a huge batch of mediocre beer before you can brew again (and trust me, even a really good beer can get tiresome after you've gone through half a case of it). You can brew more often, and it's less of a worry if you make a mistake.

On the other hand, a 1-gallon batch is small. If you make a really amazing beer, you only have 10 bottles to enjoy. And even though it's one-fifth the size of a 5-gallon batch, it's definitely not one-fifth the work. Also, little mistakes tend to be more apparent—it's especially easy to overhop 1-gallon beers, and if you use a little too much priming sugar, there's a greater risk that you'll get foaming (or bursting) bottles.

PROS AND CONS OF A 5-GALLON BATCH

Brewing 5 gallons of beer definitely gives you the best bang for your buck. The brew day is a little longer, but the trade-off is enough beer to last you and your friends a good while. Also, while 1-gallon batches usually break even on the cost of materials compared to the cost of the same amount of craft beer, brewing on a larger scale definitely starts saving you some dollars.

Brewing 5 gallons also gives you a greater margin for error. If you make a little mistake, like using too much hops or boiling a little too long, it's less noticeable in the final beer. A 5-gallon batch is more forgiving. And the con for 1-gallon brews is a pro for 5-gallon brews: when you brew 5 gallons, you get a lot of beer! You can hoard it and drink it all yourself, or share it with friends, take it to a party, or exchange it with fellow homebrewers. You can also keg your beer instead of bottling it, which saves time and labor. Plus, serving your own homebrew from a tap in your own kitchen is about the most badass thing imaginable.

On the con side for 5-gallon brews, the equipment is bigger, bulkier, and frequently more expensive. The entry cost can be steep, and unfortunately, if you skimp on good equipment, you might not be happy with either the experience of brewing or the beer you end up making. A 5-gallon batch can also be trickier to brew—you're dealing with a lot of mass, so heating it, keeping it at a steady temperature, and cooling it down can be frustrating, especially if you're new to the game. It's also difficult to brew by yourself since lifting heavy pots filled with wet grains or hot liquid is darn tricky for all but the buffest bodybuilders among us. You also need a gas stove or (even better) the outdoor space for a stand-alone burner so you can heat water and wort more quickly and keep it at a boil. Sorry, folks, but electric stoves just don't cut it power-wise. Finally, if you love the beer you brew, having a big batch is awesome, but if something went wrong or the finished beer isn't what you hoped for, you're stuck with it—or with pouring it down the drain. That's heartbreaking (been there, done that).

WHAT'S A HOMEBREWER TO DO?

Bottom line? Do what's best for you. I'm guessing there's one batch size that's calling your name more strongly than the other, and I say go with it. The pros and cons of both sizes mostly balance each other out, so decide which pros and cons are most important to you. If you're still having trouble choosing which way to go, take a look at the accompanying chart (see page 66) to help make your decision. Honestly, it's homebrew—you can't go wrong.

Also, there's nothing that says you can't do both! Brew some 1-gallon batches to get a feel for all-grain brewing or to experiment with a new recipe, then brew 5 gallons when you know you've got the recipe right. Or brew 1-gallon batches when it's just for you, but scale it up to 5 gallons if you have a party coming up.

SCALING HOMEBREW RECIPES

For the most part, you can scale recipes fairly linearly from a 1-gallon batch up to a 5-gallon batch. Yes, you can even brew 3-gallon batches or anything else in between!

You'll notice some difference in hop bitterness and flavor between 1-gallon and 5-gallon batches. A 5-gallon batch brewed with a proportionate amount of hops sometimes—but not always—tastes a bit milder and less hoppy than the 1-gallon. It depends on the kind of hops and their alpha acid level, and a few other factors too complex for this book. If you're curious and want to tinker with your recipes, look into purchasing brewing software, like BeerSmith, which helps you calculate the amount of hops to suit your taste.

Also, if you brew more than 5 gallons, some of the ingredients stop scaling so neatly. If you're heading toward bigger batches, you'll definitely want to get some brewing software to help you plan your brews.

IF YOU	THEN BREW
Live in a small apartment where space is a premium or roommates are a factor	1 gallon
Want to give homebrewing a try, but don't want to totally commit to it yet	1 gallon
Like flexibility and variety, especially in your beer fridge	1 gallon
Like flexibility and variety, especially in your beer fridge	1 gallon
Want to brew beer in the easiest, most fuss-free way possible	1 gallon
Have a tendency toward perfectionism and often fret about the details	1 gallon
Have a laissez-faire attitude and are just happy if you get something drinkable	1 gallon or 5 gallons
Have never brewed before	1-gallon or 5-gallon all-extract or partial-extract beer
Want to brew with friends	5 gallons
Want to share or trade your homebrew with your friends	5 gallons
Consider drinking beer a hobby and don't mind drinking the same thing for a while	5 gallons
Have a lot of space and like tinkering with new equipment	5 gallons
Have brewed 5 gallons of all-extract or partial-extract and are ready to step up your game	5-gallon all-grain or 1-gallon all-grain
Have brewed 1-gallon batches and are ready to step up your game	5 gallons

Pale ales are one of the most accommodating beers you can brew for the simple reason that the style tends to be a catchall for anything that doesn't quite fit the mold. In general, when we talk about pale ales, we're aiming for a beer that's light gold to amber in color with moderate, but not overly aggressive, amounts of hops and an ABV of 4% to 7%, give or take. As you can see, that description leaves a lot of room for interpretation. Brew something pale-colored that doesn't have the hoppy face-smack of an IPA? Call it a pale ale. Aiming for an amber ale that ends up more bitter than expected? Call it a pale ale. Crack open five different craft-brewed pale ales and I guarantee they will vary widely in color, aroma, and flavor.

It's for all these reasons that pale ales are great for beginners (hard to mess up) and for more experienced brewers (lots of room to play). Pale ales are actually one of my favorite styles for beer experiments. You'll notice that every recipe in this chapter has the same amount of base malts and specialty malts, but the beers they make are very different. I love swapping malts in and out of this base recipe and then switching up the hops or trying a different kind of yeast. It's a whole new pale ale every time.

>>>>> <<<<<

PALE ALES

——— [chapter 4] ———

A VERY GOOD AMERICAN PALE ALE

This pale ale is one of the most solid, dependable beers I know. It has a base of pale malts—nothing fancy—with a good dose of lightly toasted crystal malts to give it a smooth, malty flavor. On top of this, add some citrusy hops to make things interesting, and you're done. It's got some pizzazz, but nothing too challenging. For every IPA that ties your tongue in knots and every moody stout that makes you think deep thoughts, you need something easy-drinking. That something is this pale ale.

Make It Yours Stick with the malt base we have here, but have fun with the hops. While the Amarillo SMASH Ale on page 77 is a good one for testing out a single hop variety, this pale ale is a good recipe for testing combinations of hops to see how they work together.

Beers to Try Sierra Nevada Pale Ale (Sierra Nevada Brewing Co.), Dale's Pale Ale (Oskar Blues Brewing Company), Stone Pale Ale (Stone Brewing Company)

INGREDIENTS	1-GALLON	5-GALLON
White Labs California Ale yeast, Wyeast American Ale yeast, or equivalent	½ package	1 package
Pale ale malt, milled	1½ lbs (680 g)	7½ lbs (3.40 kg)
Crystal/Caramel 20 malt, milled	8 oz (227 g)	2½ lbs (1.13 kg)
Simcoe pellet hops (11.7% AA), for bittering	.10 oz (3 g)	.50 oz (14 g)
Simcoe pellet hops (11.7% AA), for flavoring	.15 oz (4 g)	.75 oz (21 g)
Irish moss	¼ tsp	1 tsp
Ahtanum pellet hops (5.6% AA), for aroma	.20 oz (5.50 g)	1 oz (28 g)
Corn sugar, for bottling	.80 oz (22 g)	4 oz (113 g)

TARGET ORIGINAL/FINAL GRAVITY: 1.052/1.012
TARGET ABV: 5.2%

Follow the master method for brewing 1-gallon or 5-gallon all-grain batches as described on pages 54–59 (5-gallon measurements in parentheses).

• Remove liquid yeast from the refrigerator and, if necessary, activate according to package instructions. Place on the counter to warm.

• Heat **1 gallon (or 3½ gallons) of water to 160°F**, then stir in the grains. Maintain a mash temperature of **148°F to 153°F** for 60 minutes. Raise the temperature of the mash to 170°F, then sparge using **1 gallon (or 3 gallons)** of 170°F water to make 1½ (or 5½) gallons wort.

• Bring to a boil over high heat. Add the Simcoe hops for bittering and boil vigorously for 40 minutes. Add the Simcoe hops for flavoring and the Irish moss and continue boiling for another 20 minutes. Add the Ahtanum hops and remove from the heat. (Total boil time: 60 minutes.)

• Cool to at least 75°F and transfer to a sanitized primary fermentation bucket. Add the yeast and aerate the wort.

• Let ferment for at least **1 week or up to 4 weeks at 70°F**; then transfer to a sanitized jug or carboy for secondary fermentation. Continue to ferment for another **2 weeks or up to 2 months at 70°F.**

• Dissolve the sugar in ¼ (or 1) cup of boiling water and let cool. Mix with the beer, bottle, and store for **2 weeks or up to a year.** Refrigerate before drinking.

Bitter Brit English-Style Pale Ale

With this beer and the Bitter Monk that follows, you can start to see how tweaking a few ingredients vastly changes the beer you're making. This recipe uses the same malt proportions as our Very Good American Pale Ale (page 71), but swaps the American pale malts for British malts as the base and uses an English variety of yeast—together these give the pale ale a milder, maltier profile. The Brits tend to shy away from hops, so I use a soft British hop to lay the bittering base, but then poke some fun at our friends across the pond with some Liberty hops from the United States.

Brew Notes If you like your pale ales on the bitter side and are brewing a 5-gallon batch, increase the bittering and flavoring hops to 1.25 ounces each.

Make It Yours Try any hops except citrusy US hops in this beer, just because that veers too far from a British-style pale ale and puts it in American territory. Woodsy Willamette hops or spicy Cluster hops both make nice riffs. You could also steep some black tea in the secondary for a few days for a truly British spin!

Beers to Try Whale's Tale Pale Ale (Cisco Brewers Inc.), Schlafly Pale Ale (The Saint Louis Brewery), St. Peter's Golden Ale (St. Peter's Brewery)

INGREDIENTS	1-GALLON	5-GALLON
White Labs London Ale yeast, Wyeast London Ale yeast, or equivalent	½ package	1 package
Maris Otter malt, milled	1½ lbs (680 g)	7½ lbs (3.40 kg)
Biscuit malt, milled	8 oz (227 g)	2½ lbs (1.13 kg)
East Kent Goldings pellet hops (7.2% AA), for bittering	.20 oz (5.5 g)	1 oz (28 g)
Liberty pellet hops (4.9% AA), for flavoring	.20 oz (5.5 g)	1 oz (28 g)
Irish moss	¼ tsp	1 tsp
Liberty pellet hops (4.9% AA), for aroma	.20 oz (5.5 g)	1 oz (28 g)
Corn sugar, for bottling	.80 oz (22 g)	4 oz (113 g)

TARGET ORIGINAL/FINAL GRAVITY: 1.054/1.014
TARGET ABV: 5.3%

Add the Liberty hops for flavoring and the Irish moss and continue boiling for another 20 minutes. Add the Liberty hops for aroma and remove from the heat. (Total boil time: 60 minutes.)

• Cool to at least 75°F and transfer to a sanitized primary fermentation bucket. Add the yeast and aerate the wort.

• Let ferment for at least **1 week or up to 4 weeks at 70°F**; then transfer to a sanitized jug or carboy for secondary fermentation. Continue to ferment for another **2 weeks or up to 2 months at 70°F**.

• Dissolve the sugar in ¼ (or 1) cup of boiling water and let cool. Mix with the beer, bottle, and store for **2 weeks or up to a year**. Refrigerate before drinking.

Follow the master method for brewing 1-gallon or 5-gallon all-grain batches as described on pages 54–59 (5-gallon measurements in parentheses).

• Remove liquid yeast from the refrigerator and, if necessary, activate according to package instructions. Place on the counter to warm.

• Heat **1 gallon (or 3½ gallons) of water to 160°F**, then stir in the grains. Maintain a mash temperature of **148°F to 153°F** for 60 minutes. Raise the temperature of the mash to 170°F, then sparge using **1 gallon (or 3 gallons)** of 170°F water to make 1½ (or 5½) gallons wort.

• Bring to a boil over high heat. Add the East Kent Goldings hops and boil vigorously for 40 minutes.

Bitter Monk Belgian-Style Pale Ale

Here's yet another direction you can go with your pale ales. Like the Bitter Brit (opposite), this Belgian-style pale ale uses the same proportions of malts as A Very Good American Pale Ale (page 71), but incorporates Belgian and German malts. These make the beer crisp and light, the perfect counterpoint to the spicy, fruity flavors brought by the Belgian saison yeast. I bring in some Mosaic hops to underscore those fruit flavors, along with Magnum hops to give the beer a bracing bitterness.

Brew Notes If you like your pale ales on the bitter side and are brewing a 5-gallon batch, increase the bittering hops to .50 ounce and the flavoring hops to 1 ounce.

Make It Yours Add some fresh summer fruit: blueberries add sweetness, while fruits like raspberries, apricots, blackberries, and kumquats take the beer in a tart and sassy direction. (Read more about adding fruit to your beers on page 166.)

Beers to Try Karma (Avery Brewing Company), Devotion Ale (The Lost Abbey), Rayon Vert Belgian-Style Pale Ale (Green Flash Brewing Co.)

INGREDIENTS	1-GALLON	5-GALLON
White Labs Saison I yeast, Wyeast Belgian Saison yeast, or equivalent	½ package	1 package
Pilsner malt (preferably Belgian pilsner), milled	1½ lbs (680 g)	7½ lbs (3.40 kg)
Munich malt, milled	8 oz (227 g)	2½ lbs (1.13 kg)
Magnum pellet hops (13.8% AA), for bittering	.07 oz (2 g)	.35 oz (10 g)
Mosaic pellet hops (11.5% AA), for flavoring	.15 oz (4 g)	.75 oz (21 g)
Irish moss	¼ tsp	1 tsp
Mosaic pellet hops (11.5% AA), for aroma	.15 oz (4 g)	.75 oz (21 g)
Corn sugar, for bottling	.80 oz (22 g)	4 oz (113 g)

TARGET ORIGINAL/FINAL GRAVITY: 1.052/1.014
TARGET ABV: 5%

Follow the master method for brewing 1-gallon or 5-gallon all-grain batches as described on pages 54–59 (5-gallon measurements in parentheses).

• Remove liquid yeast from the refrigerator and, if necessary, activate according to package instructions. Place on the counter to warm.

• Heat **1 gallon (or 3½ gallons) of water to 160°F**, then stir in the grains. Maintain a mash temperature of **148°F to 153°F** for 60 minutes. Raise the temperature of the mash to 170°F, then sparge using **1 gallon (or 3 gallons)** of 170°F water to make 1½ (or 5½) gallons wort.

• Bring to a boil over high heat. Add the Magnum hops and boil vigorously for 40 minutes. Add the Mosaic hops for flavoring and the Irish moss and continue boiling for another 20 minutes. Add the

Mosaic hops for aroma and remove from the heat. (Total boil time: 60 minutes.)

• Cool to at least 75°F and transfer to a sanitized primary fermentation bucket. Add the yeast and aerate the wort.

• Let ferment for at least **1 week or up to 4 weeks at 70°F**; then transfer to a sanitized jug or carboy for secondary fermentation. Continue to ferment for another **2 weeks or up to 2 months at 70°F**.

• Dissolve the sugar in ¼ (or 1) cup of boiling water and let cool. Mix with the beer, bottle, and store for **2 weeks or up to a year**. Refrigerate before drinking.

Pine Woods Pale Ale

How cool is it that you can literally go out into your backyard and find the ingredients to make beer? While this recipe calls for spruce tips, you can use the needles from any domestic cone-bearing pine tree: spruce, redwood, Douglas fir, and so on. The flavor of your beer also depends on when you harvest the tips. Collect them in the spring and early summer when the tips are still tender and bright green, and you'll make a beer that tastes more like soft citrus than pine. Harvest later in the season once the weather gets cold, and you'll get more resinous and piney "Christmas tree" flavors.

Brew Notes When you go out foraging, take just the first inch off the tip of the pine bough and avoid any trees that have been sprayed or treated with pesticides. Spruces, firs, redwoods, and Douglas firs are all safe for culinary purposes; do not use yew and poison hemlock.

Make It Yours Make this a full-on gruit by getting rid of the hops and adding another dose of spruce tips at the beginning of the boil. You can read more about this hop-free style of beer in the recipe for Farmers' Market Gruit on page 191. I also like this ale with some darker malts in the mix. Adding brown malts or darker Crystal malts make it more appropriate for fall and winter.

Beers to Try Alaskan Winter Ale (Alaskan Brewing Co.), Mad Scientists Series #10: Spruce Tip Ale (Sixpoint Brewery), Alba Scots Pine Ale (Williams Brothers Brewing Company)

INGREDIENTS	1-GALLON	5-GALLON
White Labs California Ale yeast, Wyeast American Ale yeast, or equivalent	½ package	1 package
Pale ale malt, milled	1½ lbs (680 g)	7½ lbs (3.40 kg)
Crystal/Caramel 20 malt, milled	8 oz (227 g)	2½ lbs (1.13 kg)
Chinook pellet hops (11.4% AA), for bittering	.15 oz (4 g)	.75 oz (21 g)
Spruce tips, rinsed of any grit, for flavoring	.75 oz (21 g)	3.75 oz (106 g)
Irish moss	¼ tsp	1 tsp
Spruce tips, rinsed of any grit, for aroma	.75 oz (21 g)	3.75 oz (106 g)
Corn sugar, for bottling	.80 oz (22 g)	4 oz (113 g)

**TARGET ORIGINAL/FINAL GRAVITY: 1.052/1.012
TARGET ABV: 5.2%**

Follow the master method for brewing 1-gallon or 5-gallon all-grain batches as described on pages 54–59 (5-gallon measurements in parentheses).

• Remove liquid yeast from the refrigerator and, if necessary, activate according to package instructions. Place on the counter to warm.

• Heat **1 gallon (or 3½ gallons) of water to 160°F**, then stir in the grains. Maintain a mash temperature of **148°F to 153°F** for 60 minutes. Raise the temperature of the mash to 170°F, then sparge using **1 gallon (or 3 gallons)** of 170°F water to make 1½ (or 5½) gallons wort.

• Bring to a boil over high heat. Add the Chinook hops and boil vigorously for 40 minutes. Add the spruce tips for flavoring and the Irish moss and continue boiling for another 20 minutes. Add the spruce tips for aroma and remove from the heat. (Total boil time: 60 minutes.)

• Cool to at least 75°F and transfer to a sanitized primary fermentation bucket. Add the yeast and aerate the wort.

• Let ferment for at least **1 week or up to 4 weeks at 70°F**; then transfer to a sanitized jug or carboy for secondary fermentation. Continue to ferment for another **2 weeks or up to 2 months at 70°F**.

• Dissolve the sugar in ¼ (or 1) cup of boiling water and let cool. Mix with the beer, bottle, and store for **2 weeks or up to a year**. Refrigerate before drinking.

Amarillo SMASH Pale Ale

No, we're not about to go Incredible Hulk on this beer—the kind of SMASH we're talking about is "Single Malt And Single Hop." This style is often used to isolate a single hop, malt, or yeast so you can understand what makes it unique, like the Amarillo hops we use here. Stripped of distracting frills, you can really home in on the flavors and characteristics of each ingredient. But even though this is a great teaching beer, never fear—it's a mighty fine drinking beer, too.

Make It Yours If your homebrewing store starts carrying a new kind of hop, this should be your go-to recipe. When subbing hops, use the hop conversion equation on page 12 or beer-brewing software to make sure the bitterness stays balanced. As a pale ale, this beer gives a fairly simple malt profile that's perfect for showcasing hops, but you can also use it to test a new variety of malt or strain of yeast.

Beers to Try Amarillo Single Hop IPA (Mikkeller), Single Hop Citra Imperial IPA (Flying Dog Brewery)

INGREDIENTS	1-GALLON	5-GALLON
White Labs California Ale yeast, Wyeast American Ale yeast, or equivalent	½ package	1 package
Pale ale malt, milled	2 lbs (907 g)	10 lbs (4.54 kg)
Amarillo pellet hops (8.2% AA), for bittering	.20 oz (5.50 g)	1 oz (28 g)
Amarillo pellet hops (8.2% AA), for flavoring	.15 oz (4 g)	.75 oz (21 g)
Irish moss	¼ tsp	1 tsp
Amarillo pellet hops (8.2% AA), for aroma	.15 oz (4 g)	.75 oz (21 g)
Corn sugar, for bottling	.80 oz (22 g)	4 oz (113 g)

TARGET ORIGINAL/FINAL GRAVITY: 1.052/1.011
TARGET ABV: 5.4%

Follow the master method for brewing 1-gallon or 5-gallon all-grain batches as described on pages 54–59 (5-gallon measurements in parentheses).

• Remove liquid yeast from the refrigerator and, if necessary, activate according to package instructions. Place on the counter to warm.

• Heat **1 gallon (or 3½ gallons) of water to 160°F**, then stir in the grains. Maintain a mash temperature of **148°F to 153°F** for 60 minutes. Raise the temperature of the mash to **170°F**, then sparge using **1 gallon (or 3 gallons)** of 170°F water to make 1½ (or 5½) gallons wort.

• Bring to a boil over high heat. Add the hops for bittering and boil vigorously for 40 minutes. Add the hops for flavoring and the Irish moss and continue boiling for another 20 minutes. Add the hops for aroma and remove from the heat. (Total boil time: 60 minutes.)

• Cool to at least 75°F and transfer to a sanitized primary fermentation bucket. Add the yeast and aerate the wort.

• Let ferment for at least **1 week or up to 4 weeks at 70°F**; then transfer to a sanitized jug or carboy for secondary fermentation. Continue to ferment for another **2 weeks or up to 2 months at 70°F**.

• Dissolve the sugar in ¼ (or 1) cup of boiling water and let cool. Mix with the beer, bottle, and store for **2 weeks or up to a year**. Refrigerate before drinking.

WHAT TO WORRY ABOUT, WHAT NOT TO WORRY ABOUT

When you first start brewing beer, everything is unfamiliar. How do you know what the "hot break" looks like? What happens if you forgot to sanitize that spoon before stirring the wort? How do you know if you're doing it right at all?

Some of these things you just need to learn by doing; the more you brew, the more these totally foreign concepts start to feel second nature. But as you head into your first few batches, I'd like to do what I can to alleviate at least some of your worries. Here is my advice for what you should worry about and when you can relax.

WORRY ABOUT cleanliness and sanitation. Errant bacteria and wild yeast are the nemesis of good beer, therefore clean and sanitized equipment should be your top priority. Don't cut corners. Fill your fermentation bucket with sanitizer and sanitize everything that will come in contact with your wort or beer: bucket lid, air lock, stirring spoons, hoses—everything. Also, remember that cleaning and sanitizing are not the same; if your equipment is still gunky from past brew days, clean it thoroughly with soap and water before sanitizing.

DON'T WORRY ABOUT accidental sanitation slipups. All this said, random accidental slipups will not ruin your beer. If you suddenly realize that you're stirring your beer with an unsanitized spoon, don't automatically dump the batch. Yes, there's a risk that you've introduced some bacteria, but if you've been paying attention to cleanliness and sanitation all along, the beer is most likely fine.

WORRY ABOUT having the right equipment. Your brew day will go so much more smoothly and be so much more fun if you have the right equipment. Get the right size brew pot. Get a big enough strainer. Get what you need to brew a batch of beer and don't try to make do with less. Start with 1-gallon batches if you're not ready to commit to the cost of 5-gallon equipment.

DON'T WORRY ABOUT having all the fancy gadgets. You don't need fancy gadgets to brew a good batch of beer. People were brewing beer way before there were heat exchangers

for cooling down the wort or refractometers for checking the sugar content. These things can help improve your beer down the road, but when you're just getting started, focus on the basics.

DON'T WORRY if the mash temperature goes a little high or low. Let's be real here: keeping a big mass of liquid and grain within a tiny temperature range on a home stove for an hour or more is not the easiest task. If your beer gets a little warm or cool, it will be fine. The extremes you need to worry about are 143°F to 158°F. Stay within this range, and you're golden. Go above or below and you won't extract enough sugar to ferment the beer; high temperatures can also extract bitter tannins from the grains. If you had trouble with high or low temperatures, mash a little longer to make sure you've extracted all the sugars you can. (See "Get Geeky with the Mash," page 102, for more details on how mash temperature affects your beer.)

DON'T WORRY if it takes more than 20 minutes to cool your wort. If it takes a little longer to cool your wort, it will mostly likely be fine. Yes, the risk of bacteria contamination increases. And yes, you might have some haziness in your finished beer. But the likelihood of bacterial contamination at a homebrewing level is pretty low even if you take an hour or more to chill your beer. And haze isn't pretty, but it won't affect your beer's flavor.

DON'T WORRY ABOUT hitting the original gravity exactly. The original gravity of your beer is an indicator of how much sugar is in the wort; it's not an indicator of how good your beer will taste or the success (or failure) of your beer. The target original gravity is an ideal situation, but it can be affected by any number of things. In fact, when you first start out, you probably won't hit the original gravity. Don't sweat it. Once you've mastered the brewing basics, then you can start closing in on that original gravity bull's-eye.

DON'T WORRY ABOUT adding too much or too little yeast. These days, packages of dry and liquid yeasts contain the perfect amount of yeast to ferment a 5-gallon batch of beer. If you're brewing 5 gallons, you can add the entire package of yeast to the beer and walk away worry-free. If you're brewing 1-gallon batches, use half the amount of yeast in the package. If you add a little more or a little less than half, it's fine. It's easy to start nerding out about the exact "pitch rate" (that is, the number of yeast cells needed to ferment a batch of beer), but at a beginner level, it's not something to fret over. If your beer ferments, it's all good.

WORRY ABOUT your beer fermenting at all. If you see zero signs of fermentation within the first few days after brewing, there's a problem. If 48 hours have passed and you haven't seen a single bubble come through the water in your air lock, it's time to read "Common Problems, Easy Solutions," page 218.

DON'T WORRY if fermentation seems to stop after the first few days. Most of the active fermentation happens in the first few days of brewing. It starts slowly on day one, then gets really active (lots of bubbles in the air lock!) for a few days, and then quickly tapers off. Don't panic if it feels like fermentation has suddenly stopped. It just means that the yeast has eaten most of the simple sugars and started working on the more complex sugars. Action slows way down at this point.

DON'T WORRY ABOUT transferring some sediment from the primary to the secondary. The main reason for transferring beer from the primary to the secondary is to move it off the thick layer of sediment that collects on the bottom after those first few frenzied days of fermentation. If you transfer a little sediment while moving the beer, it's fine. You've removed the majority and the little bit you transfer will quickly settle on the bottom of the secondary jug. It's not enough to affect the beer's flavor.

WORRY ABOUT bottling too soon. It's tempting to rush through the primary and secondary fermentation and bottle your beer early so that you can get to the fun part of drinking it. Yes, you'll get a fizzy, alcoholic beer if you do this, but you'll enjoy the flavor a lot more if you stick to the recommended

times. Some complex sugars and other compounds take a while for the yeast to break down. Your beer will also be clearer and less hazy the longer you wait to bottle. Beer can taste oddly sharp and bitter right after bottling; wait 2 to 3 weeks for this to settle. Channel your inner Buddhist and practice patience.

DON'T WORRY if you can't to transfer or bottle the beer right away. While you shouldn't bottle or drink your beer too early, most beer does fine (or improves!) if it sits a little longer than strictly necessary. Ideally, you should transfer it to the secondary within a month to avoid picking up off flavors from the sediment, but then the beer will be fine for quite a while. If you wait more than 3 months to bottle, you might have trouble with carbonation because the yeast has gone dormant; add a dose of fresh yeast when you bottle to be sure the beer carbonates.

MOST OF ALL, DON'T WORRY if your first beer isn't perfect. Like your first time doing anything new, it's highly unlikely that your first beer will go off without a hitch. Everything is new, and no amount of me explaining how to brew, or you reading about it, will replace the experience of actually brewing. You'll get better. Aim for drinkable with your first batch and move up from there.

Distance does not always make the heart grow fonder—sometimes it grows very bitter indeed. The India pale ale was originally a malty and only mildly bitter British style of beer (check out the recipe for High Seas British IPA on page 124 for the history lesson), but once it leaped the pond to the United States, the IPA turned into the uniquely bitter brew that we now know and love. In the hands of American brewers armed with American hops, IPAs shed their refined, well-mannered nature and picked up the tongue-twisting flavors of pine resin, grapefruit, and lemon zest. You would hardly recognize these two beers as cousins.

This is an extremely fun style to play with, as its popularity with both brewers and drinkers can attest. A big dose of hops makes an IPA bitter, yes, but depending on which hops you use and when you add them, your beer can also take on the flavors and aromas of sun-ripened apricots, a meadow of wildflowers, juicy pineapple, pine trees, fresh orange juice, or even lemon candy. Adding more malts also bumps up the alcohol and allows you to stuff even more hops into a bottle. Don't let "bitterness" be your only goal here; there's a great big world of IPA fun out there.

INDIA PALE ALES (IPAS)

— [chapter 5] —

A VERY GOOD IPA

If you've never brewed an IPA before, start here. This one has all the hallmarks of a classic American IPA: smooth malt backbone, bright citrusy hops, and a touch of warming alcohol. It's not going to hit you over the head with bitterness, but there are enough hops here to make you pay attention. Once you're ready for more hop fun, read through "Play with Your Hops," page 116, and go to town

Make It Yours The bitterness is fairly in check with this beer; if you like hoppier IPAs, increase the bittering hops to .35 ounce (1.75 ounces). Also, try dry-hopping this one: add a handful of Cascade hops to the secondary to give your beer a boost of aroma without any bitterness. To make this an IPA SMASH experiment, get rid of the Crystal malts and pick one single hop to use. (Check out the Amarillo SMASH Pale Ale on page 77 for more on this style of beer.)

Beers to Try Two Hearted Ale (Bell's Brewery), HopDevil Ale (Victory Brewing Company), Blind Pig IPA (Russian River Brewing Company)

Follow the master method for brewing 1-gallon or 5-gallon all-grain batches as described on pages 54–59 (5-gallon measurements in parentheses).

• Remove liquid yeast from the refrigerator and, if necessary, activate according to package instructions. Place on the counter to warm.

• Heat **1 gallon (or 4 gallons)** of water to **160°F**, then stir in the grains. Maintain a mash temperature of **148°F to 153°F** for 60 minutes. Raise the temperature of the mash to 170°F, then sparge using **1 gallon (or 2½ gallons)** of 170°F water to make 1½ (or 5½) gallons wort.

• Bring to a boil over high heat. Add the Centennial hops and boil vigorously for 40 minutes. Add the Cascade hops for flavoring and the Irish moss and continue boiling for another 20 minutes. Add the Cascade hops for aroma and remove from the heat. (Total boil time: 60 minutes.)

INGREDIENTS	1-GALLON	5-GALLON
White Labs California Ale yeast, Wyeast American Ale yeast, or equivalent	½ package	1 package
Pale ale malt, milled	2½ lbs (1.13 kg)	12½ lbs (5.67 kg)
Crystal/Caramel 40 malt, milled	4 oz (113 g)	1¼ lbs (567 g)
Centennial pellet hops (9.2% AA), for bittering	.25 oz (7 g)	1.25 oz (35.50 g)
Cascade pellet hops (6.7% AA), for flavoring	.25 oz (5.5 g)	1.25 oz (35.50 g)
Irish moss	¼ tsp	1 tsp
Cascade pellet hops (6.7% AA), for aroma	.20 oz (5.5 g)	1 oz (28 g)
Corn sugar, for bottling	.80 oz (22 g)	4 oz (113 g)

TARGET ORIGINAL/FINAL GRAVITY: 1.072/1.017
TARGET ABV: 7.4%

• Cool to at least 75°F and transfer to a sanitized primary fermentation bucket. Add the yeast and aerate the wort.

• Let ferment for at least **1 week or up to 4 weeks** at **70°F**; then transfer to a sanitized jug or carboy for secondary fermentation. Continue to ferment for another **2 weeks or up to 2 months** at 70°F.

• Dissolve the sugar in ¼ (or 1) cup of boiling water and let cool. Mix with the beer, bottle, and store for **2 weeks or up to a year**. Refrigerate before drinking.

Centennial Dry-Hopped Double IPA

A double IPA is a chicken-and-egg scenario: Are you adding more malts to get a boozier brew, which then requires more hops to keep everything balanced? Or are you bringing in more malts because you secretly want to stuff every last ounce of hops possible into your beer? (Because more hops = more better, obviously.) This double IPA is a personal favorite. Centennial hops are fantastic added at any point in the brewing process, so here I add them continuously—every 10 minutes—during the hop boil. One last dose of hops goes directly into the secondary fermenter (aka "dry hopping"), giving the beer a perfumey citrus aroma that signals all the good things still to come in the glass.

Make It Yours Go to town with the hops here. Mix and match throughout the hop boil, then add something with real aroma power when you dry-hop. This malt base can handle just about any hop or combination of hops you throw at it.

Beers to Try Founders Centennial IPA (Founders Brewing Company), Pliny the Elder (Russian River Brewing Company), Bell's Hopslam Ale (Bell's Brewing Company)

INGREDIENTS	1-GALLON	5-GALLON
White Labs California Ale yeast, Wyeast American Ale yeast, or equivalent	½ package	1 package
Pale ale malt, milled	2 lbs (907 g)	10 lbs (4.54 kg)
Crystal/Caramel 20 malt, milled	1 lb (454 g)	5 lbs (2.27 kg)
Centennial pellet hops (9.2% AA), for bittering	.25 oz (7 g)	1.25 oz (35.50 g)
Centennial pellet hops (9.2% AA), divided into 5 portions, for flavoring	.50 oz (14 g)	2.50 oz (80 g)
Irish moss	¼ tsp	1 tsp
Centennial pellet hops (9.2% AA), for aroma	.15 oz (4 g)	.75 oz (21 g)
Centennial pellet hops (9.2% AA), for dry hopping	.15 oz (4 g)	.75 oz (21 g)
Corn sugar, for bottling	.80 oz (22 g)	4 oz (113 g)

TARGET ORIGINAL/FINAL GRAVITY: 1.077/1.017
TARGET ABV: 7.9%

Follow the master method for brewing 1-gallon or 5-gallon all-grain batches as described on pages 54–59 (5-gallon measurements in parentheses).

• Remove liquid yeast from the refrigerator and, if necessary, activate according to package instructions. Place on the counter to warm.

• Heat **1 gallon (or 5 gallons) of water to 160°F**, then stir in the grains. Maintain a mash temperature of **148°F to 153°F for 60 minutes**. Raise the temperature of the mash to 170°F, then sparge using **1 gallon (or 2 gallons)** of 170°F water to make 1½ (or 5½) gallons wort.

• Bring to a boil over high heat. Add the hops for bittering and boil vigorously for 10 minutes.

• Add one portion of the hops for flavoring every 10 minutes for the next 40 minutes. Add the last addition of flavoring hops and the Irish moss and boil a final 10 minutes. Add the hops for aroma and remove from the heat. (Total boil time: 60 minutes.)

• Cool to at least 75°F and transfer to a sanitized primary fermentation bucket. Add the yeast and aerate the wort.

• Let ferment for at least **1 week or up to 4 weeks at 70°F**; then transfer to a sanitized jug or carboy for secondary fermentation. Continue to ferment for another **2 weeks or up to 2 months at 70°F**.

• Two to seven days before you plan to bottle, place the hops for dry hopping in a small sanitized mesh bag and add to the secondary. Do not let sit longer than a week.

• Dissolve the sugar in ¼ (or 1) cup of boiling water and let cool. Mix with the beer, bottle, and store for **2 weeks or up to a year**. Refrigerate before drinking.

Double-Take Black IPA

A black IPA is meant to trick your eyes and make your taste buds think twice. What you see is a malty, pitch black stout that is sure to stick to your ribs. But what you taste is a crisp, piney nose-punch of an IPA with a touch of roastiness. What makes this feat of brewing legerdemain possible? A secret ingredient called black roasted barley. A handful of this added to your favorite India pale ale and you have yourself a bona fide black IPA.

Make It Yours Use this dark-hued beer as a cover for sneaking in fruits that pair well with IPAs but would otherwise turn it a very odd color. Think blackberries, cranberries, and pomegranates. (Read more about adding fruit to your on page 166.) You could also take things one step further and add smoked malts along with the black roasted barley. Don't go too far—add just enough to get a hint of woodsy smoke.

Beers to Try Hop in the Dark (Deschutes Brewery), Back in Black (21st Amendment Brewery), DogZilla Black IPA (Laughing Dog Brewing)

INGREDIENTS	1-GALLON	5-GALLON
White Labs California Ale yeast, Wyeast American Ale yeast, or equivalent	½ package	1 package
pale ale malt, milled	2 lbs (907 g)	10 lbs (4.54 kg)
Crystal/Caramel 80 malt, milled	8 oz (227 g)	2½ lbs (1.13 kg)
Carafa II malt, milled	4 oz (113 g)	1¼ lbs (567 g)
Chinook pellet hops (11.4% AA), for bittering	.20 oz (5.5 g)	1 oz (28 g)
Chinook pellet hops (11.4% AA), for flavoring	.15 oz (4 g)	.75 oz (21 g)
Irish moss	¼ tsp	1 tsp
Ahtanum pellet hops (5.6% AA), for aroma	.20 oz (5.50 g)	1 oz (28 g)
corn sugar, for bottling	.80 oz (22 g)	4 oz (113 g)

TARGET ORIGINAL/FINAL GRAVITY: 1.070/1.015
TARGET ABV: 7.3%

Follow the master method for brewing 1-gallon or 5-gallon all-grain batches as described on pages 54–59 (5-gallon measurements in parentheses).

• Remove liquid yeast from the refrigerator and, if necessary, activate according to package instructions. Place on the counter to warm.

• Heat **1 gallon (or 4½ gallons) of water to 160°F**, then stir in the grains. Maintain a mash temperature of **148°F to 153°F** for 60 minutes. Raise the temperature of the mash to 170°F, then sparge using **1 gallon (or 2½ gallons) of 170°F** water to make 1½ (or 5½) gallons wort.

• Bring to a boil over high heat. Add the Chinook hops for bittering and boil vigorously for 40 minutes. Add the Chinook hops for flavoring and the Irish moss and continue boiling for another 20 minutes. Add the Ahtanum hops and remove from the heat. (Total boil time: 60 minutes.)

• Cool to at least 75°F and transfer to a sanitized primary fermentation bucket. Add the yeast and aerate the wort.

• Let ferment for at least **1 week or up to 4 weeks at 70°F**; then transfer to a sanitized jug or carboy for secondary fermentation. Continue to ferment for another **2 weeks or up to 2 months at 70°F**.

• Dissolve the sugar in ¼ (or 1) cup of boiling water and let cool. Mix with the beer, bottle, and store for **2 weeks or up to a year**. Refrigerate before drinking.

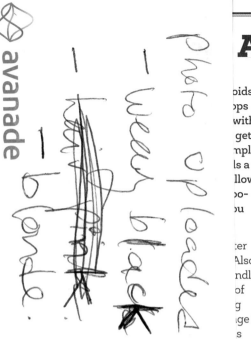
American Barleywine

INGREDIENTS	1-GALLON	5-GALLON
White Labs California IV Ale yeast, Wyeast American Ale II yeast, or equivalent, divided	1 package, divided	2 packages, divided
Light dried malt extract	.90 oz (25 g or 2 heaping Tbsps)	3.50 oz (100 g or ½ cup)
Pale ale malt, milled	3 lbs (1.36 kg)	15 lbs (6.80 kg)
Crystal/Caramel 40 malt, milled	12 oz (340 g)	3¾ lbs (1.70 kg)
Apollo pellet hops (18% AA), for bittering	.20 oz (5.50 g)	1 oz (28 g)
Apollo pellet hops (18% AA), for flavoring	.20 oz (5.50 g)	1 oz (28 g)
Irish moss	¼ tsp	1 tsp
Cascade pellet hops (6.7% AA), for aroma	.20 oz (5.5 g)	1 oz (28 g)
Corn sugar, for bottling	.70 oz (20 g)	3.50 oz (100 g)

TARGET ORIGINAL/FINAL GRAVITY: 1.097/1.025
TARGET ABV: 9.6%

oids.
ops
with
get
mplex
ls a
llow
oo-
ou

ter
Also,
ndle
of
g
ge 9).
s

before bottling, add an extra dose of yeast when you bottle to ensure carbonation.

Make It Yours Soak oak cubes in rum, brandy, or even Grand Marnier, and add them to the secondary. Or play up the fruity flavors in the finished beer by adding rum-soaked dried cherries, raisins, or apricots. (Read more about adding oak cubes and fruit to your beers on page 166.)

Beers to Try Stone Old Guardian Barley Wine (Stone Brewing Co.), Old Ruffian Barley Wine (Great Divide Brewing Company)

Follow the master method for brewing 1-gallon or 5-gallon all-grain batches as described on pages 54–59 (5-gallon measurements in parentheses).

• Using ½ (or 1) package of the yeast and the malt extract, make a yeast starter 12 to 18 hours before you plan to brew, following the instructions in "How to Make a Yeast Starter," page 16.

• Heat 1¼ (or 6 ½) gallons of water to 160°F, then stir in the grains. Maintain a mash temperature of 148°F to 153°F for 60 minutes. Raise the temperature of the mash to 170°F, then sparge using 1 gallon (or 2 gallons) of 170°F water to make 1½ (or 5½) gallons wort.

• Bring to a boil over high heat. Add the Apollo hops for bittering and boil vigorously for 40 minutes. Add the Apollo hops for flavoring and the Irish moss and continue boiling for another 20 minutes. Add the Cascade hops and remove from the heat. (Total boil time: 60 minutes.)

• Cool to at least 75°F and transfer to a sanitized primary fermentation bucket. Add the yeast starter and aerate the wort.

• Let ferment for at least **1 week or up to 4 weeks at 70°F**; then transfer to a sanitized jug or carboy for secondary fermentation. Continue to ferment for another **3 months or up to 1 year at 70°F**.

• Dissolve the sugar in ¼ (or 1) cup of boiling water and let cool. Mix ½ (or 1) package of yeast and the sugar mixture into the beer. Bottle and store for **1 month or up to a year**. Refrigerate before drinking.

Campari IPA

At The Kitchn, the homecooking website where I write and edit, we have a mild obsession with Campari. This bright red and intensely bitter herbal liqueur can be sipped on its own as an aperitif or digestif, but Campari is extra delicious when mixed with gin, prosecco, or even, say, an IPA. You'd think the combination of bitter liqueur and bitter beer would be too much bitter to handle, but this unlikely combination has become one of our favorite 5 o'clock sips. Consider this homebrewed version a bottled cocktail and sip it from coupe glasses before an al fresco summer dinner.

Make It Yours For a stronger botanical bitterness, increase the Campari to 20 ounces (or 100 ounces for 5-gallon batches). This results in more bottles of beer, so sanitize a few extra. If you're not a fan of Campari, try its milder cousin Aperol or the slightly sweeter Gran Classico.

Beer to Try Sixty-One Minute IPA (Dogfish Head Craft Brewery)

INGREDIENTS	1-GALLON	5-GALLON
White Labs California Ale yeast, Wyeast American Ale yeast, or equivalent	½ package	1 package
Pale ale malt, milled	2 lbs (907 g)	10 lbs (4.54 kg)
Biscuit malt, milled	8 oz (227 g)	2½ lbs (1.13 kg)
Bravo pellet hops (15.1% AA), for bittering	.15 oz (4 g)	.75 oz (21 g)
Chinook pellet hops (11.4% AA), for flavoring	.10 oz (3 g)	.50 oz (14 g)
Irish moss	¼ tsp	1 tsp
Chinook pellet hops (11.4% AA), for aroma	.20 oz (5.50 g)	1 oz (28 g)
Campari	10 oz (283 g)	50 oz (1.42 kg)
Corn sugar, for bottling	.80 oz (22 g)	4 oz (113 g)

TARGET ORIGINAL/FINAL GRAVITY: 1.065/1.013
TARGET ABV: 6.9%

Follow the master method for brewing 1-gallon or 5-gallon all-grain batches as described on pages 54–59 (5-gallon measurements in parentheses).

• Remove liquid yeast from the refrigerator and, if necessary, activate according to package instructions. Place on the counter to warm.

• Heat **1 gallon (or 4 gallons) of water to 160°F**, then stir in the grains. Maintain a mash temperature of **148°F to 153°F** for 60 minutes. Raise the temperature of the mash to 170°F, then sparge using **1 gallon (or 2½ gallons)** of 170°F water to make 1½ (or 5½) gallons wort.

• Bring to a boil over high heat. Add the Bravo hops and boil vigorously for 40 minutes. Add the Chinook hops for flavoring and the Irish moss and continue boiling for another 20 minutes. Add the Chinook hops for aroma and remove from the heat. (Total boil time: 60 minutes.)

• Cool to at least 75°F and transfer to a sanitized primary fermentation bucket. Add the yeast and aerate the wort.

• Let ferment for at least **1 week or up to 4 weeks at 70°F**; then transfer to a sanitized jug or carboy for secondary fermentation. Continue to ferment for another **2 weeks or up to 2 months at 70°F**.

• Dissolve the sugar in ¼ (or 1) cup of boiling water and let cool. Gently mix the Campari into the beer along with the sugar mixture before bottling. Bottle and store for **2 weeks or up to a year**. Refrigerate before drinking.

HOW TO POUR AND TASTE BEER

If you're going to brew beer, you'd better know how to drink it, proper-like. I'm not going to get all fussy on you here—if you like to drink out of the bottle or don't particularly feel like diving into a deep analysis of hop aroma, I respect that. But! I do think it's worth knowing the basics of pouring and tasting beer.

1. POUR YOUR BEER INTO A GLASS

The biggest reason to pour your beer in a glass is so that you can appreciate its aromas. Taste is actually a mix of aroma and flavor (as you know if you've ever had a head cold). If you drink from a bottle, you get only half of the experience. Plus, you put hard work into the aromas of your beer, not to mention its color and clarity! You don't want to miss these things now that the beer is done.

And as long as we're taking the trouble to pour our beer into a glass, make sure it's a clean one, okay? Remnants of other beverages muck up the flavors and prevent the foamy head from forming.

2. TILT THE GLASS AS YOU POUR

There are two ways to pour beer and both involve tilting the glass. You can tilt the glass at about a 45-degree angle from the get-go and slowly bring it upright as it fills, or you can start by pouring straight down, then tilt the glass once the head forms. Whichever option you choose, pour the beer against the side of the glass when tilting and aim a little above the surface of the liquid.

Tilting discourages foam formation and pouring straight down encourages it. Your goal with either approach is an inch or so of creamy foam on top of your beer. The foam is full of aromatic puffs of air and a big part of the overall beer-tasting experience. Personally, I like the second approach—straight down, then tilt. I like to pause midway through pouring, once the head has formed, and take a few deep sniffs while the aromas are concentrated in the glass.

3. HOLD THE SEDIMENT . . . OR NOT

Homebrews and unfiltered commercial beers have a little yeast sediment in the bottom. In general, stop pouring when there's about a half-inch of liquid left in the bottle; sediment clouds the beer and makes it taste a little different. However, there are some fun flavors in the yeast—if you like, pour it on in! Some styles, like hefeweizen, are traditionally served with the yeast sediment. I say, try your beer both ways and decide which you like best.

4. LOOK AT WHAT YOU'VE GOT

Hold your beer up to the light, preferably against a window with natural daylight. Check out its color and clarity: color is 100 percent about the malts you used in your beer; clarity is affected by factors such as whether you used clarifying agents (like Irish moss), how quickly you cooled the wort before pitching the yeast, fermentation temperature, and how much sediment was transferred to the bottles.

If you're in a note-taking mood, jot down a few thoughts: Is the beer as clear as you'd like? Does the color look as you expected it to? If not, flip back to your brew day notes and see if you can spot any errors. Maybe the store was out of a malt you wanted and you had to sub in something a shade darker, or maybe you forgot to add the Irish moss at the right time. If everything went as expected, jot down a note to try a different malt next time or tweak your brewing procedure.

5. TAKE A SNIFF

Take a few deep sniffs of your beer while the head is still thick and creamy. If you don't smell anything, try swirling the glass and then cupping your hand over it. Aromas are your indicators of how the beer will taste. Mostly, we're looking for hop aromas, which can range from citrusy to piney, earthy to floral. You might also smell some fruitiness, evidence of esters created by the yeast.

Make note of any aromas you don't like. This might be a particular hop or spice you don't care for, but bad aromas can also indicate problems in the beer. Check out "Common Problems, Easy Solutions," page 218, for answers.

6. DRINK DEEPLY

Finally! Yes! Take a sip! Let the beer wash over your entire tongue and hold it for a second before swallowing. Notice what's going on as you sip. For most beers, there's a distinct beginning, middle, and end—certain flavors you taste right off the bat at the tip of your tongue, which then change as the beer moves to the middle and sides, and the again when you swallow.

If you recall grade school science class, you'll remember that taste buds are distributed in sections around your tongue with distinct groups of sweet, sour, salty, and bitter receptors, all of which "taste" the beer differently and collectively form your overall taste experience.

Also take note of the way the beer feels in your mouth—smooth or prickly, light or heavy, silky or rough. You might sense hotness on your tongue, cheeks, or throat in a high-alcohol beer. You might notice a dryness or astringency like the dregs from a cup of tea.

None of these flavors or sensations are necessarily good or bad. Just observe them and take notes on what you like or don't like. As you get better at brewing and learn the cause-and-effect relationships, you can start to control how much or little of these flavors you create in your finished beer.

7. ENJOY YOUR BEER

Keep on sipping! As the beer warms and the carbonation lessens, new flavors emerge while others fade. Swirl your glass occasionally and check out the aromas. Notice how everything comes together: the aromas, the flavors, the feel of the beer in your mouth. Congrats, you're a bona fide beer geek now!

Brown ales are a hard style to pin down. Like a pale ale, brown ale is a bit of a catchall for any beer darker than an amber but not quite dark enough to call a porter. Browns tend to be malt-forward brews with nutty, roasty characteristics, but that doesn't mean they can't also handle some hops—especially woodsier hops from England or spicy German varieties.

I also love a brown ale as the base for spiced seasonal beers, like the Great Pumpkin Ale on page 99 or Chai-Spiced Winter Warmer on page 101. This style showcases the warm flavors of cinnamon, clove, ginger, and other baking spices so very well. It's like a tray of spiced holiday cookies in a bottle.

BROWN ALES

[chapter 6]

A VERY GOOD AMERICAN BROWN ALE

My idea of a good brown ale is something that gives a nod to the toasted brown bread flavors of a British mild ale but that pulls American hops into the party. It's a tricky balance, though: lean too much on the hops and a brown ale can taste like an off-kilter frankenbeer. In my version, high alpha-acid Columbus hops ensure a bracing bitterness against the malts while the Willamette hops lay a softer top note of deep woods evergreen.

Make It Yours If you love hops, double the amount of flavoring hops for a stronger bitterness. For an English-style brown ale, swap in English hops (East Kent Goldings and/or Fuggles) and increase the mash temperature to 154°F–158°F.

Beers to Try Smuttynose Old Brown Dog Ale (Smuttynose Brewing Company), Moose Drool Brown Ale (Big Sky Brewing Company), Indian Brown Ale (Dogfish Head Craft Brewery)

INGREDIENTS	1-GALLON	5-GALLON
White Labs British Ale yeast, Wyeast British Ale yeast, or equivalent	½ package	1 package
Pale ale malt, milled	1 lb (454 g)	5 lbs (2.27 kg)
Honey malt, milled	1 lb (454 g)	5 lbs (2.27 kg)
Crystal/Caramel 120 malt, milled	4 oz (113 g)	1¼ lbs (567 g)
Columbus pellet hops (16.3% AA), for bittering	.05 oz (1.50 g)	.25 oz (7 g)
Columbus pellet hops (16.3% AA), for flavoring	.05 oz (1.50 g)	.25 oz (7 g)
Irish moss	¼ tsp	1 tsp
Willamette pellet hops (4.7% AA), for aroma	.10 oz (3 g)	.50 oz (14 g)
Corn sugar, for bottling	.70 oz (20 g)	3.50 oz (100 g)

TARGET ORIGINAL/FINAL GRAVITY: 1.059/1.017
TARGET ABV: 5.5%

Follow the master method for brewing 1-gallon or 5-gallon all-grain batches as described on pages 54–59 (5-gallon measurements in parentheses).

• Remove liquid yeast from the refrigerator and, if necessary, activate according to package instructions. Place on the counter to warm.

• Heat **1 gallon (or 3½ gallons)** of water to **160°F**, then stir in the grains. Maintain a mash temperature of **148°F to 153°F** for 60 minutes. Raise the temperature of the mash to 170°F, then sparge using **1 gallon (or 3 gallons)** of 170°F water to make 1½ (or 5½) gallons wort.

• Bring to a boil over high heat. Add the Columbus hops for bittering and boil vigorously for 40 minutes. Add the Columbus hops for flavoring and the Irish moss and continue boiling for another 20 minutes. Add the Willamette hops and remove from the heat. (Total boil time: 60 minutes.)

• Cool to at least 75°F and transfer to the sanitized primary fermentation bucket. Add the yeast and aerate the wort.

• Let ferment for at least **1 week or up to 4 weeks at 70°F**; then transfer to a sanitized jug or carboy for secondary fermentation. Continue to ferment for another **2 weeks or up to 2 months at 70°F**.

• Dissolve the sugar in ¼ (or 1) cup of boiling water and let cool. Mix with the beer, bottle, and store for **2 weeks or up to a year**. Refrigerate before drinking.

Pecan Pie Brown Ale

I'm a huge fan of pecan pie, particularly the A+ version that my A+ husband makes every Thanksgiving. He insists he has no secrets, but the fact remains that his pecan pie woos even the severest of pie critics. I have relinquished all Thanksgiving pie–making duties to him, but I stake my own territory with this pecan-flavored beer. It's as rich and lush as a bite of pie with haunting flavors of real pecan and warm vanilla.

Brew Notes The oil from the roasted nuts prevents this beer from having much of a head, though adding flaked wheat helps. Additionally, the bittering hops are added before bringing the wort to a boil, a method called "first-wort hopping" that gives the beer a gentler bitterness. (See "Play with Your Hops," page 116, for more).

Make It Yours Do you like bourbon in your pecan pie? Add bourbon-soaked oak cubes to the secondary. Also, substitute any kind of nut that appeals to you. Nuts play well with chocolate flavors, so think about adding some cacao nibs too. (Read about adding oak cubes and spices on pages 167–68.)

Beers to Try Nut Brown Ale (Samuel Smith Brewing Co.), Messiah Nut Brown Ale (Shmaltz Brewing Company)

INGREDIENTS	1-GALLON	5-GALLON
Pecans	8 oz (227 g)	2½ lbs (1.13 kg)
White Labs British Ale yeast, Wyeast British Ale yeast, or equivalent	½ package	1 package
Maris Otter malt, milled	1½ lbs (680 g)	7½ lbs (3.40 kg)
Crystal/Caramel 60 malt, milled	8 oz (227 g)	2½ lbs (1.13 kg)
Flaked wheat	4 oz (113 g)	1¼ lbs (567 g)
Crystal/Caramel 120 malt, milled	2 oz (57 g)	10 oz (283 g)
East Kent Goldings pellet hops (7.2% AA), for bittering	.15 oz (4 g)	.75 oz (21 g)
East Kent Goldings pellet hops (7.2% AA), for flavoring	.05 oz (1.50 g)	.25 oz (7 g)
Irish moss	¼ tsp	1 tsp
Vanilla bean	1 whole	3 whole
Corn sugar, for bottling	.70 oz (20 g)	3.50 oz (100 g)

TARGET ORIGINAL/FINAL GRAVITY: 1.063/1.020
TARGET ABV: 5.7%

Follow the master method for brewing 1-gallon or 5-gallon all-grain batches as described on pages 54–59 (5-gallon measurements in parentheses).

• Preheat the oven to 350°F. Arrange the pecans on a baking sheet and roast for 8 to 12 minutes, stirring occasionally, until fragrant and slightly darkened. Coarsely chop and let cool completely.

• Remove liquid yeast from the refrigerator and, if necessary, activate according to package instructions. Place on the counter to warm.

• Heat **1 gallon (or 4 gallons) of water to 164°F**, then stir in the grains and the chopped pecans. Maintain a mash temperature of **154°F to 158°F** for 60 minutes. Raise the temperature of the mash to 170°F, then sparge using **1 gallon (or 2½ gallons)** of 170°F water to make 1½ (or 5½) gallons wort.

• Add the hops for bittering, then bring to a boil over high heat. Boil vigorously for 40 minutes. Add the hops for flavoring and the Irish moss and continue boiling for another 20 minutes. Remove from the heat. (Total boil time: 60 minutes.)

• Cool to at least 75°F and transfer to a sanitized primary fermentation bucket. Add the yeast and aerate the wort.

• Let ferment for at least **1 week or up to 4 weeks at 70°F**. When ready to transfer the beer for secondary fermentation, split the vanilla bean down its length and add it to the sanitized jug. Siphon the beer over top. Continue to ferment the beer for another **2 weeks or up to 2 months at 70°F**.

• Dissolve the sugar in ¼ (or 1) cup of boiling water and let cool. Mix with the beer, bottle, and store for **2 weeks or up to a year**. Refrigerate before drinking.

Brown Bear Seeks Honey Braggot

We all grow up sometime, and I can't help but think that all lovable bears from Pooh to Paddington eventually leave behind their honey pots and marmalade toast for something more "Papa Bear" in nature. Something like a braggot. This exceedingly old style of beer mixes honey into sweet wort to make what is essentially a beer-mead hybrid. You can base it off of any style, but I think honey and brown ales are natural companions—rather like bears and honeycomb. After all, just because a bear grows up doesn't mean he doesn't still like a little honey from time to time.

Brew Notes You'll need to make a yeast starter for this recipe to ensure good fermentation. Even so, the antiseptic properties of the honey and the high original gravity of this beer can make life difficult for the yeast. If fermentation seems sluggish in the first few days, add 1 teaspoon of yeast nutrient to the beer; it's available at any homebrew store with wine-making supplies.

Make It Yours Any beer style can be a base for a braggot, but some have more potential for awesomeness than others. Make a braggot with other brown ales, any British or Scottish ales, light lagers (especially maibock), saisons, or even very lightly hopped pale ales.

Beers to Try Biere de Miele (Rabbit's Foot Meadery), Bragget Honey Ale (Atlantic Brewing Company)

INGREDIENTS	1-GALLON	5-GALLON
White Labs British Ale yeast, Wyeast British Ale yeast, or equivalent	½ package	1 package
Light dried malt extract	.90 oz (25 g or 2 heaping tbsps)	3½ oz (100 g or ⅓ cup)
Honey	1 lb (454 g)	5 lbs (2.27 kg)
Maris Otter malt, milled	1 lb (454 g)	5 lbs (2.27 kg)
Biscuit malt, milled	8 oz (227 g)	2½ lbs (1.13 kg)
Crystal/Caramel 80 malt, milled	4 oz (113 g)	1¼ lbs (567 g)
Cluster pellet hops (6.8% AA), for bittering	.15 oz (4 g)	.75 oz (21 g)
Irish moss	¼ tsp	1 tsp
Palisade pellet hops (7.5% AA), for aroma	.15 oz (4 g)	.75 oz (21 g)
Corn sugar, for bottling	.70 oz (20 g)	3.50 oz (100 g)

TARGET ORIGINAL/FINAL GRAVITY: 1.081/1.007
TARGET ABV: 9.8%

Follow the master method for brewing 1-gallon or 5-gallon all-grain batches as described on pages 54–59 (5-gallon measurements in parentheses).

• Using the yeast, malt extract, and 1 tablespoon (or 5 tablespoons) of the honey, make a yeast starter 12 to 18 hours before you plan to brew, following the instructions in "How to Make a Yeast Starter," page 16.

• Heat **3 quarts (or 3 gallons) of water to 164°F**, then stir in the grains. Maintain a mash temperature of **154°F to 158°F for 60 minutes.** Raise the temperature of the mash to 170°F, then sparge

using **3 quarts (or 2½ gallons)** of 170°F water to make 1 gallon (or 5 gallons) wort. Stir in the remaining honey and add more 170°F water as needed to make 1½ (or 5½) gallons.

• Add the Cluster hops, then bring to a boil over high heat. Boil vigorously for 40 minutes. Add the Irish moss and continue boiling for another 20 minutes. Add the Palisade hops and remove from the heat. (Total boil time: 60 minutes.)

• Cool to at least 75°F and transfer to a sanitized primary fermentation bucket. Add the yeast starter and aerate the wort.

• Let ferment for at least **1 week or up to 4 weeks at 70°F**; then transfer to a sanitized jug or carboy for secondary fermentation. Continue to ferment for another **2 weeks or up to 2 months at 70°F.**

• Dissolve the sugar in ¼ (or 1) cup of boiling water and let cool. Mix with the beer, bottle, and store for **2 weeks or up to a year.** Refrigerate before drinking.

The Great Pumpkin Ale

A pumpkin ale can be a fine and glorious thing. Caramelizing chunks of pumpkin with brown sugar adds both flavor and fermentable sugars to a brew. Be careful when adding the spices—use a light hand. Your reward is something worthy of sipping from Halloween to Thanksgiving.

Make It Yours Not a fan of spiced beers? Brew without the spices and see what you think. Add Crystal or Saaz hops at the end of the boil for some spicy hop flavors and aromas. For more caramel flavor, boil the first runnings of the wort separately until reduced by half, then add them to the main boil. (Read more on this in "Get Geeky with the Mash," page 102.)

Beers to Try Pumking (Southern Tier Brewing Company), Pumpkick (New Belgium Brewing)

Follow the master method for brewing 1-gallon or 5-gallon all-grain batches as described on pages 54–59 (5-gallon measurements in parentheses).

• Preheat the oven to 425°F. Line a baking sheet with parchment paper. Peel the pumpkin and scoop out the seeds. Chop into pieces, toss with the brown sugar, and roast until very soft and browned, 30 to 40 minutes. Stir every 10 minutes.

• Remove liquid yeast from the refrigerator and, if necessary, activate according to package instructions. Place on the counter to warm.

• Heat **3 quarts (or 3½ gallons) of water to 160°F**, then stir in the grains and the pumpkin. Maintain a mash temperature of **148°F to 153°F** for 60 minutes. Raise the temperature of the mash to 170°F, then sparge using **1½ (or 3) gallons** of 170°F water to make 1½ (or 5½) gallons wort.

• Bring to a boil over high heat. Add the Crystal hops and boil vigorously for 40 minutes. Add the Saaz hops and the Irish moss and continue boiling for another 15 minutes. Add the cinnamon, clove(s), allspice, and nutmeg and boil another 5 minutes. Remove from the heat. (Total boil time: 60 minutes.)

• Cool to at least 75°F and transfer to a sanitized primary fermentation bucket. Add the yeast and aerate the wort.

INGREDIENTS	1-GALLON	5-GALLON
Sugar pumpkin or baking pumpkin	1½ to 2 lbs	5 lbs
Brown sugar	¼ cup (1¾ oz or 50 g)	1 cup (7 oz or 198g)
White Labs English Ale yeast, Wyeast London Ale III yeast, or equivalent	½ package	1 package
Maris Otter malt, milled	1¼ lbs (567 g)	6¼ lbs (2.84 kg)
Crystal/Caramel 20 malt, milled	8 oz (227 g)	2½ lbs (1.13 kg)
Crystal/Caramel 60 malt, milled	4 oz (113 g)	1¼ lbs (567 g)
Special B malt, milled	1 oz (28 g)	5 oz (142 g)
Chocolate malt, milled	.50 oz (14 g)	2.50 oz (71 g)
Crystal pellet hops (4.1% AA), for bittering	.20 oz (5.50 g)	1 oz (28 g)
Saaz pellet hops (2.9% AA), for flavoring	.20 oz (5.50 g)	1 oz (28 g)
Irish moss	¼ tsp	1 tsp
Cinnamon stick	½ whole	3 whole
Clove	1 whole	3 whole
Whole dried allspice berries	½ tsp	1 tsp
Freshly ground nutmeg	⅛ tsp	½ tsp
Corn sugar, for bottling	.80 oz (22 g)	4 oz (113 g)

TARGET ORIGINAL/FINAL GRAVITY: 1.055/1.019
TARGET ABV: 4.9%

• Let ferment for at least **1 week or up to 4 weeks at 70°F**; then transfer to a sanitized jug or carboy for secondary fermentation. Continue to ferment for another **2 weeks or up to 2 months at 70°F**.

• Taste the beer a few days before you plan to bottle. Add more of any of the spices, if you wish. Taste daily and bottle when the beer tastes good to you.

• Dissolve the sugar in ¼ (or 1) cup of boiling water and let cool. Mix with the beer, bottle, and store for **2 weeks or up to a year**. Refrigerate before drinking.

Chai-Spiced Winter Warmer

What's the best thing about winter? All the options for warming up once you're safe and snug inside. A mug of spicy chai tea is a personal favorite, but a pint of dark beer isn't a bad option either. I satisfy cravings for both with this winter warmer.

Brew Notes To get the most cardamom flavor, split the pods down the middle with a paring knife and crack them open a bit with your fingers before tossing everything—seeds, skin, and all—into the wort.

Make It Yours This makes a fantastic braggot, especially if you add a split vanilla bean in the secondary for a little extra warmth and sweetness. Take a look at the braggot recipe on page 98 for honey and malt ratios.

Beers to Try Great Lakes Christmas Ale (Great Lakes Brewing Company), Fireside Chat (21st Amendment Brewery).

INGREDIENTS	1-GALLON	5-GALLON
White Labs British Ale yeast, Wyeast British Ale yeast, or equivalent	½ package	1 package
Pale ale malt, milled	1¾ lbs (794 g)	8¾ lbs (3.97 kg)
Crystal/Caramel 40 malt, milled	8 oz (227 g)	2½ lbs (1.13 kg)
Crystal/Caramel 120 malt, milled	4 oz (113 g)	1¼ lbs (567 g)
Northern Brewer pellet hops (9.6% AA), for bittering	.10 oz (3 g)	.50 oz (14 g)
Crystal pellet hops (4.1% AA), for flavoring	.10 oz (3 g)	.50 oz (14 g)
Irish moss	¼ tsp	1 tsp
White cardamom pods, split	2 whole	8 whole
Peppercorns	¼ tsp	1 tsp
Cinnamon stick	½ whole	3 whole
Fresh ginger, peeled and grated	1-inch piece	3-inch piece
Clove	1 whole	3 whole
Crystal pellet hops (4.1% AA), for aroma	.15 oz (4 g)	.75 oz (21 g)
Corn sugar, for bottling	.80 oz (22 g)	4 oz (113 g)

TARGET ORIGINAL/FINAL GRAVITY: 1.064/1.018
TARGET ABV: 6.1%

Follow the master method for brewing 1-gallon or 5-gallon all-grain batches as described on pages 54–59 (5-gallon measurements in parentheses).

• Remove liquid yeast from the refrigerator and, if necessary, activate according to package instructions. Place on the counter to warm.

• Heat 1 gallon (or 4 gallons) of water to 160°F, then stir in the grains. Maintain a mash temperature of 148°F to 153°F for 60 minutes. Raise the temperature of the mash to 170°F, then sparge using 1 gallon (or 2½ gallons) of 170°F water to make 1½ (or 5½) gallons wort.

• Bring to a boil over high heat. Add the Northern Brewer hops and boil vigorously for 40 minutes. Add the Crystal hops for flavoring and the Irish moss and continue boiling for another 15 minutes. Add the cardamom, peppercorns, cinnamon, ginger, and clove(s) and boil another 5 minutes. Add the Crystal hops for aroma and remove from the heat. (Total boil time: 60 minutes.)

• Cool to at least 75°F and transfer to a sanitized primary fermentation bucket. Add the yeast and aerate the wort.

• Let ferment for at least 1 week or up to 4 weeks at 70°F; then transfer to a sanitized jug or carboy for secondary fermentation. Continue to ferment for another 2 weeks or up to 2 months at 70°F.

• Taste the beer a few days before you plan to bottle. Add more of any of the spices, if you wish. Taste daily and bottle when the beer tastes good to you.

• Dissolve the sugar in ¼ (or 1) cup of boiling water and let cool. Mix with the beer, bottle, and store for 2 weeks or up to a year. Refrigerate before drinking.

GET GEEKY WITH THE MASH

In many ways, the mash is the easiest and least technically challenging part of the brewing process. Just combine warm water with crushed grains and walk away. I don't want to overcomplicate this essentially stress-free step, but I do want to take a moment to talk about what's going on in that brew pot and how you can use this knowledge to benefit your brews.

ENZYMATIC REACTIONS IN YOUR MASH

While the mash may look like a big pot of steamy oatmeal, there's actually a lot of activity going on beneath the surface. When you mix the grains into the warm water, starches from the crushed grains start to dissolve. The dissolved starches are too long and complex to work as yeast food, so we have to allow time for enzymatic reactions to take place.

There are two enzymes that go to work once the starches are dissolved in the mash water: alpha-amylase and beta-amylase. These enzymes are naturally present in the grains and become active once you mix the grains with warm water. Their job is to chomp the long starch molecules into simple sugars and dextrins. Sugars are yeast food; yeasts aren't interested in dextrins, but they add body and sweetness to the beer. If we let the mash sit for about an hour, that's enough time for the enzymes to do their job and create a sugary feast for the yeast.

Ready for one more bit of enzyme knowledge? Okay! Alpha-amylase enzymes work best if you keep your mash temperature between 149°F and 153°F, and they stop working after about 2 hours at warmer temperatures. Meanwhile, beta-amylase enzymes prefer cooler temperatures (between 126°F and 144°F) and quit working after about an hour at temperatures above 144°F. Both enzymes work, albeit less enthusiastically, if you nudge them outside their ideal temperature zones. Since you need both

enzymes working in conjunction to get the best conversion of starch to sugar, a temperature compromise is necessary.

THE EFFECT OF MASH TEMPERATURE ON ENZYMES (AND YOUR BEER)

Despite their individual preferences, the full temperature range at which our starch-chomping enzymes reliably work is pretty big: 143°F to 158°F. Keep your mash within this range for about an hour and you'll get enough sugar to make beer. Phew!

Dial in that temperature a bit and we can start to fine-tune the effects in our finished beer. At the higher end, you produce a lot of sweet dextrins but less fermentable sugars; so beers mashed between 154°F and 158°F are sweeter and heavier-bodied with less alcohol. (Remember that sugars are what yeast eats to make alcohol; less sugar means less food for the yeast, which means less alcohol.) Conversely, beers mashed at the lower end make more sugars but less dextrins; so beers mashed between 143°F and 147°F make lighter-bodied, crisp-tasting beers with more alcohol.

As you might have noticed, there's a sweet spot in the middle. Beers mashed between 148°F and 153°F get the best of both worlds: a good amount of fermentable sugars to keep the yeast happy but also some dextrins to add body and flavor. It's a win-win, and that's why the vast majority of beers are brewed in this temperature range.

One last note: When I say that a high-temperature mash makes less alcohol and a low-temperature mash makes more, that's if we use the same recipe. A beer mashed at a high temperature can still have a high ABV if enough malts are used, and a beer mashed at a low temperature can still be sessionable if you decrease the malts.

BOILING THE FIRST RUNNINGS

There's one more way that you can increase the malty, caramel flavors in your beer without any extra fussing with temperature or worry over enzymes: boil the first runnings. The first runnings are the super concentrated wort we have when we first separate it from the grains but before we begin sparging. This undiluted wort is very rich and packed with sugars. If you boil these first runnings on their own, apart from the main wort, they will start to caramelize and develop lots of interesting toffee, nutty, and candy-like flavors.

You do this by setting aside the first ½ gallon of wort from a 1-gallon batch (or the first gallon from a 5-gallon batch) and then sparging the grains as usual. When you begin the hop boil with the main wort after sparging, also begin boiling the first runnings in a separate pot; hop only the main wort. Let the first runnings reduce until they are as syrupy and caramel-like as you desire, then pour them into the main wort and continue with the recipe.

You'll see this technique used most frequently with Scottish-style ales, like those in chapter 10, but it's a technique you can use anytime you'd like a little extra burst of caramelized candy sweetness in your beer.

BREW THE BEER YOU WANT TO DRINK

Knowing how these enzymes work and the relationship between mash temperature and the ratio of sugars to dextrins gives us the ability to make exactly the beer we want. No matter what mash temperature is given in your recipe, you can always change it, or you can try boiling the first runnings. You're the brewer, so you're in control! If you'd like a more full-bodied IPA, for instance, try bumping up the mash temperature in your next batch. Or, if you like the flavor of an IPA but want a crisper, drier mouthfeel, try mashing it around 145°F.

The chart below will help you figure out exactly how hot your strike water (the water getting mixed with the grains) should be before you add the malts in order achieve your desired final mash temperature. All calculations are based on a ratio of 1½ quarts of water to 1 pound of grain, which is the ratio used for the recipes in this book.

STRIKE TEMPERATURE	DESIRED MASH TEMPERATURE	RESULT
156°F	143°F–147°F	More fermentable sugars, less body
160°F	148°F–153°F	Balance of sugars and body
164°F	154°F–158°F	Less fermentable sugar, more body

Most of us probably think of porters and stouts as "those beers"—the ones that are dark and bitter and heavy. And, yes, some of them are. But many are silky smooth or crisp like a wafer or sweet as milk chocolate or surprisingly thirst-quenching or any number of other delicious characteristics. My point is that even though porters and stouts might look similar from the outside, they're as different as can be.

Porters came first, historically speaking. They were probably a slightly more robust version of British milds and brown ales. Stouts emerged on the scene when brewers decided to try upping the ante on their porters. The first stouts were actually called "stout porters," though the "porter" in the name was eventually dropped as stouts evolved into their own style. Today, there is still a lot of crossover between the two styles, though generally (but not always) stouts contain roasted barley or black patent malt for extra-roasty flavor and a darker color, while porters do not.

PORTERS AND STOUTS

[chapter 7]

A VERY GOOD PORTER

A good porter can be a nebulous target. You're going for something darker than a brown ale but not as opaque as a stout. You want a beer with some body but not so heavy or rich that it's no longer easily quaffable. It should be malty, certainly, but a touch of bitterness from either dark-roasted malts or bittering hops gives porters their balance. Steer toward the middle path here and I think you'll like what you get.

Make It Yours Porters make a good backdrop for flavor experimentation. Add some coconut to the secondary or throw in a handful of dried cherries. You can also make a very nice holiday beer by adding spices like cinnamon, nutmeg, and cloves. (Read more about adding fruit and spices on page 166.)

Beers to Try Black Butte Porter (Deschutes Brewing Company), Smuttynose Robust Porter (Smuttynose Brewing Company), Porter (Southern Tier Brewing Company)

INGREDIENTS	1-GALLON	5-GALLON
White Labs English Ale yeast, Wyeast London Ale yeast, or equivalent	½ package	1 package
Maris Otter malt, milled	1 lb (454 g)	5 lbs (2.27 kg)
Brown malt, milled	8 oz (227 g)	2½ lbs (1.13 kg)
Crystal/Caramel 40 malt, milled	4 oz (113 g)	1¼ lbs (567 g)
Chocolate malt, milled	1 oz (28 g)	5 oz (142 g)
East Kent Goldings pellet hops (7.2% AA), for bittering	.10 oz (3 g)	.50 oz (14 g)
East Kent Goldings pellet hops (7.2% AA), for flavoring	.10 oz (3 g)	.50 oz (14 g)
Irish moss	¼ tsp	1 tsp
East Kent Goldings pellet hops (7.2% AA), for aroma	.10 oz (3 g)	.50 oz (14 g)
Corn sugar, for bottling	.70 oz (20 g)	3.50 oz (100 g)

TARGET ORIGINAL/FINAL GRAVITY: 1.047/1.015
TARGET ABV: 4.2%

Follow the master method for brewing 1-gallon or 5-gallon all-grain batches as described on pages 54–59 (5-gallon measurements in parentheses).

• Remove liquid yeast from the refrigerator and, if necessary, activate according to package instructions. Place on the counter to warm.

• Heat **3 quarts (or 3 gallons) of water to 160°F**, then stir in the grains. Maintain a mash temperature of **148°F to 153°F** for 60 minutes. Raise the temperature of the mash to 170°F, then sparge using **1 gallon (or 3½ gallons)** of 170°F water to make 1½ (or 5½) gallons wort.

• Bring to a boil over high heat. Add the hops for bittering and boil vigorously for 40 minutes. Add the hops for flavoring and the Irish moss and continue boiling for another 20 minutes. Add the hops for aroma and remove from the heat. (Total boil time: 60 minutes.)

• Cool to at least 75°F and transfer to a sanitized primary fermentation bucket. Add the yeast and aerate the wort.

• Let ferment for at least **1 week or up to 4 weeks at 70°F**; then transfer to a sanitized jug or carboy for secondary fermentation. Continue to ferment for another **2 weeks or up to 2 months at 70°F**.

• Dissolve the sugar in ¼ (or 1) cup of boiling water and let cool. Mix with the beer, bottle, and store for **2 weeks or up to a year**. Refrigerate before drinking.

A VERY GOOD STOUT

Stouts are a solid, dependable beer, both from a drinking perspective and from a brewing perspective. This is a good style for new brewers to try because the dark color and deep-roasted flavor can hide a multitude of small mistakes, but stouts are equally beloved by veteran brewers for their versatility, adaptability, and incredible potential. A basic stout can be sweet or darkly bitter, rich or dry, sessionable or boozy, flavored with coffee and vanilla or left to stand on its own. Master a basic stout like this one and the possibilities are endless.

Make It Yours Mash this stout a little warmer if you'd like more body or cooler if you'd like it more crisp and light. Bumping up the Maris Otter malts takes this closer to an imperial stout, or swap them for pale ale malts and use US hops for an American-style stout.

Beers to Try Heart of Darkness (Magic Hat Brewing Company), Bell's Kalamazoo Stout (Bell's Brewery)

INGREDIENTS	1-GALLON	5-GALLON
White Labs London Ale yeast, Wyeast London Ale yeast, or equivalent	½ package	1 package
Maris Otter malt, milled	2 lbs (907 g)	10 lbs (4.54 kg)
Flaked barley	4 oz (113 g)	1¼ lbs (567 g)
Chocolate malt, milled	2.50 oz (71 g)	12.50 oz (354 g)
Roasted barley malt, milled	2.50 oz (71 g)	12.50 oz (354 g)
Fuggles pellet hops (5.3% AA), for bittering	.50 oz (14 g)	2.50 oz (71 g)
Irish moss	¼ tsp	1 tsp
Fuggles pellet hops (5.3% AA), for aroma	.25 oz (7 g)	1.25 oz (35.50 g)
Corn sugar, for bottling	.70 oz (20 g)	3.50 oz (100 g)

TARGET ORIGINAL/FINAL GRAVITY: 1.066/1.021
TARGET ABV: 5.9%

Follow the master method for brewing 1-gallon or 5-gallon all-grain batches as described on pages 54–59 (5-gallon measurements in parentheses).

• Remove liquid yeast from the refrigerator and, if necessary, activate according to package instructions. Place on the counter to warm.

• Heat **1 gallon (or 4 gallons) of water to 160°F**, then stir in the grains. Maintain a mash temperature of **148°F to 153°F** for 60 minutes. Raise the temperature of the mash to 170°F, then sparge using **1 gallon (or 2½ gallons)** of 170°F water to make 1½ (or 5½) gallons wort.

• Bring to a boil over high heat. Add the hops for bittering and boil vigorously for 40 minutes. Add the Irish moss and continue boiling for another 20 minutes. Add the hops for aroma and remove from the heat. (Total boil time: 60 minutes.)

• Cool to at least 75°F and transfer to a sanitized primary fermentation bucket. Add the yeast and aerate the wort.

• Let ferment for at least **1 week or up to 4 weeks** at 70°F; then transfer to a sanitized jug or carboy for secondary fermentation. Continue to ferment for another **2 weeks or up to 2 months at 70°F.**

• Dissolve the sugar in ¼ (or 1) cup of boiling water and let cool. Mix with the beer, bottle, and store for **2 weeks or up to a year**. Refrigerate before drinking.

Smoky Chipotle Porter

I admit it: the idea of a spicy beer is a little . . . strange. Even to me. But this smooth and smoky porter with its slight prickle of heat is worth a leap of faith. Chipotles are the smoked and dried version of jalapeños—a process that transforms the crunchy green peppers into wrinkled, deep-red husks while simultaneously tempering their quick burst of heat into something slow and smoldering. Just the thing for a moody beer like this one.

Brew Notes If you'd like the smoky flavor of chipotles without the heat, crack open the dried peppers and shake out the seeds before adding them to the beer.

Make It Yours Make a Mexican hot chocolate version! Add cinnamon sticks, cacao beans, and a split vanilla bean or two to the secondary. (Read more about adding spices on page 166.)

Beers to Try Pipeline Porter (Kona Brewing Company), Stone Smoked Porter (Stone Brewing Company), Alaskan Smoked Porter (Alaskan Brewing Company

INGREDIENTS	1-GALLON	5-GALLON
White Labs British Ale yeast, Wyeast British Ale yeast, or equivalent	½ package	1 package
Maris Otter malt, milled	1½ lbs (680 g)	7½ lbs (3.40 kg)
Crystal/Caramel 60 malt, milled	8 oz (227 g)	2½ lbs (1.13 kg)
Brown malt, milled	4 oz (113 g)	1¼ lbs (567 g)
Chocolate malt, milled	1 oz (28 g)	5 oz (142 g)
Magnum pellet hops (13.8% AA), for bittering	.10 oz (3 g)	.50 oz (14 g)
Mt. Hood pellet hops (6% AA), for flavoring	.05 oz (1.50 g)	.25 oz (7 g)
Irish moss	¼ tsp	1 tsp
Dried chipotle pepper, chopped, plus more to taste	1 whole	5 whole
Mt. Hood pellet hops (6% AA), for aroma	.15 oz (4 g)	.75 oz (21 g)
Corn sugar, for bottling	.70 oz (20 g)	3.5 oz (100 g)

TARGET ORIGINAL/FINAL GRAVITY: 1.061/1.020
TARGET ABV: 5.4%

Follow the master method for brewing 1-gallon or 5-gallon all-grain batches as described on pages 54–59 (5-gallon measurements in parentheses).

• Remove liquid yeast from the refrigerator and, if necessary, activate according to package instructions. Place on the counter to warm.

• Heat **1 gallon (or 4 gallons) of water to 160°F**, then stir in the grains. Maintain a mash temperature of **148°F to 153°F** for 60 minutes. Raise the temperature of the mash to 170°F, then sparge using **1 gallon (or 2½ gallons)** of 170°F water to make 1½ (or 5½) gallons wort.

• Bring to a boil over high heat. Add the Magnum hops and boil vigorously for 40 minutes. Add the Mt. Hood hops for flavoring and the Irish moss and continue boiling for another 15 minutes. Add the chipotle peppers and continue boiling for another 5 minutes. Add the Mt. Hood hops for aroma and remove from the heat. (Total boil time: 60 minutes.)

• Cool to at least 75°F and transfer to a sanitized primary fermentation bucket. Add the yeast and aerate the wort.

• Let ferment for at least **1 week or up to 4 weeks at 70°F**; then transfer to a sanitized jug or carboy for secondary fermentation. Continue to ferment for another **2 weeks or up to 2 months at 70°F**.

• Taste the beer a few days before you plan to bottle. If you'd like a stronger, hotter flavor, chop 1 chipotle pepper (or 5 peppers) and steep in just enough vodka to cover for 15 minutes, then drain and add the peppers to the beer. Taste daily and bottle when the beer tastes good to you.

• Dissolve the sugar in ¼ (or 1) cup of boiling water and let cool. Mix with the beer, bottle, and store for **2 weeks or up to a year**. Refrigerate before drinking.

All-Day Dry Irish Stout

Think all stouts are heavy and rich? Here's one that's exactly the opposite. This style of stout is called "dry" because very little sugar is left behind after fermenting, and I call it an "all-day" stout because the alcohol is low enough that you can sip a few of these over an afternoon and not need a nap. It has a clean bitterness and a roasty flavor, making it perfect for backyard barbecues and dinner parties alike.

Make It Yours For a more full-bodied stout, swap the Irish Ale yeast for English Ale yeast. You could also throw a handful or two of flaked oats into the mash. If you want to push this one toward black IPA territory, add some citrusy hops late in the boil.

Beers to Try Donnybrook Stout (Victory Brewing Co.), Guinness Extra Stout (Guinness Ltd.), Black Hawk Stout (Mendocino Brewing Company)

INGREDIENTS	1-GALLON	5-GALLON
White Labs Irish Ale yeast, Wyeast Irish Ale yeast, or equivalent	½ package	1 package
Maris Otter malt, milled	1¼ lbs (567 g)	6¼ lbs (2.84 kg)
Flaked barley	8 oz (227 g)	2½ lbs (1.13 kg)
Black barley malt, milled	4 oz (113 g)	1¼ lbs (567 g)
East Kent Goldings pellet hops (7.2% AA), for bittering	.30 oz (8.50 g)	1.50 oz (42.50 g)
Irish moss	¼ tsp	1 tsp
Corn sugar, for bottling	.60 oz (16 g)	3 oz (80 g)

TARGET ORIGINAL/FINAL GRAVITY: 1.050/1.016
TARGET ABV: 4.5%

Follow the master method for brewing 1-gallon or 5-gallon all-grain batches as described on pages 54–59 (5-gallon measurements in parentheses).

• Remove liquid yeast from the refrigerator and, if necessary, activate according to package instructions. Place on the counter to warm.

• Heat **1 gallon (or 3 gallons) of water to 164°F**, then stir in the grains. Maintain a mash temperature of **154°F to 158°F for 60 minutes**. Raise the temperature of the mash to 170°F, then sparge using **1 gallon (or 3½ gallons)** of 170°F water to make 1½ (or 5½) gallons wort.

• Bring to a boil over high heat. Add the hops and boil vigorously for 40 minutes. Add the Irish moss and continue boiling for another 20 minutes. Remove from the heat. (Total boil time: 60 minutes.)

• Cool to at least 75°F and transfer to a sanitized primary fermentation bucket. Add the yeast and aerate the wort.

• Let ferment for at least **1 week or up to 4 weeks at 70°F**; then transfer to a sanitized jug or carboy for secondary fermentation. Continue to ferment for another **2 weeks or up to 2 months at 70°F**.

• Dissolve the sugar in ¼ (or 1) cup of boiling water and let cool. Mix with the beer, bottle, and store for **2 weeks or up to a year**. Refrigerate before drinking.

Affogato Milk Stout

An affogato is an Italian dessert of vanilla ice cream topped with a shot of hot espresso. So simple, yet so perfect. Like the affogato, this beer is somehow more than the sum of its parts. It uses neither espresso beans nor vanilla beans, and yet the illusion of a creamy, coffee-like dessert is near perfect. The secret is a dose of lactose (the sugar found in milk) added to the boil. Yeast can't ferment this sugar, so it adds a touch of milky sweetness and silky body to the beer instead.

Brew Notes Be careful of serving this one to anyone with lactose intolerance.

Make It Yours Coffee lovers, add ¼ cup coarsely ground coffee to the secondary (breakfast stout!) and strain after a few days. To accentuate the sweetness in this beer, add a split vanilla bean or shredded coconut to the secondary. (Read more about adding flavoring ingredients on page 166.)

Beers to Try Milk Stout (Left Hand Brewing Company), Milkstout (Duck-Rabbit Craft Brewery), Crème Brûlée (Southern Tier Brewing Company)

INGREDIENTS	1-GALLON	5-GALLON
White Labs London Ale yeast, Wyeast London Ale yeast, or equivalent	½ package	1 package
Maris Otter malt, milled	1 lb (454 g)	5 lbs (2.27 kg)
Crystal/Caramel 60 malt, milled	8 oz (227 g)	2½ lbs (1.13 kg)
Caramunich malt, milled	8 oz (227 g)	2½ lbs (1.13 kg)
Chocolate malt, milled	2 oz (57 g)	10 oz (283 g)
Flaked oats	2 oz (57 g)	10 oz (283 g)
Flaked barley	2 oz (57 g)	10 oz (283 g)
Roasted barley, milled	1 oz (28 g)	5 oz (142 g)
Northern Brewer pellet hops (9.6% AA), for bittering	.10 oz (3 g)	.50 oz (14 g)
East Kent Goldings pellet hops (7.2% AA), for flavoring	.10 oz (3 g)	.50 oz (14 g)
Irish moss	¼ tsp	1 tsp
Lactose	4 oz (113 g)	1¼ lbs (567 g)
East Kent Goldings pellet hops (7.2% AA), for aroma	.10 oz (3 g)	.50 oz (14 g)
Corn sugar, for bottling	.70 oz (20 g)	3.50 oz (100 g)

TARGET ORIGINAL/FINAL GRAVITY: 1.071/1.018
TARGET ABV: 7%

Follow the master method for brewing 1-gallon or 5-gallon all-grain batches as described on pages 54–59 (5-gallon measurements in parentheses).

• Remove liquid yeast from the refrigerator and, if necessary, activate according to package instructions. Place on the counter to warm.

• Heat **1 gallon (or 4 gallons) of water to 164°F**, then stir in the grains. Maintain a mash temperature of **154°F to 158°F** for 60 minutes. Raise the temperature of the mash to 170°F, then sparge using **1 gallon (or 2½ gallons)** of 170°F water to make 1½ (or 5 ½) gallons wort.

• Bring the wort to a boil over high heat. Add the Northern Brewer hops and boil vigorously for 40 minutes. Add the East Kent Goldings hops for flavoring and the Irish moss and continue boiling for another 15 minutes. Add the lactose and continue boiling for another 5 minutes.

Add the East Kent Goldings hops for aroma and remove the pot from the heat. (Total boil time: 60 minutes.)

• Cool to at least 75°F and transfer to a sanitized primary fermentation bucket. Add the yeast and aerate the wort.

• Let ferment for at least **1 week or up to 4 weeks at 70°F**; then transfer to a sanitized jug or carboy for secondary fermentation. Continue to ferment for another **2 weeks or up to 2 months at 70°F**.

• Dissolve the sugar in ¼ (or 1) cup of boiling water and let cool. Mix with the beer, bottle, and store for **2 weeks or up to a year**. Refrigerate before drinking.

Boss-Level Barrel-Aged Imperial Stout

Think of the boss level of any video game. You know it's coming. Your fingers are nimble and swift. And then that boss guy knocks you out at least ten times before you catch on to his tricks. The imperial stout is the boss level of beers. It might take a few times to nail it, and even then, one boozy bottle can still knock you clear off the screen.

Brew Notes You'll need to make a yeast starter to ensure good fermentation. If aging longer than 3 months, add fresh yeast when bottling to ensure carbonation.

Make It Yours For sweeter, richer flavors in the finished beer, use English or British Ale yeast.

Beer to Try Bourbon County Brand Stout (Goose Island Beer Company)

INGREDIENTS	1-GALLON	5-GALLON
White Labs Irish Ale yeast, Wyeast Irish Ale yeast, or equivalent	½ package	1 package
Light dried malt extract	.90 oz (25 g or 2 heaping tbsps)	3.50 oz (100 g or ½ cup)
Maris Otter malt, milled	2½ lbs (1.13 kg)	12½ lbs (5.67 kg)
Crystal 120 malt, milled	8 oz (227 g)	2½ lbs (1.13 kg)
Special B malt, milled	8 oz (227 g)	2½ lbs (1.13 kg)
Wheat malt, milled	8 oz (227 g)	2½ lbs (1.13 kg)
Chocolate malt, milled	1.50 oz (43 g)	7.50 oz (213 g)
Roasted barley malt, milled	1.50 oz (43 g)	7.50 oz (213 g)
Rice hulls	2 oz (57 g)	10 oz (283 g)
Northern Brewer pellet hops (9.6% AA), for bittering	.30 oz (8.5 g)	1.50 oz (42.5 g)
Mt. Hood pellet hops (5.9% AA), for flavoring	.25 oz (7 g)	1.25 oz (35.50 g)
Irish moss	¼ tsp	1 tsp
Mt. Hood pellet hops (5.9% AA), for aroma	.25 oz (7 g)	1.25 oz (35.50 g)
Oak cubes	.50 oz (14 g)	2.50 oz (71 g)
Bourbon	2 oz (57 g)	10 oz (283 g)
Corn sugar, for bottling	.60 oz (18 g)	3.17 oz (90 g)

TARGET ORIGINAL/FINAL GRAVITY: 1.109/1.034
TARGET ABV: 10%

Follow the master method for brewing 1-gallon or 5-gallon all-grain batches as described on pages 54–59 (5-gallon measurements in parentheses).

• Using the yeast and malt extract, make a yeast starter 12 to 18 hours before you plan to brew, following the instructions on page 16.

• Heat **1¼ (or 6) gallons of water to 164°F**, then stir in the grains and rice hulls. Maintain a mash temperature of **154°F to 158°F** for 60 minutes. Raise the temperature of the mash to 170°F, then sparge using **1 gallon (or 1½ gallons)** of 170°F water to make 1½ (or 5½) gallons wort.

• Bring to a boil over high heat. Add the Northern Brewer hops and boil vigorously for 40 minutes. Add the Mt. Hood hops for flavoring and the Irish moss and continue boiling for another 20 minutes. Add the Mt. Hood hops for aroma and remove from the heat. (Total boil time: 60 minutes.)

• Cool to at least 75°F and transfer to a sanitized primary fermentation bucket. Add the yeast starter and aerate the wort.

• Let ferment for at least **1 week or up to 4 weeks at 70°F**. Meanwhile, combine the oak cubes and bourbon, and soak for at least 1 week. When ready to transfer the beer for secondary fermentation, drain the oak cubes, reserving the bourbon, and add the cubes to the sanitized jug; then siphon the beer over top. Continue to ferment for another **1 month to 1 year at 70°F**. (If aging for longer than 2 months, transfer the beer off the oak cubes, clean and sanitize the jug, and transfer the beer back into the jug.)

• Taste the beer a few days before you plan to bottle. Add some of the reserved bourbon if you wish. Taste daily and bottle when the beer tastes good to you.

• Dissolve the sugar in ¼ (or 1) cup of boiling water and let cool. Mix with the beer, bottle, and store for **2 weeks or up to a year**. Refrigerate before drinking.

PLAY WITH YOUR HOPS

Okay! Let's talk about hops! You love hoppy beers and want all hops all the time. Or maybe . . . you're more interested in getting just a dash of bitterness and no more. Whichever side of the hop spectrum you find yourself on, I promise there's a way to make it happen.

Quick recap of how hops work: Hops contain both bittering resins and aromatic oils. Resins require hot, boiling wort to properly add their bitterness to a beer, whereas the delicate oils are more likely to stick around when the hops are added at the end of the boil, or after, when things are calmer and cooler. So hops added at the beginning of brewing add bitterness but no aroma, and hops added at the end add aroma but little bitterness. Hops added in the middle add some of both.

With this in mind, here are the ways you can add hops throughout the brewing process and what flavors you can expect from each.

WHEN TO ADD HOPS

You can use any of these hopping techniques with any beer you brew. If you're following a recipe, take a look at how the recipe uses the hops and then adjust accordingly. For example, bittering hops could be added as first-wort hops instead. The three additions of bittering, flavoring, and aroma hops could be divided up for continuous hopping. Aroma hops could be saved and used for dry hopping—or for a real burst of hoppy aroma, you could double the amount of aroma hops and use half for dry hopping.

1. First-wort hopping. This refers to hops added to the wort immediately after sparging and as you heat the wort for the hop boil. Hops added at this stage have the longest contact time with the wort, which increases the overall bitterness of your beer. However, the bitterness from first-wort hopping tends to be smoother and less aggressive than that of hops added once the wort is boiling.

2. Hopping for bitterness. Bittering hops are added at the beginning of a 60- or 90-minute boil, once the wort has come to a full, rolling boil. All oils are destroyed, so these hops add straight-up bitterness with some hop flavor. As compared to first-wort hopping, this bitterness is a bit rougher and more astringent.

3. Hopping for flavor. Your opportunity for real hop flavor comes in the second half of the hop boil, 20 minutes or so before you wrap things up. There's not enough time to fully extract bitterness from these hops, and the oils that add aroma are mostly destroyed, but what's left translates on our palates as flavor. Less bitterness, more hoppiness.

4. Hopping for aroma. For hop aroma in your beer, add hops at the very end of the boil, as soon as you turn off the heat. The wort is still hot enough that some of the hop oils evaporate, but you're still left with a light, delicate aroma in your finished beer.

5. Continuous hopping. You can also add hops at regular 5- or 10-minute intervals throughout the entire hop boil, called "continuous hopping." This gives you an incredibly nuanced, balanced, and well-rounded hop profile in your finished beer. You extract something slightly different from the hops at every single stage.

6. Dry hopping. A sure-fire way to get a truly aromatic beer is to add hops during secondary fermentation, called "dry hopping." The alcohol in the beer helps extract and preserve the hop oils, and since the beer won't be heated again, all of the aromatic oils remain in the beer. Use a small mesh bag to add the hops for easier removal later on. Let the hops infuse the beer for anywhere from a few days to a week. Be careful not to let sit for too long, however, or your beer will start to taste unpleasantly vegetal.

WHAT TO HOP

Another way to play with hop flavors is simply to switch up the hops themselves. Hops cover an incredibly wide variety of flavors and aromas, as you can see in the Common Hops chart on page 12. Just by swapping a citrusy hop for a floral hop, you get a completely different profile in your beer.

You can (and should!) try combining different hop varieties. Want an IPA with both bright grapefruit and subtle pine flavors? Try a mix of Cascade and Simcoe hops. Why not? Blending hops can be challenging and risky (too many blended together and you end up with a muddy generic hop flavor), but it's also rewarding when you achieve the balance of flavors and aromas you envisioned.

When you start swapping or combining hops, don't forget to adjust the quantities according to their alpha acid percentage. Remember, alpha acid is an indicator of a hop's bittering potential; if you swap a low alpha acid hop for a high one without adjusting the amount, you'll end up with a beer that's more bitter than you intended. Use this equation for adjusting hops:

This said, using a hop with a slightly higher alpha acid or increasing the amount of bittering hops you use are both ways to bump up the bitterness of your brew. Just make sure it's what you mean to do and not an accident!

Blending and swapping hops by feel is fun, but if you want to be more scientific about it, invest in some beer brewing software like BeerSmith, ProMash, or Beer Calculus. Plugging your revised recipe into one of these programs gives you a more accurate idea of the bitterness and flavor profile.

$$\text{Grams New Hop} = \frac{\text{AA\% Original Hop x Grams Original Hop}}{\text{AA\% New Hop}}$$

Mild ales and bitter ales are the true heart of the British pub scene. These are low-alcohol, malt-forward ales—the kind of beers you might look forward to quaffing after a long day of labor and toil. Milds tend to be on the nuttier, sweeter side, while bitters tend to be slightly lighter in color and body. FYI, British bitters are not actually all that bitter. They're only considered bitter in comparison to milds, not as compared to the hoppy, truly bitter American IPAs most of us are used to. A few boozier British beers have also evolved from the milds and bitters: India pale ales, strong ales, and the big daddy of them all, barleywines.

BRITISH ALES

[chapter 8]

A VERY GOOD BRITISH MILD

Mild ales were the original session beers from the days when beer was something you drank with dinner or while hanging out with friends and not, expressly, to get tipsy. Mild ales should, in fact, be mild. The emphasis is on malts with just a smattering of hops—something completely drinkable but not boring. Roasted malts and a high mash temperature make this beer nutty-sweet and nuanced without worrying about booziness.

Make It Yours Tinker with the malts on this one. Switch out the Crystal malt for honey or biscuit malts or add in some brown malts for a touch of dry bitterness without changing the hops. Or brew as a SMASH ale with just Maris Otter malts and either East Kent Goldings or Fuggle hops.

Beers to Try Mild Winter (Goose Island Beer Co.), Black Cat (Moorhouse Brewery)

INGREDIENTS	1-GALLON	5-GALLON
White Labs British Ale yeast, Wyeast British Ale yeast, or equivalent	½ package	1 package
Maris Otter malt, milled	1¼ lbs (567 g)	6¼ lbs (2.84 kg)
Crystal/Caramel 20 malt, milled	4 oz (113 g)	1¼ lbs (567 g)
Crystal/Caramel 120 malt, milled	2 oz (57 g)	10 oz (283 g)
East Kent Goldings pellet hops (7.2% AA), for bittering	.15 oz (4 g)	.75 oz (21 g)
Fuggle pellet hops (5.3% AA), for flavoring	.15 oz (4 g)	.75 oz (21 g)
Irish moss	¼ tsp	1 tsp
Corn sugar, for bottling	.70 oz (20 g)	3.50 oz (100 g)

TARGET ORIGINAL/FINAL GRAVITY: 1.043/1.014
TARGET ABV: 3.8%

Follow the master method for brewing 1-gallon or 5-gallon all-grain batches as described on pages 54–59 (5-gallon measurements in parentheses).

• Remove liquid yeast from the refrigerator and, if necessary, activate according to package instructions. Place on the counter to warm.

• Heat **3 quarts (or 2½ gallons) of water to 164°F**, then stir in the grains. Maintain a mash temperature of **154°F to 158°F** for 60 minutes. Raise the temperature of the mash to 170°F, then sparge using **1½ (or 4) gallons** of 170°F water to make 1½ (or 5½) gallons wort.

• Bring to a boil over high heat. Add the East Kent Goldings hops and boil vigorously for 40 minutes. Add the Fuggle hops and the Irish moss and continue boiling for another 20 minutes, then remove from the heat. (Total boil time: 60 minutes.)

• Cool to at least 75°F and transfer to a sanitized primary fermentation bucket. Add the yeast and aerate the wort.

• Let ferment for at least **1 week or up to 4 weeks at 70°F**; then transfer to a sanitized jug or carboy for secondary fermentation. Continue to ferment for another **2 weeks or up to 2 months at 70°F.**

• Dissolve the sugar in ¼ (or 1) cup of boiling water and let cool. Mix with the beer, bottle, and store for **2 weeks or up to a year**. Refrigerate before drinking.

Tea Time Extra-Special Bitter (ESB)

Despite what its name implies, an extra-special bitter can seem downright tame to those of us used to having our tongues twisted by hops. This "bitter" beer aims for balance rather than a pummeling, and while it's certainly bitter enough by British standards, it's the toasty malt character and British hops that make me love the style. Those hops give this beer a tea-like bitterness that made me wonder how an ESB might taste if brewed with a few bags of actual tea. Answer: Amazing. Citrusy Amarillo hops complete the beverage morph like a squeeze of fresh lemon, making this the penultimate British brew.

Make It Yours For an extra splash of lemon in your beer tea, add .05 ounce (.25 ounce) Sorachi hops (11.9% AA) with the aroma hops. They taste a little too much like sweet lemon candy on their own but are fantastic in combination with the Amarillo hops. Also, try with other kinds of tea. A Darjeeling version, with its strong bergamot flavors, is particularly divine.

Beers to Try Fuller's ESB (Fuller Smith & Turner PLC), Hobgoblin (Wychwood Brewery Company)

INGREDIENTS	1-GALLON	5-GALLON
White Labs English Ale yeast, Wyeast London ESB Ale, or equivalent	½ package	1 package
Maris Otter malt, milled	1¾ lbs (794 g)	8¾ lbs (3.97 kg)
Crystal/Caramel 40 malt, milled	8 oz (227 g)	2½ lbs (1.13 kg)
Crystal/Caramel 80 malt, milled	2 oz (57 g)	10 oz (283 g)
East Kent Goldings pellet hops (7.2% AA), for bittering	.15 oz (4 g)	.75 oz (21 g)
Amarillo pellet hops (8.2% AA), for flavoring	.15 oz (4 g)	.75 oz (21 g)
Irish moss	¼ tsp	1 tsp
Amarillo pellet hops (8.2% AA), for aroma	.15 oz (4 g)	.75 oz (21 g)
Assam, Ceylon, or other British black tea	2.50 g (2 bags or ½ tbsp loose leaf)	12.50 g (10 bags or 2½ tbsps loose leaf)
Corn sugar, for bottling	.8 oz (22 g)	4 oz (113 g)

TARGET ORIGINAL/FINAL GRAVITY: 1.063/1.020
TARGET ABV: 5.7%

Follow the master method for brewing 1-gallon or 5-gallon all-grain batches as described on pages 54–59 (5-gallon measurements in parentheses).

• Remove liquid yeast from the refrigerator and, if necessary, activate according to package instructions. Place on the counter to warm.

• Heat **1 gallon (or 3½ gallons) of water to 160°F**, then stir in the grains. Maintain a mash temperature of **148°F to 153°F** for 60 minutes. Raise the temperature of the mash to 170°F, then sparge using **1 gallon (or 3 gallons)** of 170°F water to make 1½ (or 5½) gallons wort.

• Bring to a boil over high heat. Add the East Kent Goldings hops and boil vigorously for 40 minutes. Add the Amarillo hops for flavoring and the Irish moss and continue boiling for another 20 minutes. Add the Amarillo hops for aroma and the tea and remove from the heat. (Total boil time: 60 minutes.)

• Cool to at least 75°F and transfer to a sanitized primary fermentation bucket, straining out the tea as you transfer. Add the yeast and aerate the wort.

• Let ferment for at least **1 week or up to 4 weeks at 70°F**; then transfer to a sanitized jug or carboy for secondary fermentation. Continue to ferment for another **2 weeks or up to 2 months at 70°F**.

• Taste the beer a few days before you plan to bottle. Add more tea if you wish (use the same amount as before). Taste daily and bottle when the beer tastes good to you.

• Dissolve the sugar in ¼ (or 1) cup of boiling water and let cool. Mix with the beer, bottle, and store for **2 weeks or up to a year**. Refrigerate before drinking.

High Seas British IPA

We've come to love hops so much for their bittering power that we often forget they play another role in our beer: preservation. Hops extend the shelf life of beers beyond their normal "best by" date—something that became very important in the mid-1700s when England needed a way to keep beer fresh on the long voyage to troops in India. These beers, which became known as India pale ales, were lighter in the malts, more liberal with the hops, and a touch more boozy. And that's, apparently, how you keep soldiers happy.

Make It Yours The trademark of the British IPA is its balanced bitterness, but I give you permission to push the envelope. Stick with British hops, but bump them up if you like hoppier, bitter beers. Or use all Maris Otter malts or switch to a slightly darker Crystal malt for a sweet malt backbone.

Beers to Try 400 Pound Monkey (Left Hand Brewing Company), Great Lakes Commodore Perry IPA (Great Lakes Brewing Co.), Old Speckled Hen (Greene King PLC)

INGREDIENTS	1-GALLON	5-GALLON
White Labs London Ale yeast, Wyeast London Ale yeast, or equivalent	½ package	1 package
Pale ale malt, milled	1 lb (454 g)	5 lbs (2.27 kg)
Maris Otter malt, milled	1 lb (454 g)	5 lbs (2.27 kg)
Crystal/Caramel 20 malt, milled	8 oz (227 g)	2½ lbs (1.13 kg)
East Kent Goldings pellet hops (7.2% AA), for bittering	.30 oz (8.5 g)	1.50 oz (43 g)
Fuggle pellet hops (5.3% AA), for flavoring	.30 oz (8.5 g)	1.50 oz (43 g)
Irish moss	¼ tsp	1 tsp
Fuggle pellet hops (5.3% AA), for aroma	.25 oz (7 g)	1.25 oz (35.50 g)
Corn sugar, for bottling	.80 oz (22 g)	4 oz (113 g)

TARGET ORIGINAL/FINAL GRAVITY: 1.066/1.018
TARGET ABV: 6.3%

Follow the master method for brewing 1-gallon or 5-gallon all-grain batches as described on pages 54–59 (5-gallon measurements in parentheses).

• Remove liquid yeast from the refrigerator and, if necessary, activate according to package instructions. Place on the counter to warm.

• Heat **1 gallon (or 4 gallons) of water to 160°F**, then stir in the grains. Maintain a mash temperature of **148°F to 153°F** for 60 minutes. Raise the temperature of the mash to 170°F, then sparge using **1 gallon (or 2½ gallons)** of 170°F water to make 1½ (or 5½) gallons wort.

• Bring to a boil over high heat. Add the East Kent Goldings hops and boil vigorously for 40 minutes. Add the Fuggle hops for flavoring and the Irish moss and continue boiling for another 20 minutes. Add the Fuggle hops for aroma and remove from the heat. (Total boil time: 60 minutes.)

• Cool to at least 75°F and transfer to a sanitized primary fermentation bucket. Add the yeast and aerate the wort.

• Let ferment for at least **1 week or up to 4 weeks at 70°F**; then transfer to a sanitized jug or carboy for secondary fermentation. Continue to ferment for another **2 weeks or up to 2 months at 70°F**.

• Dissolve the sugar in ¼ (or 1) cup of boiling water and let cool. Mix with the beer, bottle, and store for **2 weeks or up to a year**. Refrigerate before drinking.

Sugar and Spice Strong Ale

Strong ales need to be on your radar. Put them there immediately. This beer bridges the gap between the milder, lower-alcohol pub beers of Great Britain and the booze bombs that are England's barleywines. But strong ales are more than just a rest stop on your way from one to the other—strong ales stand on their own. They tend to have a warm, spicy character and surprising tartness, like a spice cake made with dried fall plums.

Brew Notes The bittering hops are added before bringing the wort to a boil, known as first-wort hopping. Read more about this technique in "Play with Your Hops," page 116.

Make It Yours Strong ales like this one often have a sour component; play this up by adding some brettanomyces yeast when you transfer the beer to the secondary. Wait several months before bottling, then wait another few months before opening your first bottle. This starts to hit a good balance of sweetness and funkitude about a year after brewing.

Beers to Try Samuel Smith's Yorkshire Stingo (Samuel Smith Old Brewery), Allies Win The War! (21st Amendment Brewery), Fuller's 1845 (Fuller Smith & Turner)

INGREDIENTS	1-GALLON	5-GALLON
White Labs English Ale yeast, Wyeast British Ale II yeast, or equivalent	½ package	1 package
Maris Otter malt, milled	2¼ lbs (1.02 kg)	11¼ lbs (5.10 kg)
Crystal/Caramel 20 malt, milled	8 oz (227 g)	2½ lbs (1.13 kg)
Crystal/Caramel 80 malt, milled	4 oz (113 g)	1¼ lbs (567 g)
Special B malt, milled	2 oz (57 g)	10 oz (283 g)
Magnum pellet hops (13.8% AA), for bittering	.15 oz (4 g)	.75 oz (21 g)
Willamette pellet hops (4.7% AA), for flavoring	.15 oz (4 g)	.75 oz (21 g)
Irish moss	¼ tsp	1 tsp
Willamette pellet hops (4.7% AA), for aroma	.15 oz (4 g)	.75 oz (21 g)
Corn sugar, for bottling	.70 oz (20 g)	3.50 oz (100 g)

TARGET ORIGINAL/ FINAL GRAVITY: 1.083/1.026
TARGET ABV: 7.6%

Follow the master method for brewing 1-gallon or 5-gallon all-grain batches as described on pages 54–59 (5-gallon measurements in parentheses).

• Remove liquid yeast from the refrigerator and, if necessary, activate according to package instructions. Place on the counter to warm.

• Heat **1 gallon (or 5 gallons) of water to 160°F**; then stir in the grains. Maintain a mash temperature of **148°F to 153°F** for 60 minutes. Raise the temperature of the mash to 170°F, then sparge using **1 gallon (or 2 gallons)** of 170°F water to make 1½ (or 5½) gallons wort.

• Add the Magnum hops and then bring to a boil over high heat. Boil vigorously for 40 minutes. Add the Willamette hops for flavoring and the Irish moss and continue boiling for another 20 minutes. Add the Willamette hops for aroma and remove from the heat. (Total boil time: 60 minutes.)

• Cool to at least 75°F and transfer to a sanitized primary fermentation bucket. Add the yeast and aerate the wort.

• Let ferment for at least **1 week or up to 4 weeks at 70°F**; then transfer to a sanitized jug or carboy for secondary fermentation. Continue to ferment for another **2 weeks or up to 2 months at 70°F**.

• Dissolve the sugar in ¼ (or 1) cup of boiling water and let cool. Mix with the beer, bottle, and store for **2 weeks or up to a year**. Refrigerate before drinking.

Figgy Pudding British Barleywine

Lest you were wondering where the Brits hide their truly tipsy-making beers, let me introduce you to the barleywine. Big malts, big booze, big fun. The only thing you won't find big-ified in this beer are hops. Barleywines are celebration beers, and this one, with its dark caramelized sugars and rich fig flavors, is perfect for the Christmas table.

Brew Notes You'll need to make a yeast starter for this recipe to ensure good fermentation. Also, make sure your brew pot is big enough to handle the amount of grains. If needed, swap some of the Maris Otter malts for extract (see page 9). And since the beer is aged for several months before bottling, add an extra dose of yeast when you bottle to ensure carbonation.

Make It Yours Soak some oak cubes in port or brandy and add them to the secondary for one more layer of holiday flavor. (Read more about adding oak cubes on page 168.)

Beer to Try Our Finest Regards (Pretty Things Beer & Ale Project)

INGREDIENTS	1-GALLON	5-GALLON
White Labs High Gravity Ale yeast, Wyeast British Ale II yeast, or equivalent	1 package, divided	2 packages, divided
Light dried malt extract	.90 oz (25 g or 2 heaping tbsps)	3.50 oz (100 g or ½ cup)
Maris Otter malt, milled	3½ lbs (1.59 kg)	17½ lbs (7.94 kg)
Crystal/Caramel 80 malt, milled	2.50 oz (71 g)	12 oz (340 g)
Crystal/Caramel 120 malt, milled	2.50 oz (71 g)	12 oz (340 g)
Fuggle pellet hops (5.3% AA), for bittering	.50 oz (14 g)	2.50 oz (71 g)
East Kent Goldings pellet hops (7.2% AA), for flavoring	.25 oz (7 g)	1.25 oz (35 g)
Irish moss	¼ tsp	1 tsp
Dried figs, chopped	3 oz (85 g)	15 oz (425 g)
Muscovado or dark brown sugar	1.80 oz (55 g)	9.40 oz (266 g)
East Kent Goldings pellet hops (7.2% AA), for aroma	.25 oz (7 g)	1.25 oz (35 g)
Corn sugar, for bottling	.60 oz (18 g)	3.17 oz (90 g)

TARGET ORIGINAL/FINAL GRAVITY: 1.103/ 1.016
TARGET ABV: 11.6%

Follow the master method for brewing 1-gallon or 5-gallon all-grain batches as described on pages 54–59 (5-gallon measurements in parentheses).

• Using ½ (or 1) package of the yeast and the malt extract, make a yeast starter 12 to 18 hours before you plan to brew, following the instructions in "How to Make a Yeast Starter," page 16.

• Heat 1¼ (or 6½) gallons of water to 160°F, then stir in the grains. Maintain a mash temperature of 148°F to 153°F for 60 minutes. Raise the temperature of the mash to 170°F, then sparge using 1 gallon (or 2 gallons) of 170°F water to make 1½ (or 5½) gallons wort.

• Bring to a boil over high heat. Add the Fuggle hops for bittering and boil vigorously for 40 minutes. Add the East Kent Goldings hops and the Irish moss and continue boiling for another 20 minutes. Add the figs, muscovado sugar, and East Kent Goldings hops for aroma and remove from the heat. (Total boil time: 60 minutes.)

• Cool to at least 75°F and transfer to a sanitized primary fermentation bucket. Add the yeast starter and aerate the wort.

• Let ferment for at least **1 week or up to 4 weeks at 70°F**; then transfer to a sanitized jug or carboy for secondary fermentation. Continue to ferment for another **3 months or up to 1 year at 70°F**.

• Taste the beer a few times during secondary fermentation. Add more figs if you wish. Bottle when the beer tastes good to you. Dissolve the sugar in ¼ (or 1) cup of boiling water and let cool. Mix ½ (or 1) package of yeast and the sugar mixture into the beer. Bottle and store for **1 month or up to a year**. Refrigerate before drinking.

BREWING IN WARM WEATHER, BREWING IN COLD WEATHER

Once your brew day is finished and the lid is snapped on your fermenter, it's easy to just stick it in a closet or throw it in the garage and forget about it for a few weeks. Not so fast, buddy! Yes, your hands-on work is done for the moment, but there's one thing you still need to keep an eye on: the ambient temperature around your fermenting beer.

IT'S ALL ABOUT HAPPY YEAST

Yeast isn't happy at just any old temperature. There's a range at which it works best. For ale yeasts, like those used for most of the recipes in this book, that ideal range is 65°F to 75°F. For lager yeasts used to brew pilsners and bocks, the range is 50°F to 55°F. Specific yeast strains have more specific temperature ranges, but these are fine to use as basic guidelines.

Now before you panic because your apartment isn't air-conditioned or the only place you can store your fermenting beer is the unheated garage, know that the ideal temperature is also an average of all the hours in the day. Liquid takes a while to heat up or cool down, so if your most extreme daytime temperature and most extreme nighttime temperature average out to within the ideal range, your beer is probably fine. Also, the most delicate time for the beer is during those first few days of fermentation when the yeast is eating the majority of the sugars. After the first stage of fermentation slows, and especially once you transfer the beer to the secondary or bottle it, the yeast can handle a little more temperature swing.

WHAT HAPPENS AT HIGHER (OR LOWER) TEMPERATURES?

If you go above or below the ideal temperature range, the yeast gets stressed out, quite literally. How happy are you if you have to work when the temperature starts creeping up toward the 90s or dropping toward freezing?

At higher-than-ideal temperatures, yeasts go into a feeding frenzy and gobble up all the sugars as quickly as they can. This might sound like an okay thing, but these hot and stressed-out yeasties also produce by-products that can significantly affect the flavor of your beer. In a warm-fermented beer, you'll notice more fruity, "estery" flavors, like bananas and pears, along with some spicy "phenolic" flavors, like cloves or even plastic. Sometimes you'll also get green apple flavors from the production of acetaldehyde and buttery flavors from diacetyl. At extreme temperatures, 85°F to 95°F or even higher, the yeast produces more fusel alcohols, which can give your beer harsh, solvent-like flavors similar to grain alcohol.

The biggest risk at low temperatures is that the yeast grows sluggish or goes completely dormant. You won't notice any off flavors (in fact, colder temperatures usually result in a smoother beer with crisper flavors), but it can be tricky to get the beer to complete fermentation. At best, your beer takes longer to finish. At worst, you're left with a sugary, big-bodied beer without much alcohol.

TRICKS FOR BREWING IN WARM WEATHER

It's challenging, but not impossible, to brew decent beers once the hot, humid days of summer descend. For most of the time I've been brewing beer, I've lived in apartments without air-conditioning. Yes, I still brew during the summer, and yes, I still like the beers I brew! Here are a few tricks.

Pick your brew day wisely. Temperature is most important during the first few days of fermentation. If a heat wave just ended and you're expecting a few days of more moderate temperatures, this is the time to brew. By contrast, if the Weather Channel predicts a few days of unexpectedly high heat, it's best to hold off on brewing.

Scout out your home. If your home is anything like mine, there are rooms that seem to get warmer than others and spots that stay cooler. Scout these out and use them to your advantage. Get creative, too. Often the bathroom is the coolest room in the house, so why not stick the beer in your bathtub while it bubbles? In my home, we have a breezy, shaded landing outside our front entrance; my beers can stay quite cool there even when we have the fans on inside.

Apply cold compresses. It sounds a little bizarre, but wrapping your fermentation buckets, jugs, or carboys in damp towels can really help keep the beer at a cool temperature. It's the sweat effect: evaporating liquid keeps the beer cool. On the hottest days, tuck ice cubes or ice packs into the folds of the towel or place the whole shebang in a tub of ice water.

Some beers do just fine when brewed at warmer temperatures. The yeast might still be a bit stressed out, but the flavors created actually complement the finished beers. Saisons, many Belgian ales, and hefeweizens (provided you like bubble-gummy flavors in your hefs) are all good choices.

TRICKS FOR BREWING IN COLD WEATHER

Keeping beer warm in the winter while it ferments is usually a bit easier than keeping it cool in the summer, thankfully! Here are some ideas to try.

Find a warm spot. Scout out the warm spots in winter just the way you scouted out the cool spots in summer. Assuming you keep your house heated to 65°F or 70°F during the winter, ideally you could keep the beer in one of the main rooms of your house. If that's not an option, interior closets are a great choice. They are insulated from exterior walls and usually keep a fairly steady temperature. Close to a water heater or furnace can also work, but be careful that the beer doesn't get too warm!

Get your beer a heater. If the only spot you can store your fermenting beer is an unheated garage or somewhere similar, keep it warm with a heating pad—though, again, make sure it doesn't keep the beer too warm. Homebrewing stores also sell special temperature-controlled heaters and carboy jackets intended just for keeping jugs and carboys of beer warm.

You can also work the cool weather to your advantage! If you want to brew lagers but aren't quite ready for a whole lagering setup (see "The Real Deal with Lagers," page 206), winter is the time to experiment. Lager yeasts love cool temperatures, but make sure they stay above freezing. Especially think about brewing steam beers, doppelbocks, or other darker lagers. These turn out well (and can hide a few flaws) even if the temperature fluctuates.

IN A PERFECT WORLD . . .

In a perfect world, you would keep tight control over the temperature of your fermentation and stay in the ideal range 24/7. The only way to do this is to invest in some extra equipment. A temperature-controlled fridge, as described in "The Real Deal with Lagers," page 206, is perfect not only for lagering beers but also for controlling the fermentation temperature of ales throughout the year.

A fridge won't keep your beer warm if it's out in the garage in the middle of a Minnesota winter, though. For warming, it's best to invest in heaters and warming jackets specifically designed for beer brewing. All the equipment for both cooling and warming beer is available at most well-stocked homebrewing supply stores or online.

Don't tell the other beers, but Belgians might just be my favorite. I love their fruity flavors, which can range from tart lemons to dried plums. I love their embrace of wild yeast and the funky flavor fest that follows. I love that a Belgian beer pairs just as well with burgers and fries as it does with Thanksgiving dinner. Is there anything I don't like about them? Nope.

There is also a Belgian ale for every season: sour ales and abbey ales in the summer, darker dubbels when the weather cools, and boozy tripels to toast the New Year and take us into spring. Saisons are another Belgian beer style and a favorite of mine in warmer weather; you'll find a recipe for Watermelon Saison in chapter 13 with the session ales.

BELGIAN ALES

[chapter 9]

A VERY GOOD ABBEY ALE

An abbey ale is not something you'll likely find in entry forms for a beer competition or in descriptions of classic styles. It's more of a catchall term for Belgian-style beers that can't quite be shoehorned into the usual molds.

Consider this particular abbey ale your gateway to all Belgiany, abbeyish beers. It's a "single" to the dubbel and tripel beers in the recipes that follow. Technically speaking, it's closer to what a beer judge would call a Belgian pale ale, but it's not pale or hoppy in the usual way of pale ales. Rather, it's a ruddy amber color with soft fruity and nutty flavors and a bare whiff of spicy hops. It's one of my favorites to serve with a casual dinner, no matter what happens to be on the table.

Make It Yours Nudge this in the direction of a light-colored Belgian-style pale ale by swapping the Caramunich malts for another dose of pilsner malts or some light-roasted biscuit malts. Use a saison yeast for a more citrusy profile or add some extra hops for more bitterness and aroma.

Beers to Try Brother Thelonious (North Coast Brewing Company), Rare Vos (Brewery Ommegang), Orval Trappist Ale (Brasserie D'Orval)

INGREDIENTS	1-GALLON	5-GALLON
White Labs Abbey Ale yeast, Wyeast Belgian Abbey yeast, or equivalent	½ package	1 package
Pilsner malt (preferably Belgian pilsner), milled	1¾ lbs (794 g)	8¾ lbs (3.97 kg)
Caramunich malt, milled	8 oz (227 g)	2½ lbs (1.13 kg)
East Kent Goldings pellet hops (7.2% AA), for bittering	.15 oz (4 g)	.75 oz (21 g)
East Kent Goldings pellet hops (7.2% AA), for flavoring	.05 oz (1.50 g)	.25 oz (7 g)
Irish moss	¼ tsp	1 tsp
Saaz pellet hops (2.9% AA), for aroma	.25 oz (7 g)	1.25 oz (35.50 g)
Corn sugar, for bottling	.80 oz (22 g)	4 oz (113 g)

TARGET ORIGINAL/FINAL GRAVITY: 1.058/1.015
TARGET ABV: 5.7%

Follow the master method for brewing 1-gallon or 5-gallon all-grain batches as described on pages 54–59 (5-gallon measurements in parentheses).

• Heat **1 gallon (or 3½ gallons) of water to 154°F**, then stir in the grains. Maintain a mash temperature of **154°F to 158°F** for 60 minutes. Raise the temperature of the mash to 170°F, then sparge using **1 gallon (or 3 gallons)** of 170°F water to make 1½ (or 5½) gallons wort.

• Bring to a boil over high heat. Add the East Kent Goldings hops for bittering and boil vigorously for 40 minutes. Add the East Kent Goldings hops for flavoring and the Irish moss and continue boiling for another 20 minutes. Add the Saaz hops and remove from the heat. (Total boil time: 60 minutes.)

• Cool to at least 75°F and transfer to a sanitized primary fermentation bucket. Add the yeast and aerate the wort.

• Let ferment for at least **1 week or up to 4 weeks at 70°F**; then transfer to a sanitized jug or carboy for secondary fermentation. Continue to ferment for another **2 weeks or up to 2 months at 70°F**.

• Dissolve the sugar in ¼ (or 1) cup of boiling water and let cool. Mix with the beer, bottle, and store for **2 weeks or up to a year**. Refrigerate before drinking.

Maple Cider Dubbel

I look forward to two things once the dog days of summer roll into the cooler days of fall: darker beers and cider doughnuts. With the introduction of this dubbel into my beer calendar, I can happily take care of both cravings. Maple syrup and an apple cider reduction take the place of the traditional Belgian candi syrup and transform what is already a treat of a beer into something truly sublime. Think of the best mug of apple cider you've ever had and add notes of caramelized fruit, roasted nuts, and warm maple syrup.

Brew Notes You'll need to make a yeast starter for this recipe to ensure good fermentation.

Make It Yours If you want to push this already insane beer into the stratosphere, add some bourbon-soaked oak cubes to the secondary (see page 168). Or go the other direction and trim out the cider and maple syrup for a more traditional dubbel; sparge to make 1½ (or 5½) gallons of wort and continue with the boil as usual.

Beers to Try Allagash Dubbel (Allagash Brewing Company), Chimay Premiere Red (Beires de Chimay)

INGREDIENTS	1-GALLON	5-GALLON
White Labs Belgian Strong Ale yeast, Wyeast Belgian Abbey yeast, or equivalent	½ package	1 package
Light dried malt extract	.90 oz (25 g or 2 tbsps)	3.50 oz (100 g or ½ cup)
Pilsner malt (preferably Belgian pilsner malt), milled	2 lbs (907 g)	10 lbs (4.54 kg)
Caramunich malt, milled	8 oz (227 g)	2½ lbs (1.13 kg)
Caravienne malt, milled	4 oz (113 g)	1¼ lbs (567 g)
Special B malt, milled	.50 oz (14 g)	2.50 oz (71 g)
Apple cider	½ gallon	2½ gallons
Perle pellet hops (8.9% AA), for bittering	.10 oz (3 g)	.50 oz (14 g)
Tettanger pellet hops (3.7% AA), for flavoring	.15 oz (4 g)	.75 oz (21 g)
Grade B maple syrup	5 oz (142 g or ½ cup)	1 lb 9 oz (709 g or 2½ cups)
Irish moss	¼ tsp	1 tsp
Tettanger pellet hops (3.7% AA), for aroma	.10 oz (3 g)	.50 oz (14 g)
Corn sugar, for bottling	.7 oz (20 g)	3.50 oz (100 g)

TARGET ORIGINAL GRAVITY/FINAL: 1.095/1.016
TARGET ABV: 10.5%

Follow the master method for brewing 1-gallon or 5-gallon all-grain batches as described on pages 54–59 (5-gallon measurements in parentheses).

• Using the yeast and malt extract, make a yeast starter 12 to 18 hours before you plan to brew, following the instructions in "How to Make a Yeast Starter," page 16.

• Heat **1 gallon (or 5 gallons) of water to 160°F**, then stir in the grains. Maintain a mash temperature of **148°F to 153°F** for 60 minutes. While the grains are mashing, bring the cider to a boil in a large saucepot and reduce by half; set aside. When the mash is finished, raise the temperature to 170°F, then sparge using **3 quarts (or 2½ gallons)** of 170°F water to make 1 gallon (or 5 gallons) wort.

• Bring to a boil over high heat. Add the Perle hops and boil vigorously for 40 minutes. Add the Tettnanger hops for flavoring, the reduced cider, maple syrup, and Irish moss and continue boiling for another 20 minutes. Add the Tettnanger hops for aroma and remove from the heat. (Total boil time: 60 minutes.)

• Cool to at least 75°F and transfer to a sanitized primary fermentation bucket. Check the volume of your wort; add tap water as needed to make 1 gallon (or 5 gallons). Add the yeast starter and aerate the wort.

• Let ferment for at least **1 week or up to 4 weeks at 70°F**; then transfer to a sanitized jug or carboy for secondary fermentation. Continue to ferment for another **2 weeks or up to 2 months at 70°F**.

• Dissolve the sugar in ¼ (or 1) cup of boiling water and let cool. Mix with the beer, bottle, and store for **2 weeks or up to a year**. Refrigerate before drinking.

Tropical Island Tripel

Even monks deserve a vacation every once in a while, don't you think? I like to imagine this band of brothers returning from a jaunt to the tropics freshly inspired for their abbey brews. Surely they'd throw some coconut into their next beer and maybe the last few mangoes smuggled in with their luggage. Citra hops, juicy and fruity, would be just the thing to pull the whole brew together. A tropical tripel? Oh yes, that sounds like a vacation we *all* need.

Make It Yours Instead of mango, use pineapple, guava, or kiwi. Or try a barrel-aged effect: soak some oak cubes in rum and add them to the secondary. (Read more about adding oak cubes and fruit on page 166.)

Beers to Try Mischief (The Bruery), Golden Monkey (Victory Brewing)

INGREDIENTS	1-GALLON	5-GALLON
White Labs Belgian Golden Ale yeast, Wyeast Belgian Abbey yeast, or equivalent	½ package	1 package
Pilsner malt (preferably Belgian pilsner), milled	2½ lbs (1.13 kg)	12½ lbs (5.67 kg)
Biscuit malt, milled	2 oz (57 g)	10 oz (283 g)
Aromatic malt, milled	2 oz (57 g)	10 oz (283 g)
Citra pellet hops (12% AA), for bittering	.10 oz (3 g)	.50 oz (14 g)
Citra pellet hops (12% AA), for flavoring	.10 oz (3 g)	.50 oz (14 g)
Belgian light candi sugar	3 oz (85 g)	15 oz (425 g)
Irish moss	¼ tsp	1 tsp
Citra pellet hops (12% AA), for aroma	.15 oz (4 g)	.75 oz (21 g)
Diced fresh or frozen mango	4 oz (113 g or 1 cup)	20 oz (560 g or 5 cups)
Unsweetened flaked coconut	2.50 oz (71 g or ¾ cup)	12.50 oz (354 g or 3¾ cups)
Corn sugar, for bottling	.80 oz (22 g)	4 oz (113 g)

TARGET ORIGINAL/FINAL GRAVITY: 1.079/1.018
TARGET ABV: 8.1%

Follow the master method for brewing 1-gallon or 5-gallon all-grain batches as described on pages 54–59 (5-gallon measurements in parentheses).

• Remove liquid yeast from the refrigerator and, if necessary, activate according to package instructions. Place on the counter to warm.

• Heat **1 gallon (or 4½ gallons) of water to 164°F**, then stir in the grains. Maintain a mash temperature of **154°F to 158°F** for 60 minutes. Raise the temperature of the mash to 170°F, then sparge using **1 gallon (or 2½ gallons)** of 170°F water to make 1½ (or 5½) gallons wort.

• Bring to a boil over high heat. Add the hops for bittering and boil vigorously for 40 minutes. Add the hops for flavoring, the candi sugar, and the Irish moss and continue boiling for another 20 minutes. Add the hops for aroma and remove from the heat. (Total boil time: 60 minutes.)

• Cool to at least 75°F and transfer to a sanitized primary fermentation bucket. Add the yeast and aerate the wort.

• Let ferment for at least **1 week or up to 4 weeks at 70°F**. When ready to transfer the beer for secondary fermentation, add the mango and coconut to a sanitized jug or carboy and siphon the beer over top. Continue to ferment for another **2 weeks or up to 2 months at 70°F**.

• Taste the beer after 2 weeks. Add more mango or coconut if you wish. When ready to bottle, siphon the beer to a sanitized bucket or stockpot to separate it from the fruit and coconut. Clean and sanitize the jug, and transfer the beer back into the jug. Let stand another few days to allow any remaining solids to settle to the bottom.

• Dissolve the sugar in ¼ (or 1) cup of boiling water and let cool. Mix with the beer, bottle, and store for **2 weeks or up to a year**. Refrigerate before drinking.

Fuzzy Nose Sour Ale

Sour ales are the kind of beer you either love or hate. As you can probably guess, I fall solidly in the "love" camp. I just can't get enough of that funky, tart, nose-tickling flavor. It's unlike any other beer out there. Sours are not hard to brew, but they do take time—brettanomyces is a slow-working yeast. Give this at least a year before you open a bottle, preferably longer.

Brew Notes I highly suggest investing in a second set of equipment if you'd like to brew sour ales regularly, as the risk for contaminating other brews with brett yeast is high. If you don't, pay very careful attention to cleaning and sanitizing your equipment after using. Read "Get Funky with Sour Beers," page 140, before making this recipe.

Make It Yours Add some fruit flavor with some fruit-forward hops, like Galaxy or Mosaic, or a fruitier strain of Belgian yeast. To make an authentic gueuze-style sour ale, blend a few bottles of this batch with your next one.

Beers to Try Temptation (Russian River Brewing Company), Brute (Ithaca Brewing Company)

INGREDIENTS	1-GALLON	5-GALLON
White Labs Belgian Saison yeast, Wyeast Belgian Saison yeast, or equivalent	1 package, divided	2 packages, divided
Pilsner malt (preferably Belgian pilsner), milled	2¼ lbs (1.02 kg)	11¼ lbs (5.10 kg)
Munich malt, milled	4 oz (113 g)	1¼ lbs (567 g)
Wheat malt, milled	4 oz (113 g)	1¼ lbs (567 g)
Palisade pellet hops (7.1% AA), for bittering	.10 oz (3 g)	.50 oz (14 g)
Falconer's Flight pellet hops (9.9% AA), for flavoring	.10 oz (3 g)	.50 oz (14 g)
Irish moss	¼ tsp	1 tsp
Falconer's Flight pellet hops (9.9% AA), for aroma	.10 oz (3 g)	.50 oz (14 g)
White Labs Brettanomyces bruxellensis, Wyeast Brettanomyces bruxellensis, or equivalent	½ package	1 package
Corn sugar, for bottling	.80 oz (22 g)	4 oz (113 g)

TARGET ORIGINAL/FINAL GRAVITY: 1.073/1.021
TARGET ABV: 6.9%

Follow the master method for brewing 1-gallon or 5-gallon all-grain batches as described on pages 54–59 (5-gallon measurements in parentheses).

• Remove ½ (or 1) package of Belgian saison liquid yeast from the refrigerator and, if necessary, activate according to package instructions. Place on the counter to warm.

• Heat **1 gallon (or 4½ gallons) of water to 160°F**, then stir in the grains. Maintain a mash temperature of **148°F to 153°F** for 60 minutes. Raise the temperature of the mash to 170°F, then sparge using **1 gallon (or 2½ gallons)** of 170°F water to make 1½ (or 5½) gallons wort.

• Bring to a boil over high heat. Add the Palisade hops and boil vigorously for 40 minutes. Add the Falconer's Flight hops for flavoring and the Irish moss and continue boiling for another 20 minutes. Add the Falconer's Flight hops for aroma and remove from the heat. (Total boil time: 60 minutes.)

• Cool to at least 75°F and transfer to a sanitized primary fermentation bucket. Add the ½ (or 1) package saison yeast and aerate the wort.

• Let ferment for at least **1 week or up to 4 weeks at 70°F**. When ready to transfer the beer for secondary fermentation, let the brettanomyces yeast warm on the counter for a few hours. Add it to the sanitized jug and siphon the beer over top. Continue to ferment for another **3 months or up to 1 year at 70°F**.

• Dissolve the sugar in ¼ (or 1) cup of boiling water and let cool. Bottle **with the remaining ½ (or 1) package saison yeast** to ensure carbonation, and store for **1 month or up to several years**. Refrigerate before drinking. (This beer doesn't start to taste sour until about 1 year after brewing and improves the longer you let it sit.)

Peach Melba Sour Lambic

Sour beer + fruit = happiness. This is a well-known equation. Sours naturally have a lot of tart fruit flavors, so adding actual fruit takes things one step closer to heaven. A mix of fresh raspberries and summer peaches as found in a classic melba sauce? Heavenly to the nth degree.

Brew Notes I highly suggest investing in a second set of equipment if you'd like to brew sour ales regularly, as the risk for contaminating other brews with brett yeast is high. If you don't, pay very careful attention to cleaning and sanitizing your equipment after using. Read "Get Funky with Sour Beers," page 140, before making this recipe.

Make It Yours Just head to the farmers' market and grab some fruit! Sour cherries, strawberries, mangoes—I can't think of a single fruit that wouldn't be delicious (see page 166).

Beers to Try Raspberry Tart (New Glarus Brewing Co.), Juliet (Goose Island Beer Company)

INGREDIENTS	1-GALLON	5-GALLON
White Labs Abbey Ale yeast, Wyeast Belgian Abbey yeast, or equivalent	1 package, divided	2 packages, divided
Whole peaches	2 lbs (907 g, 4 to 5) (about 4½ cups chopped)	10 lbs (4.54 kg, about 25) (about 23 cups chopped)
Pilsner malt (preferably Belgian pilsner), milled	1½ lbs (680 g)	7½ lbs (3.40 kg)
Wheat malt, milled	12 oz (340 g)	3¾ lbs (1.70 kg)
Spalt pellet hops (4.75% AA), for bittering	.10 oz (3 g)	.50 oz (14 g)
Irish moss	¼ tsp	1 tsp
Fresh or frozen raspberries	½ lb (227 g)	2½ lbs (1.13 kg)
Spalt pellet hops (4.75 % AA), for aroma	.10 oz (3 g)	.50 oz (14 g)
White Labs Brettanomyces bruxellensis, Wyeast Brettanomyces bruxellensis, or equivalent	½ package	1 package
Corn sugar, for bottling	.80 oz (22 g)	4 oz (113 g)

TARGET ORIGINAL/FINAL GRAVITY: 1.065/ 1.012
TARGET ABV: 7%

Follow the master method for brewing 1-gallon or 5-gallon all-grain batches as described on pages 54–59 (5-gallon measurements in parentheses).

• Remove ½ (or 1) package of abbey liquid yeast from the refrigerator and, if necessary, activate according to package instructions. Place on the counter to warm.

• Peel the peaches with a vegetable peeler, then coarsely chop, discarding the pits.

• Heat **1 gallon (or 3½ gallons) of water to 160°F**, then stir in the grains. Maintain a mash temperature of **148°F to 153°F** for 60 minutes. Raise the temperature of the mash to 170°F, then sparge using **1 gallon (or 3 gallons)** of 170°F water to make 1½ (or 5½) gallons wort.

• Bring to a boil over high heat. Add the hops for bittering and boil vigorously for 40 minutes. Add the Irish moss and continue boiling for another 15 minutes. Add the peaches and raspberries, return to a boil, and continue boiling for another 5 minutes. Add the hops for aroma and remove from the heat. (Total boil time: 60 minutes.)

• Cool to at least 75°F and transfer to a sanitized primary fermentation bucket. Do not strain. Add the ½ (or 1) package abbey yeast and aerate the wort.

• Let ferment for at least **1 week or up to 4 weeks at 70°F**. When ready to transfer the beer for secondary fermentation warm the brettanomyces yeast on the counter for a few hours. Add to the sanitized jug, and carefully siphon the beer over top, leaving the fruit behind. Taste after 1 month and add more fruit if you wish. Continue to ferment for another **2 months or up to 1 year at 70°F**. If waiting longer than 2 months, transfer the beer off any added fruit.

• Dissolve the sugar in ¼ (or 1) cup of boiling water and let cool. Mix ½ (or 1) package of yeast and the sugar mixture into the beer. Bottle and store for **1 month or up to several years**. Refrigerate before drinking. (This beer starts tasting sour at 1 year and improves the longer you let it sit.)

GET FUNKY WITH SOUR BEERS

A beer with tart, sour, funky, barnyard-like flavors can be seen as either a colossal mistake or the ultimate homebrewing achievement. The difference is in whether you meant for those mouth-puckering sour flavors to appear in your brew . . . or not.

WHAT IS A SOUR BEER?

Traditionally speaking, a sour beer is one that has been fermented with wild yeasts and bacteria—those that happen to be floating around in the air as the beer is brewed or that live in the tank where it ferments. This probably sounds more like poor sanitation than good brewing practice, and in a way, it is! Think of this as intentionally poor sanitation. In the breweries that have historically produced sour beer, particularly those located near Brussels in Belgium, these wild yeasts and bacteria have been carefully cultivated to the point where they now live in the air and the walls of the breweries themselves.

This spontaneous fermentation leads to some completely unexpected flavors—green apple, sour grape, barnyard, horse, musty leather, tart fruit, and sour candy. As strange as these flavors might sound, sour beers are truly some of the most complex and intriguing beers around.

WHICH BEERS TO SOUR?

Any beer style can be used as a base for a sour beer. I like using a saison or wheat beer base because I think their simple, light malt profile shows off funky flavors in the best way possible. This said, strong ales, brown ales, and even porters can make very interesting sour beers.

Stay away from super-hoppy styles or beers with a large percentage of darkly roasted, bitter malts, however. Hop flavors often get scrubbed away during the long aging process, and bitter flavors can throw off the balance of the finished beer.

WHY YOU SHOULD GET A SECOND SET OF EQUIPMENT

Wild yeasts are pernicious and hard to kill. They survive in the nooks and crannies of your equipment, often despite your most thorough cleaning efforts. And while you might love the brett character in your latest batch of lambic, you probably won't love it in your next batch of IPA. To prevent errant and unwanted cross-contamination, I highly recommend investing in a second set of equipment for your sour beer experiments: fermentation bucket, jug or carboy, siphon and siphon hoses, air locks—the whole set.

MAKING SOUR BEERS WITH WILD YEAST AND BACTERIA

To make true homebrewed sours, you don't have to leave your fermenter open and cross your fingers. Many of the wild yeast strains and bacteria traditionally used to make sours are commercially available at homebrewing stores. Here are the usual suspects.

Brettanomyces. Brett is the big papa of the wild yeast world. It produces all those glorious funky, barnyardy flavors we love in a classic gueuze. It is slow-working, so give it plenty of time to do its job. You might not notice any brett character at all for several months after adding it to your beer, and it might take a year or more for your beer to get as funky as you like. Also, note that while brett brings the funk, it does not bring any sourness.

Lactobacillus. This bacteria puts the "sour" in sour ales. It produces lactic acid, which has a tangy, tart flavor profile. You'll recognize it from eating foods like yogurt and sauerkraut. It works a little more quickly than brett, but even so, give beers made with lactobacillus a couple of months to a year (or even longer!) to get nice and tart.

Pediococcus. This guy is in the same bacterial family as lactobacillus. In the short term, it produces buttery-tasting diacetyl along with a good amount of lactic acid, but let the beer mellow for a good long while and the yeasts in the beer eventually absorb the diacetyl. What remains is a clean, bright acidity in the beer.

Brett yeast, lactobacillus, and pediococcus can be used individually or in combination; some yeast manufacturers produce ready-made blends of all three. Brett can also be used on its own to ferment a beer, but since it's so slow to work, I recommend including another strain of regular brewer's yeast to get things going.

Add these souring agents to the beer at the start of fermentation, when transferring to the secondary, or even before bottling. Keep beers inoculated with wild yeast or bacteria in the secondary until you think they're ready to bottle—taste every few months and transfer the beer off the sediment into a clean jug every now and then. Sour beers will continue to age well for years.

Bonus idea! If you want to experiment with a sour and unsoured version of the same beer, add some brett and bacteria to half your batch of beer just before bottling.

MAKING SOUR BEERS WITH A SOUR MASH

If you're feeling impatient and don't want to wait a year or more before drinking your first sour beer, consider doing a sour mash. In principle, the idea is simple: mash your beer as normal, then let the mash sit out for a day or two until it smells and tastes sour, then sparge, boil, and ferment as usual. The sourness in the mash comes from lactobacillus strains that live on the surface of the grains. Once the grains are sparged and the wort is boiled, all the bacteria is killed. Fermentation can continue without risk of continued souring, the need for longer aging, or cross-contamination with other brews made with the same equipment.

In reality, a really good sour mash can be tricky. Along with our friend lactobacillus, other less friendly bacteria are also eager to take up residence in the warm, sultry environment of the mash. They can make the mash smell and taste like vinegar at best or vomit at worst. Yuck.

The real trick is keeping the sour mash between 115°F and 120°F until it has soured to your liking. Here's how to do it.

1. *Mash the grains. Set aside a handful of dry grain before mashing to use as a "starter" for the lactobacillus. Mash your beer as usual.*

2. *Cool and store the mash. Transfer the mash to a small container. Let it cool to 120°F, then stir in the reserved dry grain. Press some plastic wrap right up against the surface of the mash to minimize contact with the air and encourage an* anaerobic environment (which we want). Cover the container itself with another layer of plastic wrap or a lid.

3. *Keep the mash between 115°F and 120°F until soured. Place the mash somewhere warm and keep it between 115°F and 120°F. A dehydrator or bread proofing box is ideal, but wrapping the container in a towel and keeping it on a heating pad also works. Check the temperature frequently; avoid stirring the mash, as oxygen can introduce some of those nonfriendly bacteria or start some aerobic enzymatic reactions (which we don't want). Taste and smell the mash every so often; it should sour within 12 to 48 hours.*

4. *Continue brewing the beer. Once the mash has soured to your liking, sparge, proceed with the hop boil, and ferment as usual.*

If you don't want to brew right away, you can keep the sour mash in the fridge for a day or so. The cool temperature makes the bacteria slow down and prevents the mash from becoming too sour.

EXPERIMENTAL SOURS

Souring beers with wild yeast and bacteria or with a sour mash are the most typical and time-honored ways to make a sour beer, but if you have a brave and adventurous spirit, you can experiment! Wild brettanomyces live on the surface of most fruits, especially grapes—try pitching some raw fruit right into the primary. Or top off your batch with some leftover whey from cheesemaking, which has long been used to kick-start lacto-fermentation in foods.

As a final thought, look into brewing with kombucha. This tart and fizzy fermented tea is also made with a dual yeast-and-bacteria fermentation, just like sour ales, and has a lot of similar flavors. Blend bottles of kombucha with a finished beer to make a quick sour ale, or add raw kombucha (or even the scoby used to make kombucha) to the beer as it ferments.

If you've already discovered the pleasures of a robust, malty Scottish ale or the incomparable smoothness of a good Irish red, I salute you. However, if you just walked into the party, allow me to make introductions.

Scottish ales are cousins to British milds and bitters (see chapter 8), but with a heartier, maltier profile. They are low-alcohol, but they carry the weight and flavor of a bigger beer thanks to a unique step in the brewing process: the first runnings from the wort (taken before sparging) are boiled separately until they become syrupy and caramelized; then they're stirred back into the main wort. This gives Scottish ales—and their boozier kinfolk, Scotch ales and wee heavies—their signature caramelized flavor. Read more about this technique in "Get Geeky with the Mash," page 102.

Irish reds also flaunt a malty profile, but because they are mashed at a slightly lower temperature, they are also quite crisp and smooth. They also end up with a slightly higher ABV, a lighter body, and a drier finish. (See "Get Geeky with the Mash," page 102.) These beers are the definition of easy drinking, and they deserve to be appreciated beyond St. Patrick's Day.

SCOTTISH AND IRISH RED ALES

[chapter 10]

A VERY GOOD SCOTTISH ALE

This is an ale for those times when you want something malty and rich but without the booze. Like most beers from across the pond, this one doesn't have much concern for hops; there are just enough in the boil to keep the beer from being cloying. Also, don't confuse this beer with Scotch ales or wee heavies—those are the brawny, grown-up versions of this relatively polite and demure Scottish ale.

Brew Notes The rich, sugary first runnings from the wort are boiled separately for this beer; read the directions carefully.

Make It Yours For an extra layer of complexity in this super-malty brew, add a few bags of black tea during the secondary and let them infuse for a few days. This adds a soft, gentle bitterness along with some floral tea flavors and aromas. If you use tea in both the boil and the secondary, skip the hops altogether to make a gruit-style Scottish ale!

Beers to Try Robert the Bruce Scottish Ale (Three Floyds Brewing Company), Odell 90 Shilling Ale (Odel Brewing Company), Hibernator (Long Trail Brewing Company)

INGREDIENTS	1-GALLON	5-GALLON
White Labs Edinborough yeast, Wyeast Scottish Ale yeast, or equivalent	½ package	1 package
Maris Otter malt, milled	1½ lbs (680 g)	7½ lbs (3.40 kg)
Crystal/Caramel 80 malt, milled	2 oz (57 g)	10 oz (283 g)
Roasted barley malt, milled	.50 oz (14 g)	2.50 oz (71 g)
East Kent Goldings pellet hops (7.2% AA), for bittering	.10 oz (3 g)	.50 oz (14 g)
East Kent Goldings pellet hops (7.2% AA), for flavoring	.10 oz (3 g)	.50 oz (14 g)
Irish moss	¼ tsp	1 tsp
Corn sugar, for bottling	.70 oz (20 g)	3.50 oz (100 g)

TARGET ORIGINAL/FINAL GRAVITY: 1.045/1.015
TARGET ABV: 3.9%

Follow the master method for brewing 1-gallon or 5-gallon all-grain batches as described on pages 54–59 (5-gallon measurements in parentheses).

• Remove liquid yeast from the refrigerator and, if necessary, activate according to package instructions. Place on the counter to warm.

• Heat **3 quarts (or 3 gallons) of water to 164°F**, then stir in the grains. Maintain a mash temperature of **154°F to 158°F** for 60 minutes. Raise the temperature of the mash to 170°F. To collect the first runnings, drain **½ (or 1) gallon** of liquid from the mash and set aside. Sparge as usual using **1 gallon (or 3½ gallons)** of 170°F water, to make 1 gallon (or 5 gallons) wort.

• Bring to a boil over high heat. Add the hops for bittering and boil vigorously for 40 minutes.

Meanwhile, bring the first runnings to a boil in a large saucepot (be attentive for boil-overs!) and reduce by half. Add the reduced first runnings, the hops for flavoring, and the Irish moss to the wort and continue boiling for another 20 minutes. Remove from the heat. (Total boil time: 60 minutes.)

• Cool to at least 75°F and transfer to a sanitized primary fermentation bucket. Check the volume of your wort; add tap water as needed to make 1 gallon (or 5 gallons). Add the yeast and aerate the wort.

• Let ferment for at least **1 week or up to 4 weeks at 70°F**; then transfer to a sanitized jug or carboy for secondary fermentation. Continue to ferment for another **2 weeks or up to 2 months at 70°F**.

• Dissolve the sugar in ¼ (or 1) cup of boiling water and let cool. Mix with the beer, bottle, and store for **2 weeks or up to a year**. Refrigerate before drinking.

A VERY GOOD IRISH RED ALE

Drinking a good Irish red feels like settling in with a very good, very old friend, one who doesn't mind it when you kick off your shoes under the table or steal a fry from his plate. It's a beer that's as easy to love as it is to drink: toasty malts, crisp finish, smooth going down. Go on, have another. No need to stand on ceremony here.

Make It Yours Citrus flavors make a nice contrast to the crisp, though malty, character of this beer. Trade the British hops for some American West Coast hops or add some lemon peel to the secondary.

Beers to Try Conway's Irish Ale (Great Lakes Brewing Company), Irish Ale (Boulevard Brewing Company), Harpoon Celtic Ale (Harpoon Brewery)

INGREDIENTS	1-GALLON	5-GALLON
White Labs Irish Ale yeast, Wyeast Irish Ale yeast, or equivalent	½ package	1 package
Maris Otter malt, milled	2 lbs (907 g)	10 lbs (4.54 kg)
Crystal/Caramel 40 malt, milled	4 oz (113 g)	1¼ lbs (567 g)
Roasted barley malt, milled	.50 oz (14 g)	2.50 oz (71 g)
Fuggles pellet hops (5.3% AA), for bittering	.15 oz (4 g)	.75 oz (21 g)
Fuggles pellet hops (5.3% AA), for flavoring	.15 oz (4 g)	.75 oz (21 g)
Irish moss	¼ tsp	1 tsp
Corn sugar, for bottling	.80 oz (22 g)	4 oz (113 g)

TARGET ORIGINAL/FINAL GRAVITY: 1.054/1.015
TARGET ABV: 5.1%

Follow the master method for brewing 1-gallon or 5-gallon all-grain batches as described on pages 54–59 (5-gallon measurements in parentheses).

• Remove liquid yeast from the refrigerator and, if necessary, activate according to package instructions. Place on the counter to warm.

• Heat **1 gallon (or 3½ gallons) of water to 156˚F**, then stir in the grains. Maintain a mash temperature of **142˚F to 147˚F for 60 minutes**. Raise the temperature of the mash to 170˚F, then sparge using **1 gallon (or 3 gallons)** of 170˚F water to make 1½ (or 5½) gallons wort.

• Bring to a boil over high heat. Add the hops for bittering and boil vigorously for 40 minutes. Add the hops for flavoring and the Irish moss and continue boiling for another 20 minutes. Remove from the heat. (Total boil time: 60 minutes.)

• Cool to at least 75˚F and transfer to a sanitized primary fermentation bucket. Add the yeast and aerate the wort.

• Let ferment for at least **1 week or up to 4 weeks at 70˚F**; then transfer to a sanitized jug or carboy for secondary fermentation. Continue to ferment for another **2 weeks or up to 2 months at 70˚F.**

• Dissolve the sugar in ¼ (or 1) cup of boiling water and let cool. Mix with the beer, bottle, and store for **2 weeks or up to a year**. Refrigerate before drinking.

Day Hiker Irish Red

Is it just me or does *nothing* taste better after a long hike than a cold beer? Especially if you happen to be sitting outside in a camp chair at the time, and especially if you discover a handful of trail mix still left in your pocket? This beer captures that moment exactly. It's crisp and smooth, smelling of forest and moss and fresh air. A handful of dried currants added to the boil gives this malty beer a slight berry flavor that completes the picture nicely.

Make It Yours If you like Flanders red ales with their interesting mix of sweet, fruity, and sour flavors, give this a little souring action. Add some lactobacillus culture along with the yeast and let sit for a month or two in the secondary before bottling. It should start showing some sour character about 6 months after brewing.

Beers to Try Hot Red Ale (Aviator Brewing Company), Lobstah Killah from Slumbrew (Sommerville Brewing Company), Irish Setter Red (Thirsty Dog Brewing Company)

INGREDIENTS	1-GALLON	5-GALLON
White Labs Irish Ale yeast, Wyeast Irish Ale yeast, or equivalent	½ package	1 package
Maris Otter malt, milled	1½ lbs (680 g)	7½ lbs (3.40 kg)
Crystal 20 malt, milled	4 oz (113 g)	1¼ lbs (567 g)
Crystal 40 malt, milled	4 oz (113 g)	1¼ lbs (567 g)
Roasted barley malt, milled	.50 oz (14 g)	2.50 oz (71 g)
Northern Brewer pellet hops (9.6% AA), for bittering	.10 oz (3 g)	.50 oz (7 g)
Northern Brewer pellet hops (9.6% AA), for flavoring	.05 oz (1.5 g)	.25 oz (14 g)
Irish moss	¼ tsp	1 tsp
Dried black currants	3 oz (84 g)	15 oz (425 g)
Corn sugar, for bottling	.80 oz (22 g)	4 oz (113 g)

TARGET ORIGINAL/FINAL GRAVITY: 1.054/1.014
TARGET ABV: 5.3%

Follow the master method for brewing 1-gallon or 5-gallon all-grain batches as described on pages 54–59 (5-gallon measurements in parentheses).

• Remove liquid yeast from the refrigerator and, if necessary, activate according to package instructions. Place on the counter to warm.

• Heat **1 gallon (or 3½ gallons) of water to 156°F**, then stir in the grains. Maintain a mash temperature of **142°F to 147°F** for 60 minutes. Raise the temperature of the mash to 170°F, then sparge using **1 gallon (or 3 gallons)** of 170°F water to make 1½ (or 5½) gallons wort.

• Bring to a boil over high heat. Add the hops for bittering and boil vigorously for 40 minutes. Add the hops for flavoring and the Irish moss and continue boiling for another 15 minutes. Add the currants and continue boiling for another 5 minutes. Remove from the heat. (Total boil time: 60 minutes.)

• Cool to at least 75°F and transfer to the sanitized primary fermentation bucket. Add the yeast and aerate the wort.

• Let ferment for at least **1 week or up to 4 weeks at 70°F**; then transfer to a sanitized jug or carboy for secondary fermentation. Continue to ferment for another **2 weeks or up to 2 months at 70°F**.

• Taste the beer a few days before you plan to bottle. If you'd like a stronger currant flavor, steep 1½ (or 7½) ounces currants in just enough vodka to cover for 15 minutes, then drain and add to the beer. Taste daily and bottle when the beer tastes good to you.

• Dissolve the sugar in ¼ (or 1) cup of boiling water and let cool. Mix with the beer, bottle, and store for **2 weeks or up to a year**. Refrigerate before drinking.

Caramel-Coconut Wee Heavy

Call them Samoas or call them Caramel deLites, either way this Girl Scout cookie is my kryptonite. In the midst of withdrawal after the most recent cookie season, I realized that the flavors of my beloved Samoas would make a fantastic wee heavy. This super-sized version of a Scottish ale is well known for its seductive caramel and milk chocolate flavors. I help things along by adding shredded coconut and roasted cacao nibs to the brew.

Brew Notes The rich, sugary first runnings from the wort are boiled separately for this beer; read the directions carefully.

Make It Yours Use this beer as a base for all your dessert-meets-beer fantasies. Swap the coconut and cacao nibs for fresh peaches to make Peach Pie Ale. (Or ripe fall apples to make Apple Pie Ale!) (See "Adding Fruits, Spices, and Other Fun Things to Beer," page 166, for more.)

Beers to Try Dirty Bastard (Founders Brewing Company), Wee Heavy (Belhaven Brewery)

INGREDIENTS	1-GALLON	5-GALLON
White Labs Edinborough yeast, Wyeast Scottish Ale yeast, or equivalent	½ package	1 package
Maris Otter malt, milled	2½ lbs (1.13 kg)	12½ lbs (5.67 kg)
Crystal/Caramel 60 malt, milled	8 oz (227 g)	2½ lbs (1.13 kg)
Special B malt, milled	1 oz (28 g)	5 oz (142 g)
East Kent Goldings pellet hops (7.2% AA), for bittering	.15 oz (4 g)	.75 oz (21 g)
East Kent Goldings pellet hops (7.2% AA), for flavoring	.10 oz (3 g)	.50 oz (14 g)
Irish moss	¼ tsp	1 tsp
Unsweetened flaked coconut	2.50 oz (71 g or ¾ cup)	12.50 oz (354 g or 3¾ cups)
Roasted cacao nibs	1 oz (28 g or scant ¼ cup)	5 oz (142 g or 1¼ cups)
Corn sugar, for bottling	.70 oz (20 g)	3.5 oz (100 g)

TARGET ORIGINAL/FINAL GRAVITY: 1.082/1.025
TARGET ABV: 7.6%

Follow the master method for brewing 1-gallon or 5-gallon all-grain batches as described on pages 54–59 (5-gallon measurements in parentheses).

• Remove liquid yeast from the refrigerator and, if necessary, activate according to package instructions. Place on the counter to warm.

• Heat **1 gallon (or 5 gallons) of water to 164°F**, then stir in the grains. Maintain a mash temperature of **154°F to 158°F** for 60 minutes. Raise the temperature of the mash to 170°F. To collect the first runnings, drain ½ **(or 1) gallon** of liquid from the mash and set aside. Sparge as usual using **1 gallon (or 2½ gallons)** of 170°F water, to make 1 gallon (or 5 gallons) wort.

• Bring to a boil over high heat. Add the hops for bittering and boil vigorously for 40 minutes. Meanwhile, bring the first runnings to a boil in a large saucepot (be attentive for boil-overs!) and reduce by half. Add the first runnings, the hops for flavoring, and the Irish moss to the wort and continue boiling for another 20 minutes. Remove from the heat. (Total boil time: 60 minutes.)

• Cool to at least 75°F and transfer to a sanitized primary fermentation bucket. Check the volume of your wort; add tap water as needed to make 1 gallon (or 5 gallons). Add the yeast and aerate the wort.

• Let ferment for at least **1 week or up to 4 weeks at 70°F**. When ready to transfer the beer for secondary fermentation, add the coconut and cacao nibs to a sanitized jug and siphon the beer over top. Let sit for at least **2 weeks or up to 1 month at 70°F**. Taste occasionally and add more coconut or cacao nibs if desired. When ready to bottle, siphon the beer off the solids into a sanitized bucket or stockpot. Clean and sanitize the jug, and transfer the beer back into the jug. Let stand another few days to allow any remaining solids to settle to the bottom.

• Dissolve the sugar in ¼ (or 1) cup of boiling water and let cool. Mix with the beer, bottle, and store for **2 weeks or up to a year**. Refrigerate before drinking.

Smoke & Scotch Ale

Any fellow scotch lovers out there? This one's for you. It's another grown-up version of a Scottish ale, but it's less candy-sweet and a touch more bitter than a wee heavy. It also gets a double dose of smokiness: first with some smoked malts in the mash and then with scotch-soaked oak cubes in the secondary.

Brew Notes You'll need to make a yeast starter for this recipe to ensure good fermentation. The rich, sugary first runnings from the wort are boiled separately for this beer; read the directions carefully.

Make It Yours Nix the booze-soaked oak cubes for a solid, malty Scotch ale with a hint of campfire. Add some spruce tips à la Pine Woods Pale Ale (page 74) for a deep woods fantasy.

Beers to Try Old Chub (Oskar Blues), Claymore Scotch Ale (Great Divide Brewing Company)

Follow the master method for brewing 1-gallon or 5-gallon all-grain batches as described on pages 54–59 (5-gallon measurements in parentheses).

• Using the yeast and malt extract, make a yeast starter 12 to 18 hours before you plan to brew, following the instructions in "How to Make a Yeast Starter," page 16.

• Heat **1 gallon (or 5 gallons)** of water to **164°F,** then stir in the grains. Maintain a mash temperature of **154°F to 158°F** for 60 minutes. Raise the temperature of the mash to 170°F. To collect the first runnings, drain ½ **(or 1) gallon** of liquid from the mash and set aside. Sparge as usual using **1 gallon (or 2 gallons)** of 170°F water, to make 1 gallon (or 5 gallons) wort.

• Bring to a boil over high heat. Add the East Kent Goldings hops and boil vigorously for 40 minutes. Meanwhile, in a large saucepot bring the first runnings to a boil (be attentive for boil-overs!) and reduce by half. Add the first runnings, the Willamette hops for flavoring, and the Irish moss to the wort and continue boiling for another 20 minutes. Add the Willamette hops for aroma and remove from the heat. (Total boil time: 60 minutes.)

INGREDIENTS	1-GALLON	5-GALLON
White Labs Edinborough yeast, Wyeast Scottish Ale yeast, or equivalent	½ package	1 package
Light dried malt extract	.90 oz (25 g or 2 heaping tbsps)	3.50 oz (100 g or ½ cup)
Maris Otter malt, milled	2½ lbs (1.13 kg)	12½ lbs (5.67 kg)
Crystal/Caramel 80 malt, milled	4 oz (113 g)	1¼ lbs (567 g)
Smoked malt, milled	2 oz (57 g)	10 oz (283 g)
Roasted barley malt, milled	1 oz (28 g)	5 oz (142 g)
East Kent Goldings pellet hops (7.2% AA), for bittering	.15 oz (4 g)	.75 oz (21 g)
Willamette pellet hops (4.7% AA), for flavoring	.15 oz (4 g)	.75 oz (21 g)
Irish moss	¼ tsp	1 tsp
Willamette pellet hops (4.7% AA), for aroma	.15 oz (4 g)	.75 oz (21 g)
Oak cubes	½ oz (14 g)	2½ oz (71 g)
Laphroaig Scotch Whisky, or equivalent	2 oz (57 g)	10 oz (283 g)
Corn sugar, for bottling	.70 oz (20 g)	3.50 oz (100 g)

TARGET ORIGINAL/FINAL GRAVITY: 1.079/1.015
TARGET ABV: 8.5%

• Cool to at least 75°F and transfer to a sanitized primary fermentation bucket. Check the volume; add tap water as needed to make 1 gallon (or 5 gallons). Add the yeast starter and aerate the wort.

• Let ferment for at least **1 week or up to 4 weeks at 70°F.** Meanwhile, soak the oak cubes in scotch for at least 1 week. When ready to transfer the beer for secondary fermentation, drain the oak cubes, reserving the scotch. Add the cubes to a sanitized jug and siphon the beer over top. Continue to ferment for another **2 weeks or up to 2 months at 70°F.** Taste the beer a few days before you plan to bottle. Add some of the reserved scotch if you wish. Dissolve the sugar in ¼ (or 1) cup of boiling water and let cool. Mix with the beer, bottle, and store for **2 weeks or up to a year.** Refrigerate before drinking.

TEN SMALL HABITS THAT WILL MAKE YOU A BETTER BREWER

Becoming a successful homebrewer isn't just about learning how to mash grains and bottle beer; it's also in the details. These are things that don't seem important as you're mastering the basic skills but that can really make a difference as you become a bona fide homebrewer.

HABIT 1:
CLEAN EQUIPMENT RIGHT AWAY

The last thing you probably want to do at the end of a long brew day or after bottling a huge batch of beer is clean up, but trust me, you'll be happier if you do. The longer you wait, the stickier and gummier the beer residue becomes and the harder it is to clean. This goes for empty beer bottles after a party, too. Not only does prompt attention to cleaning duties make your life easier, it makes your housemates happier, too, and thus more likely to support future homebrewing efforts.

HABIT 2:
SET A TIMER FOR EVERYTHING

This is to say, don't look at your kitchen clock and think you'll remember to add the next batch of hops in 40 minutes. You won't. (Been there, done that.) Always, always, always set a timer—for the mash, for the hop boil, for cooling down the wort. Small variances in how long you mash your grains or boil your hops make a big difference in the final flavor and character of your beer, so paying attention to timing really matters.

HABIT 3:
SET OUT EQUIPMENT AND INGREDIENTS AHEAD OF TIME

Rather than waiting until your timer dings to dig out the strainer or measure the next dose of hops, get those things done up front. I usually line up the brew day ingredients on my counter in the order in which I'll be adding them and move down the line as I go. Same with equipment.

HABIT 4:
DOUBLE-CHECK THE ALPHA ACID OF YOUR HOPS BEFORE BREWING

A hop's alpha acid percentage (AA%) is a measure of bittering power, and it is not a fixed thing. The AA% can vary widely from batch to batch and variety to variety, so before you brew, it's always good to check the AA% of the hops you bought versus the AA% of the hops in the recipe—this is triple-true if you're using a different hop than the recipe calls for. The AA% is printed on the outside of your hops package. If it differs from the recipe, recalculate how much hops you should use using the formula in "Play with Your Hops" on page 116.

HABIT 5:
TASTE THE BEER AT EVERY STAGE

Get into the habit of tasting the beer at every stage of the game. Sip a little of the wort before you add the yeast, taste again when you transfer it to the secondary, again when you're bottling, and, of course, when you pour your first glass. Not only does this give you insight into how sugary wort becomes delicious beer, but it also helps you keep tabs on how the beer is doing. You can spot potential problems, decide if it needs longer aging, choose to add dry hops for more aroma, or make any number of small decisions to refine your beer.

HABIT 6:
BE AWARE OF ROOM TEMPERATURE

Stay on top of the ambient temperature where you're storing your fermenting beer. As we talked about in "Brewing in Warm Weather, Brewing in Cold Weather" on page 128, ales like an ambient temperature of around 70°F and lagers like an ambient temperature of around 50°F. Don't forget that your beer is in the garage when a summer heat wave hits or when you get an early fall freeze. Move your beer where it will be close to its ideal temperature.

HABIT 7:
LABEL AND DATE YOUR BOTTLES

Six months from now when you discover a dusty bottle at the back of the cupboard, you won't remember whether this was your IPA or the barleywine. Save yourself a round of mystery beer and label that bottle! Adding the date also reminds you how old the beer is and lets you decide whether an about-to-expire beer should be enjoyed immediately or if an age-it-for-months beer needs a little more time. I'm a low-fuss gal, so I usually make labels using masking tape, though chalk pens also work well. If you're feeling fancy, you can design your own beer labels and print them out on sticky paper.

HABIT 8:
BE COOL WITH SUBSTITUTIONS

Substitutions are part of the game with home-brewing; you just have to roll with it! Brewing ingredients and equipment are more widely available than ever, but even so, not every home-brewing store carries exactly the same thing or has an item in stock when you need it. More likely than not, there's a close substitute for whatever you need. Ask for help, use your best judgment, and be cool with switcharoos.

HABIT 9:
TAKE NOTES ON EVERY BREW

Keep a beer log and take notes on every beer you make. Jot down the brew date, what recipe you followed, anything you changed, things that went wrong (or right!), gravity readings, and tasting notes. This record helps you home in on what makes one beer more successful than another and enables you to repeat your favorite beers. Your beer log also helps keep you organized if you're brewing multiple beers at once.

HABIT 10:
ENJOY THE BEER YOU BREW

This might sound pretty obvious and a little silly, but it's important to enjoy the beer you brew. Your homebrew might not be perfect or exactly what you were going for, but hey, it's beer! And you brewed it! Don't get so fixated on the technical details that you forget to take a moment to pat yourself on the back and really enjoy this beer you've spent so much time and effort making.

There's no mistaking a wheat beer. That hazy glow in the glass, the fluffy cap of foam, the smooth and silky feel in your mouth: all these signs point to wheat. The amount of wheat in the beer can vary based on style or brewer's whim, but 25 percent to 75 percent of the total grain bill is usual. Any less and the beer becomes more of a pale ale with some wheaty qualities; any more and you might have fermentation troubles since wheat lacks sufficient enzymes to totally convert starch into fermentable sugar.

The recipes in this chapter are your introduction to the wheat beer family, from a traditional hefeweizen to a witbier brewed with lavender and orange peels. I like brewing a few of these beers in late spring so that I can stock my beer fridge with fizzy, thirst-quenching wheat beers all summer long.

WHEAT BEERS

[chapter 11]

A VERY GOOD WHEAT BEER (HEFEWEIZEN)

Since the amount of wheat in a wheat beer can vary, let's start with something super basic: a 50-50 mix of wheat and barley malts. This blend makes a beer with good wheaty characteristics—foamy head, crisp flavors, creamy mouthfeel—that's also a breeze to brew (too much wheat can make things tricky).

German hefeweizens are traditionally made with a 50-50 blend, so that's what we're aiming for here. Pilsner malts (a kind of barley malt) make hefeweizens extra light and crisp, while a classic hefeweizen yeast adds notes of bananas and cloves. It's a lush summer brew, perfect for the hottest days.

Make It Yours Fresh apricots, mangoes, peaches, raspberries, and blueberries all make a very fun wheat beer. Take your pick of whatever is in season, chop it up, and add it right to the pot in the last 5 minutes of the boil. (Read more about adding fruit on page 166.)

Beers to Try Franziskaner Hefe-Weisse (Spaten-Franziskaner-Bräu), Dancing Man Wheat (New Glarus Brewing Company), Paulaner Hefe-Weissbier (Paulaner Brauerei)

INGREDIENTS	1-GALLON	5-GALLON
White Labs Hefeweizen Ale yeast, Wyeast German Wheat yeast, or equivalent	½ package	1 package
Pilsner malt, milled	1 lb (454 g)	5 lbs (2.27 kg)
Wheat malt, milled	1 lb (454 g)	5 lbs (2.27 kg)
Saaz pellet hops (2.9% AA), for bittering	.20 oz (5.50 g)	1 oz (28 g)
Irish moss	¼ tsp	1 tsp
Saaz pellet hops (2.9% AA), for aroma	.15 oz (4 g)	.75 oz (21 g)
Corn sugar, for bottling	.80 oz (22 g)	4 oz (113 g)

TARGET ORIGINAL/FINAL GRAVITY: 1.055/1.014
TARGET ABV: 5.4%

Follow the master method for brewing 1-gallon or 5-gallon all-grain batches as described on pages 54–59 (5-gallon measurements in parentheses).

• Remove liquid yeast from the refrigerator and, if necessary, activate according to package instructions. Place on the counter to warm.

• Heat **3 quarts (or 3½ gallons) of water to 160°F**, then stir in the grains. Maintain a mash temperature of **148°F to 153°F** for 60 minutes. Raise the temperature of the mash to 170°F, then sparge using **1½ (or 3) gallons** of 170°F water to make 1½ (or 5½) gallons wort.

• Bring to a boil over high heat. Add the hops for bittering and boil vigorously for 40 minutes. Add the Irish moss and continue boiling for another 20 minutes. Add the hops for aroma and remove from the heat. (Total boil time: 60 minutes.)

• Cool to at least 75°F and transfer to the sanitized primary fermentation bucket. Add the yeast and aerate the wort.

• Let ferment for at least **1 week or up to 4 weeks at 70°F**; then transfer to a sanitized jug or carboy for secondary fermentation. Continue to ferment for another **2 weeks or up to 2 months at 70°F**.

• Dissolve the sugar in ¼ (or 1) cup of boiling water and let cool. Mix with the beer, bottle, and store for **2 weeks or up to a year**. Refrigerate before drinking.

Sweet-Tart Berliner Weisse

On a sultry summer afternoon, a Berliner weisse like this one could give any icy glass of lemonade a run for its money. This tart, low-alcohol German beer is thirst-quenching with a capital "T." It's brewed with a smaller percentage of wheat—about 40% this time—but that's still enough for this beer to have some wheat character. We also give it some *Lactobacillus delbrueki*, a lactic acid–producing bacteria that makes the beer extra tart. Berliner weisse is often served with sweet fruit syrup drizzled into the glass to help cut the sour—try this if you feel so inclined!

Brew Notes Unlike sour ales or lambics where wild yeast and bacteria are added after primary fermentation, here the wild yeast and commercial yeast are added at the same time. This speeds up the souring process and gives the beer some unique flavors. (Read up on sour ales on page 140.) If aging longer than 3 months, add fresh yeast when bottling to ensure carbonation.

Make It Yours Since Berliner weisses are often served with fruit syrup, why not add the fruit to begin with? Try pomegranates, rhubarb, blackberries, strawberries, and peaches—any of these are bound to be delicious. (Read more about adding fruit on page 166.)

Beers to Try Festina Peche (Dogfish Head Craft Brewery), Hottenroth (The Bruery), Justin Blabaer (Evil Twin Brewing)

INGREDIENTS	1-GALLON	5-GALLON
White Labs Belgian Wit yeast, Wyeast German Ale yeast, or equivalent	½ package	1 package
White Labs Lactobacillus delbrueki, Wyeast Lactobacillus, or equivalent	½ package	1 package
Pilsner malt, milled	12 oz (340 g)	3¾ lbs (1.70 kg)
Wheat malt, milled	8 oz (227 g)	2½ lbs (1.13 kg)
Northern Brewer pellet hops (9.6% AA), for bittering	.05 oz (1.50 g)	.25 oz (7 g)
Palisade pellet hops (7% AA), for flavoring	.05 oz (1.50 g)	.25 oz (7 g)
Irish moss	¼ tsp	1 tsp
Palisade pellet hops (7% AA), for aroma	.15 oz (4.5 g)	.75 oz (21 g)
Corn sugar, for bottling	.80 oz (22 g)	4 oz (113 g)

TARGET ORIGINAL/FINAL GRAVITY: 1.034/1.006
TARGET ABV: 3.7%

Follow the master method for brewing 1-gallon or 5-gallon all-grain batches as described on pages 54–59 (5-gallon measurements in parentheses).

• Remove liquid yeast and lactobacillus from the refrigerator and, if necessary, activate according to package instructions. Place on the counter to warm.

• Heat **3 quarts (or 2½ gallons) of water to 156°F**, then stir in the grains. Maintain a mash temperature of **142°F to 147°F for 60 minutes**. Raise the temperature of the mash to 170°F, then sparge using **1½ (or 4) gallons** of 170°F water to make 1½ (or 5½) gallons wort.

• Bring to a boil over high heat. Add the Northern Brewer hops and boil vigorously for 40 minutes. Add the Palisade hops for flavoring and the Irish moss and continue boiling for another 20 minutes. Add the Palisade hops for aroma and remove from the heat. (Total boil time: 60 minutes.)

• Cool to at least 75°F and transfer to a sanitized primary fermentation bucket. Add the yeast and lactobacillus and aerate the wort.

• Let ferment for at least **1 week or up to 4 weeks at 70°F**; then transfer to a sanitized jug or carboy for secondary fermentation. Continue to ferment for another **month or up to 6 months at 70°F**.

• Dissolve the sugar in ¼ (or 1) cup of boiling water and let cool. Mix with the beer, bottle, and store for **2 weeks or up to a year**. Refrigerate before drinking.

Salty Dog Gose

Gose beers are sour, citrusy, and oh yeah, salty. Salty? That's right, this near-forgotten German wheat beer is traditionally brewed with a dash of salt. It's not so much that you think you're sipping seawater, but it's just enough to add a surprising savory note. I also tip the scales in favor of wheat for a little extra lushness and use a sour mash method to give it a twang. Just for good measure, I throw some grapefruit peels into the secondary as an ode to my favorite Salty Dog cocktail.

Brew Notes This is a multiday brew. Timing is important so plan accordingly.

Make It Yours If you're not up for making the sour mash, brew this beer as normal but add some lactobacillus culture when you pitch the yeast. Read more about it and other souring methods in "Get Funky with Sour Beers" on page 140.

Beer to Try Leipziger Gose (Gasthause & Gosebrauerei Bayerischer Bahnhof)

INGREDIENTS	1-GALLON	5-GALLON
Wheat malt, milled	1 lb (454 g)	5 lbs (2.27 kg)
Pilsner malt, milled	12 oz (340 g)	3¾ lbs (1.70 kg)
White Labs California Ale yeast, Wyeast American Ale yeast, or equivalent	½ package	1 package
Ahtanum pellet hops (6% AA), for bittering	.05 oz (1.50 g)	.25 oz (7 g)
Ahtanum pellet hops (6% AA), for flavoring	.05 oz (1.50 g)	.25 oz (7 g)
Irish moss	¼ tsp	1 tsp
Ahtanum pellet hops (6% AA), for aroma	.10 oz (3 g)	.50 oz (14 g)
Maldon or other sea salt	5 g (1½ tsps)	25 g (2½ tbsps)
Yellow grapefruit	1	5
Corn sugar, for bottling	.80 oz (22 g)	4 oz (113 g)

TARGET ORIGINAL/FINAL GRAVITY: 1.049/1.009
TARGET ABV: 5.2%

Follow the master method for brewing 1-gallon or 5-gallon all-grain batches as described on pages 54–59 (5-gallon measurements in parentheses).

• Remove ¼ (or 1) cup of the raw grains and set aside. Heat **3 quarts (or 3½ gallons) of water to 156°F**, then stir in the remaining grains. Maintain a mash temperature of **142°F to 147°F** for 60 minutes. **Do not sparge.**

• Let the mash cool to **120°F**. Stir in the reserved grains, then transfer to a small glass or plastic storage container. Press plastic wrap against the top of the mash and cover with a lid. Keep between **115°F and 120°F** for 1 to 2 days, until the mash starts to smell sour. (See page 140 for more details.)

• When the sour mash is ready, remove liquid yeast from the refrigerator, and if necessary, activate according to package instructions. Place on the counter to warm.

• Transfer the mash to the pot and set over medium-high heat. Raise the temperature of the mash to 170°F, then sparge using **1½ (or 3) gallons** of 170°F water to make 1½ (or 5½) gallons wort.

• Bring to a boil over high heat. Add the hops for bittering and boil vigorously for 40 minutes. Add the hops for flavoring and the Irish moss and continue boiling for another 20 minutes. Add the hops for aroma and the salt and remove from the heat. (Total boil time: 60 minutes.)

• Cool to at least 75°F and transfer to a sanitized primary fermentation bucket. Add the yeast and aerate the wort. Let ferment for at least **1 week or up to 4 weeks at 70°F**. When ready to transfer the beer for secondary fermentation, use a vegetable peeler to remove just the outer peel (none of the pith) from the grapefruit(s). Add the peels to the sanitized jug and siphon the beer over top. Continue to ferment for another **2 weeks or up to 2 months at 70°F**.

• Taste the beer a few days before you plan to bottle. Add more grapefruit peels if you wish. Taste daily and bottle when the beer tastes good to you.

• Dissolve the sugar in ¼ (or 1) cup of boiling water and let cool. Mix with the beer, bottle, and store for **2 weeks or up to a year**. Refrigerate before drinking.

American Summer Wheat Ale

This wheat ale is almost the twin of A Very Good Wheat Beer (page 159)—same amount of malts, same 50-50 split of barley and wheat. The difference is that this one goes all-American: American pale malts, American hops, and an American yeast strain. The result is a completely different beer: one that's as clear as a hefeweizen is hazy and that sings with bright, snappy, citrusy flavors. The addition of lemon peels and spicy grains of paradise make this beer even more perfect for the hottest days of summer.

Make It Yours If you're a card-carrying member of the Hophead Club, add some more to this beer. Cluster hops are fairly mild, so change them out for any of the West Coast powerhouse hops: Cascade, Centennial, or Columbus.

Beers to Try Samuel Adams Summer Ale (Boston Beer Company), Gumballhead (Three Floyds Brewing Co.), A Little Sumpin' Sumpin' Ale (Lagunitas Brewing Company)

INGREDIENTS	1-GALLON	5-GALLON
White Labs California Ale yeast, Wyeast American Wheat, or equivalent	½ package	1 package
Pale ale malt, milled	1 lb (454 g)	5 lbs (2.27 kg)
Wheat malt, milled	1 lb (454 g)	5 lbs (2.27 kg)
Cluster pellet hops (7% AA), for bittering	.20 oz (5.5 g)	1 oz (28 g)
Irish moss	¼ tsp	1 tsp
Cluster pellet hops (7% AA), for aroma	.10 oz (3 g)	.50 oz (14 g)
Grains of paradise, crushed	½ tsp	2½ tsps
Lemon	½ whole	2½ whole
Corn sugar, for bottling	.80 oz (22 g)	4 oz (113 g)

TARGET ORIGINAL/FINAL GRAVITY: 1.055/1.012
TARGET ABV: 5.6%

Follow the master method for brewing 1-gallon or 5-gallon all-grain batches as described on pages 54–59 (5-gallon measurements in parentheses).

• Remove liquid yeast from the refrigerator and, if necessary, activate according to package instructions. Place on the counter to warm.

• Heat **3 quarts (or 3½ gallons) of water to 160°F**, then stir in the grains. Maintain a mash temperature of **148°F to 153°F** for 60 minutes. Raise the temperature of the mash to 170°F, then sparge using **1½ (or 3) gallons** of 170°F water to make 1½ (or 5½) gallons wort.

• Bring to a boil over high heat. Add the hops for bittering and boil vigorously for 40 minutes. Add the Irish moss and continue boiling for another 20 minutes. Add the hops for aroma and grains of paradise and remove from the heat. (Total boil time: 60 minutes.)

• Cool to at least 75°F and transfer to a sanitized primary fermentation bucket. Add the yeast and aerate the wort.

• Let ferment for at least **1 week or up to 4 weeks at 70°F**. When ready to transfer the beer for secondary fermentation, use a vegetable peeler to remove just the outer peel (none of the pith) from the lemon. Add the peels to a sanitized jug and siphon the beer over top. Continue to ferment for another **2 weeks or up to 2 months at 70°F**.

• Taste the beer a few days before you plan to bottle. Add more grains of paradise or lemon peels if you wish. Taste daily and bottle when the beer tastes good to you.

• Dissolve the sugar in ¼ (or 1) cup of boiling water and let cool. Mix with the beer, bottle, and store for **2 weeks or up to a year**. Refrigerate before drinking.

Lavender-Orange Witbier

Instead of using malted wheat, let's try something different and brew this witbier and use unmalted flaked wheat. This gives an ultra-creamy mouthfeel and a hazy appearance, while still adding some sugars for the yeast to eat. Witbiers are traditionally brewed with dried bitter orange peels and coriander, but I like to make mine with fresh sweet orange peels and dried lavender buds. Be careful of using too much lavender, though; it can make the beer taste unpleasantly soapy.

Brew Notes Do not mill the flaked wheat, flaked oats, or rice hulls for this recipe; they will turn the mash gummy, making it impossible to separate out the sweet beer wort. Also, don't fret when your beer turns out cloudy—it's supposed to be that way!

Make It Yours If lavender isn't to your liking, you can cut it out completely and have a perfectly amazing brew. Or replace it and the sweet orange peel with the traditional crushed coriander and dried bitter orange peel. Or get creative with spices like cardamom, grains of paradise, or heck, even juniper berries. (Read more about adding spices on page 166.)

Beer to Try Allagash White (Allagash Brewing Co.)

INGREDIENTS	1-GALLON	5-GALLON
White Labs Belgian Witbier yeast, Wyeast Belgian Witbier, or equivalent	½ package	1 package
Belgian pilsner malt, milled	1 lb (454 g)	5 lbs (2.27 kg)
Flaked wheat (unmalted)	12 oz (340 g)	3¾ lbs (1.70 kg)
Flaked oats	2 oz (57 g)	10 oz (283 g)
Rice hulls	1.50 oz (43 g)	7.50 oz (213 g)
Hallertauer pellet hops (4% AA), for bittering	.20 oz (5.50 g)	1 oz (28 g)
Hallertauer pellet hops (4% AA), for aroma	.15 oz (4 g)	.75 oz (21 g)
Medium-size oranges	2 whole	8 whole
Dried lavender buds	½ to 2 tsps	1 to 3 tbsps
Corn sugar, for bottling	.80 oz (22 g)	4 oz (113 g)

TARGET ORIGINAL/FINAL GRAVITY: 1.049/1.011
TARGET ABV: 5%

Follow the master method for brewing 1-gallon or 5-gallon all-grain batches as described on pages 54–59 (5-gallon measurements in parentheses).

• Remove liquid yeast from the refrigerator and, if necessary, activate according to package instructions. Place on the counter to warm.

• Heat **3 quarts (or 3½ gallons) of water to 160°F**, then stir in the grains and rice hulls. Maintain a mash temperature of **148°F to 153°F for 60 minutes**. Raise the temperature of the mash to 170°F, then sparge using **1½ (or 3) gallons** of 170°F water to make 1½ (or 5½) gallons wort.

• Bring to a boil over high heat. Add the hops for bittering and boil vigorously for 60 minutes. Add the hops for aroma and remove from the heat. (Total boil time: 60 minutes.)

• Cool to at least 75°F and transfer to a sanitized primary fermentation bucket. Add the yeast and aerate the wort.

• Let ferment for at least **1 week or up to 4 weeks at 70°F**. When ready to transfer the beer for secondary fermentation, use a vegetable peeler to remove just the outer peel (none of the pith) from the oranges. Add the peels to a sanitized jug and siphon the beer over top. Continue to ferment for another **2 weeks or up to 2 months at 70°F**.

• A few days before you plan to bottle, add ½ teaspoon (or 1 tablespoon) of lavender buds in a sanitized mesh bag to the jug. Wait two days, then taste the beer and add more lavender or orange peels if you wish. Taste daily and bottle or remove the lavender when the beer tastes good to you. Do not let it continue to sit on the lavender once you like the way it tastes or it will become increasingly bitter.

• Dissolve the sugar in ¼ (or 1) cup of boiling water and let cool. Mix with the beer, bottle, and store for **2 weeks or up to a year**. Refrigerate before drinking.

ADDING FRUITS, SPICES, AND OTHER FUN THINGS TO BEER

As a general rule, if it's in your kitchen and you think it would taste good in your beer, it's fair game. Fresh fruits, fresh herbs, dried spices, flaked coconut, cacao nibs, nuts . . . the sky's the limit. My mantra is "If you can imagine it, you can brew it."

WHEN TO ADD FRUITS AND SPICES

Two points in the brewing process work well for adding fruits, spices, and other flavoring ingredients: at the end of the hop boil and during the secondary. Adding the ingredient at the end of the hop boil extracts a little more flavor, but since the activity of the yeast during the first few days of fermentation tends to scrub away more delicate flavors and aromas, you're typically left with a softer, subtler flavor in your beer. Also, fruits sometimes have a slightly cooked flavor when added during the boil. On the plus side, adding the ingredient to the boil sterilizes it, so there's zero risk of contamination.

If you add the ingredient during the secondary, more of the delicate flavors and aromas are retained, plus the alcohol now present in the beer helps extract essential oils and stabilize the flavors. The flavor of the ingredient is typically stronger, cleaner, and more front-and-center in the finished beer. However, you run some risk of contaminating your beer with outside bacteria and wild yeast.

Whenever you add ingredients like fruits and spices to beer, it's a bit of a flavor gamble. These ingredients have different strengths and flavors depending on how ripe they are (in the case of fruit), how fresh they are (in the case of spices), and their overall quality. In all cases, my advice is to start with less than you think you need. Once the beer is in the secondary, taste it every few days and add more if you think the beer needs it. Use a small mesh bag to hold your ingredient so that you can pull it out when you think the beer is perfect.

SAFELY ADDING FRUITS, SPICES, AND OTHER INGREDIENTS

If you add the ingredient to the boil, you don't need to worry about sterilizing: the boiling liquid takes care of it for you. You can strain the ingredient from the beer before fermenting, or let it hang out in the beer as it ferments in the primary. Either way, there isn't a big risk of contamination.

Adding ingredients to the secondary is another issue. Theoretically, any beer projected to be over 5% ABV has enough alcohol to take care of any bacteria or wild yeast you might introduce with a new ingredient. It's a risk but a relatively minor one. As long as your fruits are scrubbed clean before being chopped, and as long as spices are relatively fresh, you should be fine to add them right to the beer.

If you'd rather be safe than sorry, you can sterilize ingredients before adding them. Simmer fruits for a few minutes to kill off any bacteria. Herbs, spices, and other dry ingredients can be steeped in liquor—vodka has a neutral flavor that won't affect your beer, though you could also steep in bourbon, tequila, or anything else. Steep for a few minutes and then either drain the ingredient from the liquor before adding it or add both to the beer (for slightly more booze!).

BRING ON THE FLAVOR!

Now that we have the technical stuff out of the way, let's talk about the fun stuff. Here are some ideas for ways to add flavor and aroma to your brews.

Fruits. You can choose among fresh fruit, dried fruit, fruit puree, fruit extract, and fruit juice. Most often, I use whole fresh fruit at peak season or frozen whole fruit. I find that you get a fuller, more rounded flavor from real whole fruit. Start with 1 to 2 cups of chopped fruit for a 1-gallon batch and 5 to 10 cups for a 5-gallon batch. Dried fruit gives softer fruit flavors; I like using it when I want a subtle hint of fruit in a beer's flavor profile but not a full-blown fruit beer. Dried fruit is also great for adding fruit flavor to darker beers since the juices in fresh fruit can sometimes make dark beers taste watery. With dried fruit, start with ½ to 1 cup for a 1-gallon batch and 2½ to 5 cups for a 5-gallon batch.

Fruit puree is also fine to use; it has the added bonus of already being sterile, so there's no worry of introducing foreign bacteria or yeast to the brew. However, puree often has a cooked flavor that, to my taste, makes it a less desirable way to go. Use 1 to 2 cups for a 1-gallon batch and 5 to 10 cups for a 5-gallon batch. Extracts are my last choice; the commercial kinds always taste faintly artificial to me, though you could make one yourself by steeping fruit in vodka for a few days. Use 1½ tablespoons for a 1-gallon batch and ½ cup for a 5-gallon batch.

Any fruit can be used in your beer, but give real thought to how the flavor of the fruit and the flavor of the beer will marry. Light beers, like witbiers and saisons, work wonderfully as backdrops for anything from delicate blueberries and pineapple to more bold-tasting blackberries and cherries. Darker beers, like porters and stouts, need a strong, flavorful fruit for any of that fruit flavor to come through; try dried cherries or figs.

Citrus fruit is a slightly different flavoring situation. The most flavorful oils are in the skin, but you want to avoid the bitter white pith below. Use a vegetable peeler to cut away long strips of the peel while leaving the pith behind, and add those strips to the beer. Citrus juice has a delicate flavor that can often disappear into a beer or make it taste watery, though I sometimes like adding a little just before bottling for a burst of citrusy flavor.

The vegetable world is also open to you, though be warned that vegetal flavors translate less well in beers than fruit flavors. A lot has been done with fresh jalapeños and other chile peppers. They can add a nice spicy flavor to saisons and pilsners. (Don't forget dried chiles, too—the Smoky Chipotle Porter on page 111 is one of my favorite recipes in the book!) Cucumbers are starting to pop up in lighter beers, like pilsners and kölsches. And, of course, pumpkins and butternut squashes can be used to make true pumpkin ales once the fall comes. Beyond these tried-and-true veggies, you're in uncharted territory. Proceed with a heavy dose of caution.

Herbs and spices. Herbs! Basil, rosemary, thyme, mint, and all their herbaceous companions are welcome to the beer party. I also include fresh ingredients like lemongrass and ginger in this category. Stick to fresh herbs because their flavor comes through much better in the finished beer; dried herbs tend to taste uniformly bitter.

Spices! There's fantastic flavoring potential hiding in your spice drawer. Spices like cinnamon, cardamom, cloves, allspice, black peppercorns, and nutmeg are the usual suspects for a great winter warmer or pumpkin ale. Grains of paradise are the darling of many brewers for their unique peppery, woodsy, citrusy flavor. Go crazy with coriander seeds, dried chile peppers, fennel seeds, dried lavender, juniper berries, or anything else you can get your hands on.

Be cautious when adding both fresh herbs and dried spices to your beer. A little can go an extremely long way. If in doubt about what an herb or spice tastes like (or how they will taste when combined), steep a teaspoon in a glass of hot water and give it a taste before throwing it in your beer.

Baking ingredients. Items in your baking cupboard, like cacao nibs, coffee beans, shredded coconut, and vanilla beans, are another way to flavor your beer. So many beers are halfway to tasting like delicious baked goods anyway, and these ingredients just help things along. In fact, use your favorite cookie or bar as inspiration for your next brew—that's how I ended up with my Caramel-Coconut Wee Heavy (page 151) and Pecan Pie Brown Ale (page 96).

I like the flavor best when these ingredients are added to the secondary, where the alcohol in the fermented beer can help strip the essential oils and other flavor components from the ingredients. As with the herbs and spices, add a little to begin with, taste the beer after a few days, and add more to taste.

Tea. Sachets of tea work a lot like hops and can add many of the same flavors. A good black tea adds earthy, woodsy flavors and a soft touch of bitterness, while a jasmine green tea adds floral aromas and an alluring sweetness. Herbal tea blends can also be a shortcut to fruity and spicy flavors.

Add tea to your beer either at the very end of the boil along with the aroma hops or to the secondary. Avoid boiling the tea—this can give your beer overly bitter and astringent flavors.

Nuts. The flavor of nuts is all in the oil, but this can present problems since oil can make a beer taste overly slick and prevent foam from forming. Adding flaked wheat helps bring back some foam, but my feeling is that the trade-off is worth it for the occasional batch of truly nutty beer.

Roast the nuts until they smell delicious and then chop them into tiny pieces—if you grind them in a food processor, be sure not to process them so long that you make nut butter. Add the nuts to the mash, the boil, or the secondary for a nutty kick. You can also make a nut extract by steeping roasted and chopped nuts in vodka until infused to your liking (usually a few weeks); strain out the nuts and add the flavored vodka to the secondary.

Oak cubes and chips. Short of buying your own oak barrel, oak cubes and chips are the best way for us homebrewers to get a "barrel-aged" flavor in our beers. You don't need much: ½ ounce for a 1-gallon batch and 2½ ounces for a 5-gallon batch. They can make your beer taste a bit bland and pencil-woody on their own, so both cubes and chips are almost always soaked in liquor before being added to the beer. Bourbon has been the liquor of choice for barrel-aging for years, but times are a-changin'! Get creative with Merlot, Chardonnay, port wine, mescal or tequila, scotch, brandy, or whatever other liquors you have in your cabinet.

This oaky character tends to work best in higher-alcohol beers, like barleywines and imperial stouts, but that's not a hard-and-fast rule. Always add wood cubes or chips to the secondary and let them soak with the beer for at least a week or up to 2 months. Wood chips infuse the beer a little more quickly, so if you're using them, taste your beer every so often to make sure the oaky flavor doesn't get too strong. More darkly charred cubes also add more of that charred flavor to your beer.

A dose of rye malts gives beer a crisp, somewhat spicy, rough-around-the-edges character. At the same time, rye beers tend to feel smooth to the point of being slick in the mouth. I love this contrast of flavor and texture.

Roggenbiers and sahtis, like the two in this chapter, are traditional rye beers, but rye malts can be used to add complexity and a touch of intrigue to almost any style of beer. Don't make rye more than 50 percent of the grain bill, though; rye malts don't have hulls like barley malts do, so they can make a mash gummy and difficult to sparge if used in too great an amount. Adding rice hulls can help lighten the mash if you want to go wild and experiment with adding more.

RYE ALES

————— [chapter 12] —————

A VERY GOOD RYE PALE ALE

If you're wondering what the fuss over rye ales is all about, this recipe is a good place to start. It riffs on "A Very Good Pale Ale" (page 71), replacing half the pale ale malts in the base with rye malts and a touch of wheat. In many ways, it's your basic pale ale—crisp flavors, golden color, super-easy to drink—but the rye adds a spicy, rough-edged character that you just can't get anywhere else. Rye ales are the John Wayne of beers—smooth-talking and slick, with just enough grit to make you pay attention.

Make It Yours Play with the proportions of pale malts to rye malts, upping the rye to bring out more of that spicy, rough rye character or lowering it for less. A 100% rye would make a very sticky, gummy mash, but . . . you could always try it! If you do, throw in some rice hulls to make life easier when it comes time to sparge.

Beers to Try Righteous Ale (Sixpoint Brewery), Rye Pale Ale (Terrapin Beer Co.), Full Moon Pale Rye Ale (Real Ale Brewing Company)

INGREDIENTS	1-GALLON	5-GALLON
White Labs American Ale yeast, Wyeast American Ale yeast, or equivalent	½ package	1 package
Pale ale malt, milled	1 lb (454 g)	5 lbs (2.27 kg)
Rye malt, milled	1 lb (454 g)	5 lbs (2.27 kg)
Wheat malt, milled	4 oz (113 g)	1¼ lbs (567 g)
Columbus pellet hops (16.3% AA), for bittering	.10 oz (3 g)	.50 oz (14 g)
Saaz pellet hops (2.9% AA), for flavoring	.10 oz (3 g)	.50 oz (14 g)
Irish moss	¼ tsp	1 tsp
Saaz pellet hops (2.9% AA), for aroma	.10 oz (3 g)	.50 oz (14 g)
Corn sugar, for bottling	.8 oz (22 g)	4 oz (113 g)

TARGET ORIGINAL/FINAL GRAVITY: 1.054/1.012
TARGET ABV: 5.5%

Follow the master method for brewing 1-gallon or 5-gallon all-grain batches as described on pages 54–59 (5-gallon measurements in parentheses).

• Remove liquid yeast from the refrigerator and, if necessary, activate according to package instructions. Place on the counter to warm.

• Heat **1 gallon (or 3½ gallons) of water to 160°F**, then stir in the grains. Maintain a mash temperature of **148°F to 153°F** for 60 minutes. Raise the temperature of the mash to 170°F, then sparge using **1 gallon (or 3 gallons)** of 170°F water to make 1½ (or 5½) gallons wort.

• Bring to a boil over high heat. Add the Columbus hops and boil vigorously for 40 minutes. Add the Saaz hops for flavoring and the Irish moss and continue boiling for another 20 minutes. Add the Saaz hops for aroma and remove from the heat. (Total boil time: 60 minutes.)

• Cool to at least 75°F and transfer to a sanitized primary fermentation bucket. Add the yeast and aerate the wort.

• Let ferment for at least **1 week or up to 4 weeks at 70°F**; then transfer to a sanitized jug or carboy for secondary fermentation. Continue to ferment for another **2 weeks or up to 2 months at 70°F**.

• Dissolve the sugar in ¼ (or 1) cup of boiling water and let cool. Mix with the beer, bottle, and store for **2 weeks or up to a year**. Refrigerate before drinking.

Dark Pumpernickel Roggenbier

When rye ales first came on the craft beer scene, I kept expecting them to taste more like their cousins, those hearty Northern European rye breads. I was always a little disappointed when they did not. A beer with the dark moodiness and earthy, bittersweet flavor of a loaf of pumpernickel—that was the rye beer I wanted to drink! When you're a homebrewer, ideas like these can become a reality; if you can't find it at the grocery store, you brew it yourself.

Brew Notes White Lab's Hefeweizen IV and Wyeast's Belgian Wheat yeast both help boost the alcohol level in this beer, plus they give it a clove-like spiciness without the banana flavor of regular hefeweizen yeast. If you have trouble finding these, hefeweizen yeast is fine to use; just keep the fermentation temperature around 65°F to 70°F to limit the banana-like esters the yeast produces.

Make It Yours For deeper, more caramelized flavors, boil the first runnings, as for A Very Good Scottish Ale on page 145. Or add a dose of brettanomyces and see how it develops. Sourdough Rye Ale, anyone?

Beers to Try Rugbrod (The Bruery), Roguenbier Rye Ale (Rogue Ales)

INGREDIENTS	1-GALLON	5-GALLON
White Labs Hefeweizen IV yeast, Wyeast Belgian Wheat, or equivalent	½ package	1 package
Rye malt, milled	1 lb (454 g)	5 lbs (2.27 kg)
Vienna malt, milled	1 lb (454 g)	5 lbs (2.27 kg)
Biscuit malt, milled	4 oz (113 g)	1¼ lbs (567 g)
Flaked wheat	4 oz (113 g)	1¼ lbs (567 g)
Chocolate malt, milled	1.50 oz (43 g)	8 oz (227 g)
Cluster pellet hops (6.8% AA), for bittering	.20 oz (5.50 g)	1 oz (28 g)
Mt. Hood pellet hops (5.9% AA), for flavoring	.10 oz (3 g)	.50 oz (14 g)
Irish moss	¼ tsp	1 tsp
Mt. Hood pellet hops (5.9% AA), for aroma	.15 oz (4 g)	.75 oz (21 g)
Corn sugar, for bottling	.70 oz (20 g)	3.50 oz (100 g)

TARGET ORIGINAL/FINAL GRAVITY: 1.062/1.014
TARGET ABV: 6.3%

Follow the master method for brewing 1-gallon or 5-gallon all-grain batches as described on pages 54–59 (5-gallon measurements in parentheses).

• Remove liquid yeast from the refrigerator and, if necessary, activate according to package instructions. Place on the counter to warm.

• Heat **1 gallon (or 4½ gallons) of water to 160°F**, then stir in the grains. Maintain a mash temperature of **148°F to 153°F for 60 minutes.** Raise the temperature of the mash to 170°F, then sparge using **1 gallon (or 2½ gallons)** of 170°F water to make 1½ (or 5½) gallons wort.

• Bring to a boil over high heat. Add the Cluster hops and boil vigorously for 40 minutes. Add the Mt. Hood hops for flavoring and the Irish moss and continue boiling for another 20 minutes. Add the Mt. Hood hops for aroma and remove from the heat. (Total boil time: 60 minutes.)

• Cool to at least 75°F and transfer to a sanitized primary fermentation bucket. Add the yeast and aerate the wort.

• Let ferment for at least **1 week or up to 4 weeks at 70°F**; then transfer to a sanitized jug or carboy for secondary fermentation. Continue to ferment for another **2 weeks or up to 2 months at 70°F.**

• Dissolve the sugar in ¼ (or 1) cup of boiling water and let cool. Mix with the beer, bottle, and store for **2 weeks or up to a year.** Refrigerate before drinking.

Finnish Juniper Rye Sahti Ale

Imagine this: batches of hearty ale made not in a brewer's shiny kettle but in hollowed-out logs over outdoor fires; brews flavored not with handfuls of hops but with boughs of berry-laden juniper. Intriguing, right? These sahti ales are a very old Finnish brew made in the days when beer was safer to drink than water and people used what they could find to make the ales taste good—in this case, citrusy, piney juniper. In my modern version of this ancient ale, I use dried juniper berries (which are easier to find and more reliable for brewing) and add Simcoe hops for an extra kick of pine flavor.

Brew Notes You'll need to make a yeast starter for this recipe to ensure good fermentation. Look for dried juniper berries at health food stores or through vendors like Penzeys Spices (see the Recommended Resources section on page 226). Do not use fresh juniper berries unless you're certain they are safe to eat.

Make It Yours Try a hybrid sahti–spruce tip ale, using some elements from this beer and some from the Pine Woods Pale Ale on page 74.

Beer to Try Sah'tea (Dogfish Head Craft Brewery)

INGREDIENTS	1-GALLON	5-GALLON
White Labs Hefeweizen IV yeast, Wyeast Belgian Wheat, or equivalent	½ package	1 package
Light dried malt extract	.90 oz (25 g or 2 heaping tbsps)	3.50 oz (100 g or ½ cup)
Pale ale malt, milled	2 lbs (907 g)	10 lbs (4.54 kg)
Rye malt, milled	1 lb (454 g)	5 lbs (2.27 kg)
Caramunich malt, milled	8 oz (227 g)	2½ lbs (1.13 kg)
Special B malt, milled	2 oz (57 g)	10 oz (283 g)
Dried juniper berries	1.06 oz (30 g or 6 tbsps)	5 oz (142 g or 1¾ cups)
Simcoe pellet hops (11.7% AA), for bittering	.10 oz (3 g)	.50 oz (14 g)
Simcoe pellet hops (11.7% AA), for flavoring	.05 oz (1.50 g)	.25 oz (7 g)
Irish moss	¼ tsp	1 tsp
Simcoe pellet hops (11.7% AA), for aroma	.05 oz (1.50 g)	.25 oz (7 g)
Corn sugar, for bottling	.70 oz (20 g)	3.50 oz (100 g)

TARGET ORIGINAL GRAVITY: 1.088/1.023
TARGET ABV: 8.6%

Follow the master method for brewing 1-gallon or 5-gallon all-grain batches as described on pages 54–59 (5-gallon measurements in parentheses).

• Using the yeast and malt extract, make a yeast starter 12 to 18 hours before you plan to brew, following the instructions in "How to Make a Yeast Starter," page 16.

• Heat **1 gallon (or 6 gallons) of water to 164°F**, then stir in the grains and 4 tablespoons (or 1¼ cups) of the juniper berries. Maintain a mash temperature of **154°F to 158°F** for 60 minutes. Raise the temperature of the mash to 170°F, then sparge using **1 gallon (or 1½ gallons)** of 170°F water to make 1½ (or 5½) gallons wort.

• Bring to a boil over high heat. Add the hops for bittering and boil vigorously for 40 minutes. Add the hops for flavoring, 1 tablespoon (or ¼ cup) of the juniper berries, and the Irish moss and continue boiling for another 20 minutes. Add the hops for aroma and the remaining 1 tablespoon (or ¼ cup) of juniper berries and remove from the heat. (Total boil time: 60 minutes.)

• Cool to at least 75°F and transfer to a sanitized primary fermentation bucket. Add the yeast starter and aerate the wort.

• Let ferment for at least **1 week or up to 4 weeks at 70°F**; then transfer to a sanitized jug or carboy for secondary fermentation. Continue to ferment for another **2 weeks or up to 2 months at 70°F**.

• Taste the beer a few days before you plan to bottle. Add more juniper berries if you wish. Taste daily and bottle when the beer tastes good to you. Dissolve the sugar in ¼ (or 1) cup of boiling water and let cool. Mix with the beer, bottle, and store for **2 weeks or up to a year**. Refrigerate before drinking.

No Apologies Imperial Rye Ale

I wanted to push rye to the limits with a big beer and see what kind of trouble this malt could get into. The answer, as you can probably guess, is a *lot*. This brash, bold imperialized ale is not messing around. Bravo and Delta hops are right for the job—besides sounding tough, they stand up to the malts with a satisfying burst of spicy herbal flavor. If you need fortification for an epic adventure, this is the beer you want.

Brew Notes You'll need to make a yeast starter for this recipe to ensure good fermentation.

Make It Yours For an extra burst of bright hop aroma, dry-hop this beer in the secondary with another round of Delta hops. Also think about dividing the hops into equal doses and continuously hopping every 10 minutes during the boil for a more complex hop character.

Beers to Try Hop Rod Rye (Bear Republic Brewing Co.), Rye-On-Rye (Boulevard Brewing Co.)

INGREDIENTS	1-GALLON	5-GALLON
White Labs California Ale yeast, Wyeast American Ale yeast, or equivalent	½ package	1 package
Light dried malt extract	.90 oz (25 g or 2 heaping tbsps)	3.50 oz (100 g or ½ cup)
Pale ale malt, milled	1½ lbs (680 g)	7½ lbs (3.40 kg)
Rye malt, milled	1¼ lbs (567 g)	6¼ lbs (2.84 kg)
Munich malt, milled	8 oz (227 g)	2½ lbs (1.13 kg)
Crystal/Caramel 60 malt, milled	4 oz (113 g)	1¼ lbs (567 g)
Rice hulls	2 oz (57 g)	10 oz (283 g)
Bravo pellet hops (15.1% AA), for bittering	.35 oz (8.50 g)	1.75 oz (42.5 g)
Bravo pellet hops (15.1% AA), for flavoring	.15 oz (3 g)	.75 oz (21 g)
Delta pellet hops (4.4% AA), for flavoring	.25 oz (7 g)	1.25 oz (35.50 g)
Irish moss	¼ tsp	1 tsp
Delta pellet hops (4.4% AA), for aroma	.25 oz (7 g)	1.25 oz (35.50 g)
Corn sugar, for bottling	.70 oz (20 g)	3.5 oz (100 g)

TARGET ORIGINAL/FINAL GRAVITY: 1.085/1.019
TARGET ABV: 8.8%

Follow the master method for brewing 1-gallon or 5-gallon all-grain batches as described on pages 54–59 (5-gallon measurements in parentheses).

• Using the yeast and malt extract, make a yeast starter 12 to 18 hours before you plan to brew, following the instructions in "How to Make a Yeast Starter," page 16.

• Heat **1 gallon (or 6 gallons) of water to 160°F**, then stir in the grains and rice hulls. Maintain a mash temperature of **148°F to 153°F for 60 minutes.** Raise the temperature of the mash to 170°F, then sparge using **1 gallon (or 1½ gallons)** of 170°F water to make 1½ (or 5½) gallons wort.

• Bring to a boil over high heat. Add the Bravo hops for bittering and boil vigorously for 40 minutes. Add the Bravo and Delta hops for flavoring and the Irish moss and continue boiling for another 20 minutes. Add the Delta hops for aroma and remove from the heat. (Total boil time: 60 minutes.)

• Cool to at least 75°F and transfer to a sanitized primary fermentation bucket. Add the yeast starter and aerate the wort.

• Let ferment for at least **1 week or up to 4 weeks at 70°F**; then transfer to a sanitized jug or carboy for secondary fermentation. Continue to ferment for another **2 weeks or up to 2 months at 70°F.**

• Dissolve the sugar in ¼ (or 1) cup of boiling water and let cool. Mix with the beer, bottle, and store for **2 weeks or up to a year.** Refrigerate before drinking.

Red Eye Chicory Rye Porter

No visit to New Orleans is complete without two things: getting so swept up in the jazz bands and crazy energy of the French Quarter that the sun comes up before you've gone to bed, and finding a cup of chicory coffee to chase away the haze of a long night out. Chicory has a roughness and a warm spiciness that coffee does not, and it works terrifically in this dark rye ale. (Also, if chicory just isn't your thing, no worries—this beer is terrific with regular coffee beans.) Consider this the coffee porter of the rye family; I recommend it to begin—or end—a night on the town.

Brew Notes Chicory, a blend of chicory and coffee, or regular coffee beans can all be used in this recipe.

Make It Yours Soak some oak cubes in rye whiskey (of course) and add them to the secondary for a boozy spin. Hair of the dog? Why not! (Read more about adding oak cubes on page 168.)

Beers to Try Chicory Stout (Dogfish Head Craft Brewery), Coffee Bender (Surly Brewing Company)

INGREDIENTS	1-GALLON	5-GALLON
White Labs English Ale yeast, Wyeast London Ale yeast, or equivalent	½ package	1 package
Rye malt, milled	1 lb (454 g)	5 lbs (2.27 kg)
Munich malt, milled	1 lb (454 g)	5 lbs (2.27 kg)
Crystal/Caramel 80 malt, milled	4 oz (113 g)	1¼ lbs (567 g)
Brown malt, milled	4 oz (113 g)	1¼ lbs (567 g)
Rice hulls	1 oz (28 g)	5 oz (142 g)
Northern Brewer pellet hops (9.6% AA), for bittering	.05 oz (1.5 g)	.25 oz (7 g)
Northern Brewer pellet hops (9.6% AA), for flavoring	.05 oz (1.5 g)	.25 oz (7 g)
Irish moss	¼ tsp	1 tsp
Ground chicory	2 oz (57 g or ½ cup)	10 oz (283 g or 2½ cups)
Corn sugar, for bottling	.70 oz (20 g)	3.50 oz (100 g)

TARGET ORIGINAL/FINAL GRAVITY: 1.059/1.019
TARGET ABV: 5.3%

Follow the master method for brewing 1-gallon or 5-gallon all-grain batches as described on pages 54–59 (5-gallon measurements in parentheses).

• Remove liquid yeast from the refrigerator and, if necessary, activate according to package instructions. Place on the counter to warm.

• Heat **1 gallon (or 4 gallons) of water to 160°F**, then stir in the grains and rice hulls. Maintain a mash temperature of **148°F to 153°F for 60 minutes**. Raise the temperature of the mash to 170°F, then sparge using **1 gallon (or 2½ gallons)** of 170°F water to make 1½ (or 5½) gallons wort.

• Bring to a boil over high heat. Add the hops for bittering and boil vigorously for 40 minutes. Add the hops for flavoring and the Irish moss and continue boiling for another 20 minutes. Remove from the heat. (Total boil time: 60 minutes.)

• Cool to at least 75°F and transfer to a sanitized primary fermentation bucket. Add the yeast and aerate the wort.

• Let ferment for at least **1 week or up to 4 weeks at 70°F**; then transfer to a sanitized jug or carboy for secondary fermentation. Continue to ferment for another **2 weeks or up to 2 months at 70°F**.

• The day before bottling, add the chicory to the secondary in a sanitized bag. Infuse for 24 hours, then bottle immediately with the sugar mixture; prolonged contact with the chicory can make the beer taste bitter.

• Dissolve the sugar in ¼ (or 1) cup of boiling water and let cool. Mix with the beer, bottle, and store for **2 weeks or up to a year**. Refrigerate before drinking.

FIVE EASY WAYS TO LEVEL-UP YOUR BREW GAME

Sadly, it's true: you can't always be brewing new beer. There will be weekends when you'd love to be making—or at least drinking—more homebrew, but all your jugs and buckets are occupied and your latest batch of bottled beer isn't quite ready for sipping. But don't think of this downtime as wasted; think of it as an opportunity to improve your brewing in other ways. Here are a few ideas.

1. DRINK BEER

My personal favorite educational pastime! Stretch your beer-tasting experience and try a different style of beer than you normally drink. Start a beer journal and take notes on what you like or don't like about the beer you're drinking. Challenge yourself to pick apart the malt profile or hops that were used without looking at the label. Invite some friends over and hold a blind tasting of several beers. It's not "drinking beer"; it's "training your palate."

2. HOLD A HOPS TASTING

Pour a little hot water into several cups and add a few hop pellets of different varieties to each one. Let the hops steep for a few minutes and then inhale the aromas. Take a sip, too. This gives you an idea of what each kind of hop is all about. Mix a few hop varieties together to see how their aromas combine—you're not risking a whole batch of beer with your experiments, so you can really go wild.

3. CHEW ON SOME GRAINS

Yes, malted grains are edible on their own, and chewing them can help you understand what makes grains different—or similar. I particularly like comparing grains that are roasted to nearly the same degree, like Crystal 40 and Caramunich malts. They're similar . . . but definitely different. As with hops, you can also make a quick tea by steeping cracked grains and experimenting with different combinations.

4. GO TO A HOMEBREW CLUB MEETING

Homebrew clubs are everywhere, and they're always eager for enthusiastic new homebrewers to join their ranks. Clubs usually meet once a month, and activities range from homebrew tasting nights and guest speakers to brewery outings and group brew days. If you have trouble finding one, ask at your local homebrew store or start one yourself!

5. READ A BOOK

Nothing like a good book. Some of these I read (and reread) to improve my brew game; others I read to inspire it:

The Complete Joy of Homebrewing by Charlie Papazian. This is one of the original books (if not the original) on homebrewing. The information he includes on basic brewing methods and the science of brewing is priceless. Bonus points go to Papazian for making dry, science-y material incredibly accessible and fun to read.

The Drunken Botanist by Amy Stewart. Anything you've ever wanted to know about the ingredients used to make beers, wines, and liquors, from agave to walnuts, is in this book. Besides being a captivating read about distillable plants through-out history, I've found inspiration in this book for new flavors and ingredients to try.

The Complete Beer Course by Joshua M. Bernstein. If you're unsure of the difference between an English IPA and an American IPA or between a Belgian dubbel and a tripel, Joshua Bernstein will set you straight. Even if you feel pretty confident ordering from a beer menu, I think you'll be surprised at what new facts you learn! This book is also a great reference for learning the typical flavors, ingredients, or methods used in traditional beers. (Also, check out Bernstein's book on the history of craft brewing, *Brewed Awakening*.)

Designing Great Beers by Ray Daniels. This one gets a little technical, so wait to pour yourself a beer until break time. But if you're curious about the nitty-gritty details of brewing science, this is the book you want. It covers everything from calculating the grain bill to the pitching rate for yeast and all subjects in between.

Principles of Brewing Science by George Fix. As with *Designing Great Beers*, do not read this one if you've already had a beer or two. It dives into the chemistry of beer brewing, covering things like the role of waterborne ions in the mash

and the science of beer haze. Yeah, heavy stuff! But it will make you feel like a smarty-pants once you read it.

Sacred and Herbal Healing Beers by Stephen Harrod Buhner. This book is a fascinating look at traditional and ancient beers crafted long before the German Reinheitsgebot established its more refined definition of the beverage. Buhner focuses primarily on the history and traditional uses for various brews, but there's enough detail to piece together our own modern-day versions.

A session ale isn't a style in the way that a stout or an IPA is. Rather, it's a term used for beers that are "sessionable," which is to say, low enough in alcohol that you can drink a few over the course of a few hours (i.e., a "drinking session") without winding up passed out under the table. Session beers can be any style, any color, any level of hoppiness—but by common agreement among brewers and drinkers, session beers need to be less than 5% ABV.

My aim in this chapter is to show you the breadth of beers that can either be made sessionable (like Riding Lawn Mower Pale Ale on page 186) or that are naturally sessionable by their style (like the Lemonade Stand Shandy on page 189). Also, flip back through the other chapters: you'll find plenty of other "session" beers in these pages, like the All-Day Dry Irish Stout on page 112 and A Very Good British Mild on page 121.

SESSION ALES

[chapter 13]

A VERY GOOD SESSION ALE

This is my "house" session ale and what you're likely to get if you stop by in the late afternoon while I'm making dinner. It's based on A Very Good British Mild (page 121), but it kicks up the hops quite a bit. Think of it as an American mild. I like it for those moments when I'm ready to call it a day but still want to keep my wits about me.

Make It Yours A session beer can be anything you want it to be. Take any beer in this book and scale down the malts, and you can probably make a decent session ale. If you want to tweak this recipe first, start with the malts. Swap the Maris Otter malts for pale ale malts or pilsner malts and get an entirely different beer.

Beers to Try Bitter Brewer (Surly Brewing), Brawler's Pugilist-Style Ale (Yards Brewing Company)

INGREDIENTS	1-GALLON	5-GALLON
White Labs English Ale yeast, Wyeast London Ale yeast, or equivalent	½ package	1 package
Maris Otter malt, milled	1 lb (454 g)	5 lbs (2.27 kg)
Crystal 40 malt, milled	8 oz (227 g)	2½ lbs (1.13 kg)
Columbus pellet hops (16% AA), for bittering	.05 oz (1.50 g)	.25 oz (7 g)
Columbus pellet hops (16% AA), for flavoring	.05 oz (1.50 g)	.25 oz (7 g)
Irish moss	¼ tsp	1 tsp
Columbus pellet hops (16% AA), for aroma	.05 oz (1.50 g)	.25 oz (7 g)
Corn sugar, for bottling	.80 oz (22 g)	4 oz (113 g)

TARGET ORIGINAL/FINAL GRAVITY: 1.040/1.015
TARGET ABV: 3.3%

Follow the master method for brewing 1-gallon or 5-gallon all-grain batches as described on pages 54–59 (5-gallon measurements in parentheses).

• Remove liquid yeast from the refrigerator and, if necessary, activate according to package instructions. Place on the counter to warm.

• Heat **3 quarts (or 2½ gallons) of water to 164°F**, then stir in the grains. Maintain a mash temperature of **154°F to 158°F** for 60 minutes. Raise the temperature of the mash to 170°F, then sparge using **1½ (or 4) gallons** of 170°F water to make 1½ (or 5½) gallons wort.

• Bring to a boil over high heat. Add the hops for bittering and boil vigorously for 40 minutes. Add the hops for flavoring and the Irish moss and continue boiling for another 20 minutes. Add the hops for aroma and remove from the heat. (Total boil time: 60 minutes.)

• Cool to at least 75°F and transfer to a sanitized primary fermentation bucket. Add the yeast and aerate the wort.

• Let ferment for at least **1 week or up to 4 weeks at 70°F**; then transfer to a sanitized jug or carboy for secondary fermentation. Continue to ferment for another **2 weeks or up to 2 months at 70°F**.

• Dissolve the sugar in ¼ (or 1) cup of boiling water and let cool. Mix with the beer, bottle, and store for **2 weeks or up to a year**. Refrigerate before drinking.

Riding Lawn Mower Pale Ale

It's Saturday. It's sunny and warm outside. I'm sure you'd rather be sitting on the porch with a beer than sitting on your mower with the sun on your neck. But this is why riding lawn mowers were invented: so you could hold a crisp, lightly hopped beer in one hand and turn the wheel with the other. This is also why session beers were invented: so you can keep that wheel steady and earn yourself another one once the job is done.

Make It Yours Hop time! Pick some favorites and have at it. Go citrusy with Centennial or Cascade hops, or fruity with Mosaic or Galaxy hops. All are good choices. You can play with the malts, too, but if you want to keep the beer sessionable, watch that you don't bump up the ABV.

Beers to Try All Day IPA (Founder's Brewing), Bitter American Extra Pale Ale (21st Amendment Brewery), Levitation Ale (Stone Brewing Co.)

INGREDIENTS	1-GALLON	5-GALLON
White Labs California Ale yeast, Wyeast American Ale yeast, or equivalent	½ package	1 package
Pale ale malt, milled	1½ lbs (680 g)	7½ lbs (3.40 kg)
Crystal/Caramel 20 malt, milled	4 oz (113 g)	1¼ lbs (567 g)
Northern Brewer pellet hops (9.6% AA), for bittering	.15 oz (4.50 g)	.75 oz (21 g)
Willamette pellet hops (4.7% AA), for flavoring	.15 oz (4.50 g)	.75 oz (21 g)
Irish moss	¼ tsp	1 tsp
Willamette pellet hops (4.7% AA), for aroma	.10 oz (3 g)	.50 oz (14 g)
Corn sugar, for bottling	.80 oz (22 g)	4 oz (113 g)

TARGET ORIGINAL/FINAL GRAVITY: 1.045/1.009
TARGET ABV: 4.7%

Follow the master method for brewing 1-gallon or 5-gallon all-grain batches as described on pages 54–59 (5-gallon measurements in parentheses).

• Remove liquid yeast from the refrigerator and, if necessary, activate according to package instructions. Place on the counter to warm.

• Heat **3 quarts (or 3 gallons)** of water to **160°F**, then stir in the grains. Maintain a mash temperature of **148°F to 153°F** for 60 minutes. Raise the temperature of the mash to 170°F, then sparge using **1½ (or 3½) gallons** of 170°F water to make 1½ (or 5½) gallons wort.

• Bring to a boil over high heat. Add the Northern Brewer hops and boil vigorously for 40 minutes. Add the Willamette hops for flavoring and the Irish moss and continue boiling for another 20 minutes. Add the Willamette hops for aroma and remove from the heat. (Total boil time: 60 minutes.)

• Cool to at least 75°F and transfer to a sanitized primary fermentation bucket. Add the yeast and aerate the wort.

• Let ferment for at least **1 week or up to 4 weeks** at **70°F**; then transfer to a sanitized jug or carboy for secondary fermentation. Continue to ferment for another **2 weeks or up to 2 months at 70°F**.

• Dissolve the sugar in ¼ (or 1) cup of boiling water and let cool. Mix with the beer, bottle, and store for **2 weeks or up to a year**. Refrigerate before drinking.

Watermelon Saison

A saison is the perfect blueprint for a fruit-infused beer like this: the Belgian yeast already gives the beer plenty of lush, fruity flavors, so by adding actual fruit, we nudge it one step further. Plus, a saison is meant to be a midsummer thirst quencher for scorching hot days, so keeping the alcohol low means we get more of them.

Brew Notes Use only super-ripe watermelons at the height of the season. Anything else and your beer will taste watery. Since the sugar content of watermelons can vary, the final ABV might be a bit higher or lower than expected.

Make It Yours I also love a simple, straight-up saison—no fruity frills. To do this, increase the pilsner malts to 1¼ (or 6¼) pounds and sparge to make a preboil wort volume of 1½ (or 5½) gallons. If you're not a fan of watermelon but like the idea of fruit, think about peaches and raspberries. These have less juice than watermelons, so sparge as just described for the fruit-free saison and add the fruit in the last 5 minutes of the boil. (Read more about adding fruit on page 166.)

Beers to Try Hell or High Watermelon Wheat Beer (21st Amendment Brewery), Hennepin Farmhouse Saison (Brewery Ommegang)

INGREDIENTS	1-GALLON	5-GALLON
White Labs Belgian Saison 1 Ale yeast, Wyeast Belgian Saison yeast, or equivalent	½ package	1 package
Seedless watermelon	1 (5 to 6 lbs)	5 (5 to 6 lbs) or 2 (12 to 16 lbs)
Pilsner malt, milled	12 oz (340 g)	3¼ lbs (1.59 kg)
Munich malt, milled	8 oz (227 g)	2½ lbs (1.13 kg)
Wheat malt, milled	4 oz (113 g)	1¼ lbs (567 g)
Hallertauer pellet hops (4.8% AA), for bittering	.25 oz (7 g)	1.25 oz (35.50 g)
Hallertauer pellet hops (4.8% AA), for flavoring	.10 oz (3 g)	.50 oz (14 g)
Irish moss	1 tsp	1 tsp
Hallertauer pellet hops (4.8% AA), for aroma	.10 oz (3 g)	.50 oz (14 g)
Corn sugar, for bottling	.80 oz (22 g)	4 oz (113 g)

TARGET ORIGINAL/FINAL GRAVITY: 1.050/1.012
TARGET ABV: 5.0%

Follow the master method for brewing 1-gallon or 5-gallon all-grain batches as described on pages 54–59 (5-gallon measurements in parentheses).

• Remove liquid yeast from the refrigerator and, if necessary, activate according to package instructions. Place on the counter to warm.

• Wash the watermelon thoroughly. Cut into slices, then trim away the rinds. Chop the rinds into large pieces and refrigerate. Chop the fruit into large pieces and puree in a blender or food processor until liquefied. Measure to make 2 quarts (or 2½ gallons); add water if needed and refrigerate.

• Heat **3 quarts (or 3½ gallons) of water to 160°F**, then stir in the grains. Maintain a mash temperature of **148°F to 153°F for 60 minutes**. Raise the temperature of the mash to 170°F, then sparge

using ½ gallon (or 2 gallons) of 170°F water to make 3 quarts (or 3 gallons) wort.

• Bring to a boil over high heat. Add the hops for bittering and boil vigorously for 40 minutes. Add the hops for flavoring and the Irish moss and continue boiling for another 15 minutes. Add the watermelon puree and the rinds and let the wort return to a boil; then continue boiling for another 5 minutes. Add the hops for aroma and remove from the heat. (Total boil time: 60 minutes.)

• Cool to at least 75°F and transfer to a sanitized primary fermentation bucket. Do not strain. Add the yeast and aerate the wort.

• Let ferment for at least **1 week or up to 4 weeks at 70°F**; then transfer to a sanitized jug or carboy for secondary fermentation, leaving behind the rinds. Continue to ferment for another **2 weeks or up to 2 months at 70°F**.

• Dissolve the sugar in ¼ (or 1) cup of boiling water and let cool. Mix with the beer, bottle, and store for **2 weeks or up to a year**. Refrigerate before drinking.

Lemonade Stand Shandy

Shandies get a lot of flack for being girly or "not real beer," but this beer-loving lady would like to stand up for them. Made right, this hybrid of beer and lemonade can be downright delightful. Think of it like balancing an equation: the beer side mellows out the tongue-twisting nature of the lemon and adds a touch of sweetness, while the lemon side keeps the beer crisp and light. It's my top choice for summer picnics and beach bonfires.

Make It Yours Want something closer to sweetened lemonade? Bump up the malts a bit and mash at a slightly higher temperature. It's also fun to throw some fruits or herbs into the secondary. Think: Strawberry-Basil Lemonade, Ginger Lemonade, and Pink Raspberry Lemonade. (Read more about adding fruit and herbs on page 166.)

Beers to Try UFO Big Squeeze Shandy (Harpoon Brewing Company), Sam Adams Porch Rocker (Boston Beer Company, Leinenkugel's Summer Shandy (Jacob Leinenkugel Brewing Company)

INGREDIENTS	1-GALLON	5-GALLON
White Labs California Ale yeast, Wyeast American Ale yeast, or equivalent	½ package	1 package
Pilsner malt, milled	1 lb (454 g)	5 lbs (2.27 kg)
Vienna malt, milled	8 oz (227 g)	2½ lbs (1.13 kg)
Apollo pellet hops (18% AA), for bittering	.05 oz (1.50 g)	.25 oz (7 g)
Sorachi pellet hops (12% AA), for flavoring	.10 oz (3 g)	.50 oz (14 g)
Irish moss	¼ tsp	1 tsp
Sorachi pellet hops (12% AA), for aroma	.10 oz (3 g)	.50 oz (14 g)
Lemon juice	¼ to ¾ cup	1 to 4 cups
Corn sugar, for bottling	.80 oz (22 g)	4 oz (113 g)

TARGET ORIGINAL/FINAL GRAVITY: 1.040/1.007
TARGET ABV: 4.3%

Follow the master method for brewing 1-gallon or 5-gallon all-grain batches as described on pages 54–59 (5-gallon measurements in parentheses).

• Remove liquid yeast from the refrigerator and, if necessary, activate according to package instructions. Place on the counter to warm.

• Heat **3 quarts (or 2½ gallons) of water to 156°F**, then stir in the grains. Maintain a mash temperature of **142°F to 147°F** for 60 minutes. Raise the temperature of the mash to 170°F, then sparge using **1½ (or 4) gallons** of 170°F water to make 1½ (or 5½) gallons wort.

• Bring to a boil over high heat. Add the Apollo hops and boil vigorously for 40 minutes. Add the Sorachi hops for flavoring and the Irish moss and continue boiling for another 20 minutes. Add the Sorachi hops for aroma and remove from the heat. (Total boil time: 60 minutes.)

• Cool to at least 75°F and transfer to a sanitized primary fermentation bucket. Add the yeast and aerate the wort.

• Let ferment for at least **1 week or up to 4 weeks at 70°F**; then transfer to a sanitized jug or carboy for secondary fermentation. Continue to ferment for another **2 weeks or up to 2 months at 70°F.**

• When ready to bottle, dissolve the sugar in ¼ (or 1) cup of boiling water and let cool. Mix with the beer, along with ¼ (or 1) cup of the lemon juice. Taste and add more lemon juice as desired. Bottle and store for **2 weeks or up to a year.** Refrigerate before drinking.

Farmers' Market Gruit

Gruits are old; seriously old. This style of ale is usually credited to the Scots but was in fact brewed throughout Europe for centuries before hops came on the scene. Every brewer's gruit was a little different, though many recorded recipes contained bog myrtle, yarrow, and wild rosemary in addition to other herbs, spices, and botanicals. Since wandering the farmers' market is the modern-day equivalent of foraging for most of us, I based this broody ale on herbs commonly and easily found there.

Brew Notes Fresh herbs are tricky to use, as I discovered the first . . . and second . . . and third time I tried brewing this beer. Use too much and your beer ends up tasting like cough drops. Use too little and there's no balance. Learn from my trial and error: start with a little and add more in the secondary if needed. I also discovered that adding herbs to the mash instead of the boil gives the beer a more mild, pleasing bitterness. I used fairly leafy, full stems of herbs in my brew; if your stems are more sparse, adjust the amount accordingly.

Make It Yours I stuck to the more common herbs found at farmers' markets, but I wholeheartedly encourage you to play with others you find! Keep your eye out for yarrow—not something you'll often find but not impossible. Also, ask your market's flower sellers if they carry bog myrtle; this isn't often used for culinary purposes but is sometimes found in flower arrangements..

Beers to Try Grozet (Williams Bros. Brewing Co.), Lips for Faith Gruit (New Belgium Brewing)

Follow the master method for brewing 1-gallon or 5-gallon all-grain batches as described on pages 54–59 (5-gallon measurements in parentheses).

• Remove liquid yeast from the refrigerator and, if necessary, activate according to package instructions. Place on the counter to warm.

• Heat **3 quarts (or 3½ gallons) of water to 164°F**, then stir in the grains and the rosemary, thyme, and oregano. Maintain a mash temperature of

INGREDIENTS	1-GALLON	5-GALLON
White Labs London Ale yeast, Wyeast London Ale yeast, or equivalent	½ package	1 package
Pale ale malt, milled	1 lb (454 g)	5 lbs (2.27 kg)
Crystal 60 malt, milled	8 oz (227 g)	2½ lbs (1.13 kg)
Caramunich malt, milled	4 oz (113 g)	1¼ lbs (567 g)
Fresh rosemary	2-inch piece	5-inch piece
Fresh thyme	1 (4-inch) sprig	5 (4-inch) sprigs
Fresh oregano	2-inch piece	2 (5-inch) pieces
Irish moss	¼ tsp	1 tsp
Corn sugar, for bottling	.80 oz (22 g)	4 oz (113 g)

TARGET ORIGINAL/FINAL GRAVITY: 1.044/1.014
TARGET ABV: 3.9%

154°F to 158°F for 60 minutes. Raise the temperature of the mash to 170°F, then sparge using **1½ (or 3) gallons** of 170°F water to make 1½ (or 5½) gallons wort.

• Bring to a boil over high heat and boil vigorously for 40 minutes. Add the Irish moss and continue boiling for another 20 minutes. Remove from the heat. (Total boil time: 60 minutes.)

• Cool to at least 75°F and transfer to a sanitized primary fermentation bucket. Add the yeast and aerate the wort.

• Let ferment for at least **1 week or up to 4 weeks at 70°F**; then transfer to a sanitized jug or carboy for secondary fermentation. Continue to ferment for another **2 weeks or up to 2 months at 70°F.**

• Taste the beer a few days before you plan to bottle. Add more herbs if you wish. Taste daily and bottle when the beer tastes good to you.

• Dissolve the sugar in ¼ (or 1) cup of boiling water and let cool. Mix with the beer, bottle, and store for **2 weeks or up to a year**. Refrigerate before drinking.

HOW TO DESIGN YOUR OWN HOMEBREW

My philosophy is that if you can imagine it, you can brew it. Whether you want to make the most perfect, true-to-style Bohemian pilsner or a triple-hopped jalapeño-honey saison, as long as you can close your eyes and imagine how it will taste, you can make it happen. Brew the beer you want to drink.

TINKER WITH AN EXISTING RECIPE

You don't have to dive headfirst into the deep end the very first time you want to design your own beer. You can test the waters—and gain some experience—by taking a recipe that sounds good to you and tweaking one or two things about it.

What to tweak and how? That's what we've been building toward all through this book! Now is the time to bring it all together.

Change the malts. Simply increasing or decreasing the base malts in a recipe increases or decreases its ABV. Swapping one base malt for another, or tinkering with the specialty malts, also totally changes the flavor, character, and color of the finished beer. Go back to chapter 1 and read the Malts section (page 6) for more details on malt profiles.

Change the hops. Hops are like candy—there are lots of different kinds and they're all good. Switch the hops and you have a new beer. You can also play around with adding hops at different stages in the brewing process. Read more about this in "Play with Your Hops," page 116.

Change the yeast. You can keep the entire recipe as is but change the yeast, and you'll find yourself with a very different beer. Different varieties of yeast can make beer fruitier, sweeter and maltier, more crisp, or even more dry (less sweet). Any yeast can be used to ferment any beer; read the descriptions and choose a variety that fits the kind of beer you're in the mood to drink. Take a look back at the Yeast section in chapter 1 on page 14 for more details.

Change the mash temperature. Adjusting the temperature at which you mash your grains results in more or less sugars in your beer, which translates into more or less alcohol and more or less body once fermentation is complete. It's a small change but one of the ways to customize a brew to your tastes. Brush up on mash logistics by reading "Get Geeky with the Mash," page 102.

Change the fermentation temperature. Brew the same beer in the middle of summer and again in the middle of winter, and you'll wind up with two surprisingly different beers. If you have a temperature-controlled refrigerator, you can try this any time just by adjusting the thermostat. Find out more about how the ambient temperature can affect your finished beer in "Brewing in Warm Weather, Brewing in Cold Weather," page 128.

Add some fruit or spices. Start with just a little of whatever extra ingredient you want to add, taste the beer down the road, and add more if you think it needs it. Remember, you can always add more, but you can never take it away. For more on this topic, take a look at "Adding Fruits, Spices, and Other Fun Things to Beer," page 166.

MAKE YOUR OWN RECIPE

Feeling ready to forge out on your own? Fantastic! Welcome to the club! Designing a really good beer takes some patience and a stiff upper lip—don't expect to brew The Perfect Beer with your very first batch. More likely, you'll brew a pretty good beer, which you'll then tweak a little to make a slightly better beer, which then gets further tweaked until you find yourself with the beer of your dreams.

Designing your own beer doesn't necessarily mean starting from scratch or walking into your local homebrewing store and making up something on the spot. Let me share a few best practices to set you on your way.

Imagine your beer. The first step to designing a new beer is imagining it. Close your eyes and actually imagine how this fictional beer tastes and feels in your mouth. I'm completely serious here. Don't make a beer just because you think it sounds cool; you should have an idea of how you want it to taste before you go about making it. If you need to, try a few beers that are similar to the one you're thinking of brewing to help you form a better picture.

Don't reinvent the wheel. No need to start from square one when generations of brewers have already gone to the trouble of refining some basic combinations of malts and hops. Pale ales, stouts, pilsners—consider classic beers like these to be jumping-off points for your own brews. Build on or tinker with their components to develop your own recipes.

Think it through. A good recipe starts with malts and hops, but it doesn't end there. Think through the whole brewing process: the temperature of the mash, the yeast you'll use, the temperature at which the beer will ferment, whether you'll add dry hops or fruit in the secondary, and so on. All these decisions are what make your beer distinctly yours. Thinking them through in advance means that you brew the beer you want instead of a beer that's an accident. Take a look at the chart on page 194 to help you get started.

Use brewing software. You don't have to play guessing games or puzzle your way through complicated brewing textbooks to design good beer. A lot of good, affordable software is out there for you to use. Typically, these programs have you choose a basic style and enter your ingredients. Then they help you adjust the particulars to make sure you're creating a beer with the exact flavor, hoppiness, and color you're hoping for. I used BeerSmith to help design all the beers in this book. ProMash and Beer Calculus are two others that are very

highly rated. By the time this book comes out, I'm sure there will be more. Find one that makes sense to you and use it.

Write it down. Once you have your recipe, be sure to write it down. If you're using brewing software, you can often store all the details for your beer right in the program itself. If not (or if you're just old-school like me), make sure to write down all the details about your recipes in a beer journal. Use this when you go to the homebrewing store to pick up ingredients, for easy reference on your brew day, and to record notes as you go. There is no greater tragedy than brewing a beer off-the-cuff that ends up being amazing and then having no way to make it again.

DIY HOMEBREW CHEAT SHEET

YOU GET THIS....	FROM THIS...	SO DO THIS...
Alcohol	The amount of sugars in the beer	Home in on the amount of base malts, the mash temperature, and any added sugars (like Belgian candi sugar)
Body	The mash temperature and any adjunct grains	Mash warmer and/or add wheat and flaked oats for more body; mash cooler and/or use rice or flaked corn for a lighter body
Color	The combination of grains	Use more specialty grains for darker beers; use fewer or lightly-roasted specialty grains for lighter beers
Foaminess and Head Retention	The mash temperature, the grains used, and adjuncts	Use a 2-step infusion mash for better head retention (see page 206); add flaked wheat or wheat malts for head retention; flaked oats (in large quantities) and nuts can kill beer foam
Malty Flavor	The combination of grains	Pay careful attention to your grain bill
Bitterness	Hops added at the beginning of boil; some darkly roasted malts	Calculate the amount of hops carefully. Generally, more hops mean more bitterness. High alpha acid hops will create more bitterness.
Hop Flavor	Hops added in the middle of brewing	Choose flavorful hops and calculate the amount carefully
Hop Aroma	Hops added at the end of brewing and/or in the secondary (as dry hops)	Choose aromatic hops and be sure not to boil them. Use equal or slightly more hops than used for flavoring.
Fruity, Estery Flavors	The yeast and the fermentation temperature	Choose yeasts based on the amount of fruitiness you'd like. Higher fermentation temperatures will make the yeast character more pronounced.

As with session beers, gluten-free beers aren't a style but rather a subgroup of beers, in this case those made without barley or wheat. Come again, you say? Beer without barley or wheat? Yes, gluten is a protein found in foods made with barley, wheat, and many other grains, and folks with celiac disease or gluten intolerance can suffer quite badly when they eat foods containing it—and that includes the bit of gluten that can make its way through the brewing process.

But beer is the beverage of the people, and as a beer-loving gal, I don't want any of my friends to go without. To make a gluten-free beer, we just need to get a little creative. Sorghum syrup can be used in place of malt extract, and with it, we can actually get pretty darn close to duplicating a great many favorite brews, like the pale ale and the saison in this chapter. If you also expand your definition of "beer" to encompass all delightfully fizzy, mildy alcoholic beverages, then we get to include things like ciders and honey sparklers in our happy, gluten-free embrace.

>>>>> <<<<<

GLUTEN-FREE BEERS

——— [chapter 14] ———

A VERY GOOD GLUTEN-FREE PALE ALE

Sorghum has a flavor that's somewhere between barley malt extract and wildflower honey. It's sweet enough to pour over your oatmeal but with an interesting musky, grainy undertone. If you've never had it before, try a small spoonful before you brew with it—it's good! In a simple pale ale like this one, I like matching the earthy flavor of sorghum with woodsy, herbal hops like Chinook and Willamette.

Brew Notes Be sure to use dry yeast. Liquid yeast is cultured in a grain-based medium and introduces gluten into the beer. Dry yeast is cultured differently and is gluten free.

Make It Yours The best way to tweak this pale ale is to take a trip down the hop aisle and pick a few that sound good to you. Add little doses of hops continuously through the boil or throw a handful of dry hops into the secondary. See "Play with Your Hops," page 116, for more hoppy ideas.

Beers to Try Omission Pale Ale (Widmer Brothers Brewing Company), Pale Ale (Harvester Brewing), Geary's Pale Ale (DL Geary Brewing Company)

Follow the master method for brewing 1-gallon or 5-gallon all-grain batches as described on pages 40–49 (5-gallon measurements in parentheses).

• In a large stockpot over high heat, warm 1½ (or 5½) gallons of water to simmering; then add the sorghum extract and stir to dissolve.

• Bring to a boil over high heat. Add the Chinook hops for bittering and boil vigorously for 40 minutes. Add the Chinook hops for flavoring and the Irish moss and continue boiling for another 20 minutes. Add the Willamette hops and remove from the heat. (Total boil time: 60 minutes.)

• Cool to at least 75°F and transfer to a sanitized primary fermentation bucket. Add the yeast and aerate the wort.

INGREDIENTS	1-GALLON	5-GALLON
Sorghum extract	1½ lbs (680 g)	7½ lbs (3.40 kg)
Chinook pellet hops (11.4% AA), for bittering	.10 oz (3 g)	.50 oz (14 g)
Chinook pellet hops (11.4% AA), for flavoring	.10 oz (3 g)	.50 oz (14 g)
Irish moss	¼ tsp	1 tsp
Willamette pellet hops (4.7% AA), for aroma	.15 oz (4 g)	.75 oz (21 g)
Safale US-05 dry yeast, or equivalent	½ package	1 package
Corn sugar, for bottling	.80 oz (22 g)	4 oz (113 g)

TARGET ORIGINAL/FINAL GRAVITY: 1.054/1.013
TARGET ABV: 5.4%

• Let ferment for at least **1 week or up to 4 weeks at 70°F**; then transfer to a sanitized jug or carboy for secondary fermentation. Continue to ferment for another **2 weeks or up to 2 months at 70°F.**

• Dissolve the sugar in ¼ (or 1) cup of boiling water and let cool. Mix with the beer, bottle, and store for **2 weeks or up to a year.** Refrigerate before drinking.

Gluten-Free Saison

Sorghum and honey are perfect playmates for a saison-style beer without the gluten. The finished beer is champagne-like in character with a soft and luscious fruitiness from the Belgian-style yeast. This beer needs a citrusy hop to add some brightness, and Amarillo steps up to the job with panache.

Brew Notes Be sure to use dry yeast. Liquid yeast is cultured in a grain-based medium and introduces gluten into the beer. Dry yeast is cultured differently and is gluten free.

Make It Yours Play with the ratios of sorghum to honey. For a lighter, crisper ale, increase the honey and decrease the sorghum. For something maltier, do the opposite.

Beers to Try Quest Tripel Ale (Green's Gluten-Free Ales), Celia Saison (Ipswich Brewery)

INGREDIENTS	1-GALLON	5-GALLON
Sorghum extract	1 lb (454 g)	5 lbs (2.27 kg)
Wildflower honey	8 oz (227 g)	2½ lbs (1.13 kg)
Magnum pellet hops (13.8% AA), for bittering	.05 oz (1.5 g)	.25 oz (7 g)
Amarillo pellet hops (8.2% AA), for flavoring	.10 oz (3 g)	.50 oz (14 g)
Irish moss	¼ tsp	1 tsp
Amarillo pellet hops (8.2% AA), for aroma	.10 oz (3 g)	.50 oz (14 g)
Safbrew T-58 dry yeast, or equivalent	½ package	1 package
Corn sugar, for bottling	.80 oz (22 g)	4 oz (113 g)

TARGET ORIGINAL/FINAL GRAVITY: 1.053/1.004
TARGET ABV: 6.4%

Follow the master method for brewing 1-gallon or 5-gallon all-grain batches as described on pages 40–49 (5-gallon measurements in parentheses).

• In a large stockpot over high heat, warm 1½ (or 5½) gallons of water to simmering; then add the sorghum and honey and stir to dissolve.

• Bring to a boil over high heat. Add the Magnum hops and boil vigorously for 40 minutes. Add the Amarillo hops for flavoring and the Irish moss and continue boiling for another 20 minutes. Add the Amarillo hops for aroma and remove from the heat. (Total boil time: 60 minutes.)

• Cool to at least 75°F and transfer to a sanitized primary fermentation bucket. Add the yeast and aerate the wort.

• Let ferment for at least **1 week or up to 4 weeks at 70°F**; then transfer to a sanitized jug or carboy for secondary fermentation. Continue to ferment for another **2 weeks or up to 2 months at 70°F**.

• Dissolve the sugar in ¼ (or 1) cup of boiling water and let cool. Mix with the beer, bottle, and store for **2 weeks or up to a year**. Refrigerate before drinking.

Gluten-Free Chocolate Porter

Two challenges to making a gluten-free porter or stout are matching the roasty flavor of dark malts and creating a beer with some body. The first is managed with a combination of molasses and dark candi sugar (available at homebrewing stores). They work together to mimic the familiar porter-like flavors of bittersweet chocolate, burnt sugar, and roasted nuts. I throw in some cacao nibs for one more chocolate burst. As for giving the porter some heft, I turn to gluten-free oats. These help thicken the beer the way a pot of oatmeal thickens on the stove.

Brew Notes Be sure to use dry yeast. Liquid yeast is cultured in a grain-based medium and introduces gluten into the beer. Dry yeast is cultured differently and is gluten free.

Make It Yours Make this into a bock-style beer with some lager yeast. Keep the fermentation temperature below 50°F for the first few weeks and then 40°F for a few more weeks. (See "The Real Deal with Lagers," page 206.) As a bock, the beer keeps the chocolate flavor from the cacao but picks up a smooth, malt-forward character.

Beer to Try Brown Ale (New Planet Gluten-Free Beer)

INGREDIENTS	1-GALLON	5-GALLON
Gluten-free steel-cut oats	4 oz (113 g)	1¼ lbs (567 g)
Sorghum extract	16 oz (454 g)	5 lbs (2.27 kg)
Dark candi sugar (D-180 or equivalent)	8 oz (227 g)	2½ lbs (1.13 kg)
Molasses	2 oz (57 g)	10 oz (283 g)
Cluster pellet hops (6.8% AA), for bittering	.20 oz (5.5 g)	1 oz (28 g)
East Kent Goldings pellet hops (7.2% AA), for flavoring	.20 oz (5.5 g)	1 oz (28 g)
Irish moss	¼ tsp	1 tsp
East Kent Goldings pellet hops (7.2% AA), for aroma	.10 oz (3 g)	.50 oz (14 g)
Roasted cacao nibs, roughly ground	2 oz (57 g or ½ cup)	10 oz (283 g or 2½ cups)
Safale US-04 dry yeast, or equivalent	½ package	1 package
Corn sugar, for bottling	.80 oz (22 g)	4 oz (113 g)

TARGET ORIGINAL/FINAL GRAVITY: 1.060/1.004
TARGET ABV: 7.4%

Follow the master method for brewing 1-gallon or 5-gallon all-grain batches as described on pages 40–49 (5-gallon measurements in parentheses).

• In a large stockpot bring **2 quarts (or 2 gallons) of water to a boil**; then add the oats. Reduce heat to low and simmer for 1 hour, until the oats are completely mushy and the water is creamy. Strain out the oat solids and add enough water to the liquid to make **1½ (or 5½) gallons**. Bring to a simmer; then add the sorghum, candi sugar, and molasses and stir to dissolve.

• Bring to a boil over high heat. Add the Cluster hops and boil vigorously for 40 minutes. Add the East Kent Goldings hops for flavoring and the Irish moss and continue boiling for another 20 minutes.

Add the East Kent Goldings hops for aroma and the cacao nibs and remove from the heat. (Total boil time: 60 minutes.)

• Cool to at least 75°F and transfer to a sanitized primary fermentation bucket. Add the yeast and aerate the wort.

• Let ferment for at least **1 week or up to 4 weeks at 70°F**; then transfer to a sanitized jug or carboy for secondary fermentation. Continue to ferment for another **2 weeks or up to 2 months at 70°F**.

• Taste the beer a few days before you plan to bottle. Add more cacao nibs if you wish. Taste daily and bottle when the beer tastes good to you.

• Dissolve the sugar in ¼ (or 1) cup of boiling water and let cool. Mix with the beer, bottle, and store for **2 weeks or up to a year**. Refrigerate before drinking.

Jasmine Honey Sparkler

Sweet, syrupy mead isn't the only thing you can make with honey. Mix the honey with a little more water from the get-go and you can make a light, refreshing sparkler like this one. Honey changes in unexpected ways once it ferments with yeast. It loses much of its sticky sweetness, yet its essential "honeyness" remains. I love the subtle floral aroma and flavor that jasmine tea adds here. It's the kind of refined sip you could serve at a brunch or a classy backyard party.

Brew Notes Be sure to use dry yeast. Liquid yeast is cultured in a grain-based medium and introduces gluten into the beer. Dry yeast is cultured differently and is gluten free. You can find yeast nutrient with the wine-making supplies at any homebrewing store.

Make It Yours Honey pairs so well with so many things—just take a look at your spice cupboard for other infusing ideas. A honey-ginger sparkler made with freshly grated ginger would be amazing, as would an infusion of almost any summer fruit. (Read more about adding spices and fruit on page 166.) For a drier, extremely crisp sparkler, use champagne yeast.

Beer to Try White Jasmine Sparkling Tea (Golden Star Tea)

INGREDIENTS	1-GALLON	5-GALLON
Wildflower honey	1 lb (454 g)	5 lbs (2.27 kg)
Safale US-04 dry yeast, or equivalent	½ package	1 package
Yeast nutrient	1 tsp	5 tsps
Jasmine green tea	5 g (4 bags or 1 tbsp loose-leaf)	25 g (20 bags or 5 tbsps loose-leaf)
Corn sugar, for bottling	.80 oz (22 g)	4 oz (113 g)

TARGET ORIGINAL/FINAL GRAVITY: 1.042/1.004
TARGET ABV: 5%

• A few days before you plan to bottle, place the jasmine tea in a small sanitized mesh bag and add to the secondary. Taste daily and bottle when the beer tastes good to you.

• Dissolve the sugar in ¼ (or 1) cup of boiling water and let cool. Mix with the beer, bottle, and store for **2 weeks or up to a year**. Refrigerate before drinking.

Follow the master method for brewing 1-gallon or 5-gallon all-grain batches as described on pages 40–49 (5-gallon measurements in parentheses).

• In a large stockpot over high heat, warm **1 gallon (or 5 gallons) of water** to a simmer. Remove from the heat and stir in the honey to dissolve. Return to high heat, bring to a boil, and boil for 5 minutes.

• Cool to at least 75°F and transfer to a sanitized primary fermentation bucket. Add the yeast and the yeast nutrient, and aerate the wort.

• Let ferment for at least **1 week or up to 4 weeks at 70°F**; then transfer to a sanitized jug or carboy for secondary fermentation. Continue to ferment for another **2 weeks or up to 2 months at 70°F**.

Hoppy Hard Cider

Hard ciders today are nothing like those toothachingly sweet fizz-bombs we used to sip back in college. Today's ciders, especially homebrewed versions, are crisp and clean, refreshingly effervescent, and absolutely bursting with fresh apple flavor. We can even borrow a friend from the beer world and add hops to our ciders! Used here, hops are best if boiled only briefly with the cider, with an additional scoop of dry hops added during secondary fermentation for a bright aroma. Ciders are also naturally gluten-free.

Brew Notes Be sure to use dry yeast. Liquid yeast is cultured in a grain-based medium and introduces gluten into the beer. Dry yeast is cultured differently and is gluten free.

Make It Yours If you find raw, unpasteurized cider, try spontaneously fermenting it. You don't need to do anything—just put it in a jug with an air lock and leave it at room temperature. It will start to ferment in a few days. This is a gamble; you might end up with something totally disgusting, but there's an equal chance you'll end up with something surprisingly delicious.

Beers to Try Grasshop-ah (Colorado Cider Company), Dry Hopped Cider (Finnriver Cidery), Yakima Dry-Hopped Cider (Tieton Ciderworks)

INGREDIENTS	1-GALLON	5-GALLON
Pasteurized apple cider	1 gallon	5 gallons
Cascade pellet hops (6.7% AA), for flavoring	.20 oz (5.50 g)	1 oz (28 g)
Safale US-05 dry yeast, or equivalent	½ package	1 package
Cascade pellet hops (6.7% AA), for dry hopping	.25 oz (7 g)	1.25 oz (35.50 g)
Corn sugar, for bottling	.80 oz (22 g)	4 oz (113 g)

TARGET ORIGINAL/FINAL GRAVITY: 1.060/1.007
TARGET ABV: 7%

• Let ferment for at least **1 week or up to 4 weeks at 70°F**; then transfer to a sanitized jug or carboy for secondary fermentation. Continue to ferment for another **2 weeks or up to 2 months at 70°F**.

• Two to seven days before you plan to bottle, place the hops for dry hopping in a small sanitized mesh bag and add to the secondary. Do not let sit longer than a week.

• Dissolve the sugar in ¼ (or 1) cup of boiling water and let cool. Mix with the beer, bottle, and store for **2 weeks or up to a year**. Refrigerate before drinking.

Follow the master method for brewing 1-gallon or 5-gallon all-grain batches as described on pages 40–49 (5-gallon measurements in parentheses).

• Bring ½ gallon (or 2½ gallons) of the cider to a rapid simmer over medium-high heat. Add the hops for flavoring and simmer for **30 minutes**. Remove from the heat and stir in the remaining cider with a sanitized spoon.

• Cool to at least 75°F and transfer to the sanitized primary fermentation bucket. Add the yeast and aerate the wort.

THE REAL DEAL WITH LAGERS

Contrary to what you might think or may have heard, lagers are not all that hard to brew. In terms of the straight-up brewing mechanics—mashing, sparging, boiling, and so on—lagers are not all that different from ales. Where lagers do require extra TLC is during fermentation: most lagers need to be kept around 50°F during the first active stage of fermentation and then around 40°F for secondary fermentation. Not only are these temperatures ideal for cold-loving lager yeasts, but cooler fermentation temperatures result in a crisper, smoother, cleaner beer.

SETTING UP A LAGERING FRIDGE

Unless you have a handy cave nearby or a basement with steady sub-50°F temperatures, I highly recommend investing in a special fridge for brewing lagers. Lagers brewed at warmer temperatures or temperatures that fluctuate tend to have more ale-like characteristics: rough, fruity flavors instead of crisp, clean malt and hop flavors. They just aren't the same.

Luckily, setting up a lagering fridge isn't very hard and doesn't have to be that expensive. You need two things: a fridge and a temperature controller.

A full-size kitchen fridge is ideal if you're brewing 5-gallon batches and have the extra space for it. A mini-fridge works well if you have limited space or are just brewing 1-gallon batches. In my mini-fridge, I can fit two 1-gallon batches at a time or one 5-gallon batch with all the shelves removed. When you go shopping, double-check the dimensions of the fridge and make sure it fits the number and size of the containers you plan to use.

A temperature controller is a gadget that keeps the temperature very steady and very exact. Most fridges don't get warm enough to properly lager beers, so the temperature controller overrides the fridge's settings. Temperature controllers are available at most homebrewing stores and online. Buy the best that you can afford.

To use most temperature controllers, you plug the fridge into the controller and then the controller into the wall. A temperature probe wired to the controller goes inside the fridge to monitor the temperature—you can either drill a hole through the wall of the fridge or snake the probe under the

rubber seal on the door. Make sure the probe is positioned toward the middle of the fridge so it gets an average reading. Then just set the controller to your desired temperature.

The controller overrides all of the fridge's temperature settings, including the settings in the freezer. You won't be able to use the freezer for storing hops or frozen foods, but you can use the fridge for chilling beer! Ideal serving temperature for most craft beers is between 40°F and 55°F, a little warmer than regular fridge temperatures, so keeping them cold in a lagering fridge is perfect.

THE DECOCTION MASH: A RELIC OF LAGERS PAST

Lagers were originally brewed with a technique called "decoction mashing." This was (and still is) a laborious and time-intensive process that involved adding portions of boiled mash to the main mash at regular intervals in order to raise the temperature of the mash in a series of controlled steps. The benefit was that you didn't need a thermometer to know the mash was proceeding properly—a very handy thing in the days before the thermometer was invented. Decoction mashing was also necessary to fully extract the sugars and essential yeast nutrients from "undermodified" malts. These malts were (and still are) easier and cheaper to produce but more difficult to ferment.

Thanks to the invention of the thermometer and more affordable "fully modified" malts, we no longer need to rely on decoction mashing to make a good lager. Any malts you buy at a homebrewing store these days will be fully modified; if you do encounter undermodified malts, they should be labeled as such.

USING A 2-STEP INFUSION MASH FOR BETTER LAGERS

A full-on decoction mash may no longer be necessary for brewing lagers, but there are some benefits to a slightly modified mash technique. If we let the mash rest for about 30 minutes at around 130°F before bringing it up to usual mashing temperatures, we can develop some extra nutrients for the yeast (helpful when fermenting at low temperatures) as well as some proteins that help foam quality. This "2-step infusion mash," as it's technically called, also makes a more stable finished beer with less risk of haziness.

The 2-step infusion can be used for any beer (ale or lager) and is especially helpful when brewing lagers, but it's also not strictly necessary. You can brew a good lager following the same technique as outlined in the master method on pages 54–59. Consider the 2-step infusion mash an alternative technique that gives you extra mojo for making a truly outstanding beer.

If you want to try a 2-step infusion, here's how to do it:

• Measure 1 quart of water for every pound of grain in your recipe. In a large stockpot over high heat, warm the water to 138°F. Pour all the grains into the water and stir off the heat, checking the temperature of the mash with an instant-read thermometer, until it falls between 130°F and 135°F. Cover the pot with a lid and let the mash rest for 30 minutes. Check the temperature occasionally and warm it for a minute or two if necessary to keep the mash within the temperature range. (If you're doing a 1-gallon batch, you can keep the grains in a warm oven while they mash.)

• Close to the end of the 30-minute mash, measure ½ quart of water for every 1 pound of grain and pour it into a separate pot. Warm until just below boiling, around 200°F. When the 30-minute mash has finished, stir this water into the mash to raise the temperature to 148°F to 153°F. Check the temperature with an instant-read thermometer; if necessary, stir to cool the mash or turn on the heat to raise the temperature so that the mash is within the proper range.

• Cover the pot and mash the grains for 60 minutes. Check the temperature every 15 minutes; if it drops below 148°F, set the pot on the burner for just a minute or two to warm it up again. If it's too warm, stir the mash off the heat for a few minutes to bring the temperature down.

• After an hour, the grains are mashed. If you had trouble with high or low temperatures, give the mash another 15 minutes to make sure you've extracted all the sugar. Proceed with the mash-out and sparge as usual.

SIX WEEKS TO MAKE A LAGER, MINIMUM

Lager yeasts love the cold, but it also makes them slower when it comes to converting sugars into alcohol. At the very least, let the beer spend 2 weeks in the primary and 4 weeks in the secondary before bottling, though extending the secondary fermentation to 2 or 3 months can give you even better results.

Also, don't worry if you don't see as much activity during primary fermentation as you do for your ales. Once a lager's fermentation gets going, you'll see a bubble or two in the air lock every minute, at most. It might feel disturbingly slow, but that's just the lager yeast working at its own pace and helping to make you the best lager possible.

THE DIACETYL REST, OR "NO BUTTER IN MY LAGER, THANKS"

One last step is necessary for brewing good lager, and it's called the "diacetyl rest." Diacetyl is a chemical created during the brewing process that causes a buttery or butterscotch-like flavor in the finished beer (though it's not otherwise harmful; a small amount of it is acceptable in some ale beer styles, like Scottish ales and English brown ales). Diacetyl is usually consumed by the yeast at ale fermentation temperatures but can sometimes remain in the beer after the cool fermentation of a lager.

To make sure no diacetyl remains in a finished lager, all we need to do is raise the temperature of the beer to 60°F for 2 days after the primary fermentation has finished and before cooling it down for the longer secondary fermentation. This is easy enough to do in a temperature-controlled fridge just by increasing the temperature setting. You can also remove the beer from the fridge and let it sit at cool room temperature.

PUT IT ALL TOGETHER

Put all these pieces together and I promise you'll make a wonderful lager. The first time can feel a bit intimidating, but once you have a lager fridge established and get the feel for some of the differences between lagers and ales, it's no biggie. Start with the lagers in the next chapter—they are some of my all-time favorites—and then you'll be ready to tackle anything.

The beauty of a good lager is its simplicity. Pare things down to a few malts, a dash of mild hops, and a good lager yeast and you get a beer of incredible clarity with clean, crisp flavors and perfect balance. This simplicity is also its challenge: there's nowhere to hide mistakes when you brew a lager. Every choice you make (or don't make) during brewing is apparent in the finished beer. Intimidating? A bit. But it also sounds like the kind of dare we homebrewing types love to accept.

Before brewing any lagers, I highly recommend investing in a lagering fridge and temperature controller, like the setup described in "The Real Deal with Lagers," page 206. While you can brew a lager without temperature control, you aren't likely to be as happy with the results, especially if your aim is an authentic Bohemian pilsner or German bock. Relying on cool temperatures in your basement or any other area of your house leaves you with less control over the beer and gives you inconsistent results.

LAGERS

[chapter 15]

A VERY GOOD PILSNER

This is not the pilsner that you most likely drank by the keg back in college. A true German or Czech pilsner is about as far removed from that as the moon is from blue cheese. The pilsner I'm sharing here is slightly more Czech in nature with a clean, sweet malt profile, a subtle but perceptible hop bitterness, and a crisp finish. It's a beer to make again and again.

Brew Notes You'll need to make a yeast starter for this recipe to ensure good fermentation Also, this beer has a 90-minute boil, so plan your brew day accordingly. I highly recommend investing in a lagering fridge and temperature controller (see page 206).

Make It Yours I love a hoppy pilsner. Increase all the hops by .05 (or .25) ounce for very happy, hoppy results. Swap the German hops for some American hops for a West Coast–style pilsner.

Beers to Try Prima Pils (Victory Brewing Company), Scrimshaw Pilsner (North Coast Brewing Company)

Follow the master method for brewing 1-gallon or 5-gallon all-grain batches as described on pages 54–59 (5-gallon measurements in parentheses).

• Using the yeast and malt extract, make a yeast starter 12 to 18 hours before you plan to brew, following the instructions in "How to Make a Yeast Starter," page 16.

• Heat **3 quarts (or 3 gallons) of water to 160°F**, then stir in the grains. Maintain a mash temperature of **148°F to 153°F** for 60 minutes. (Alternatively, do a 2-step infusion mash as described on page 206.) Raise the temperature of the mash to 170°F, then sparge using **1½ (or 3½) gallons** of 170°F water to make 1¾ (or 6) gallons wort.

• Bring to a boil over high heat. Add the Hallertauer and Saaz hops for bittering and boil vigorously for 60 minutes. Add the Saaz and Hallertauer hops for flavoring and the Irish moss and continue boiling for another 30 minutes. Add the Saaz hops

INGREDIENTS	1-GALLON	5-GALLON
White Labs German Lager yeast, Wyeast Czech Pils lager yeast, or equivalent	½ package	1 package
Light dried malt extract	.90 oz (25 g or 2 heaping tbsps)	3.50 oz (100 g or ½ cup)
German pilsner malt, milled	1½ lbs (680 g)	7½ lbs (3.40 kg)
Vienna malt, milled	4 oz (113 g)	1¼ lbs (567 g)
Black Patent malt, milled	Pinch	.50 oz (14 g)
Hallertauer pellet hops (4.3% AA), for bittering	.15 oz (4 g)	.75 oz (21 g)
Saaz pellet hops (3% AA), for bittering	.15 oz (4 g)	.75 oz (21 g)
Saaz pellet hops (3% AA), for flavoring	.10 oz (3 g)	.50 oz (14 g)
Hallertauer pellet hops (4.3% AA), for flavoring	.05 oz (1.5 g)	.25 oz (7 g)
Irish moss	¼ tsp	1 tsp
Saaz pellet hops (3% AA), for aroma	.20 oz (5.5 g)	1 oz (28 g)
Corn sugar, for bottling	.80 oz (22 g)	4 oz (113 g)

TARGET ORIGINAL/FINAL GRAVITY: 1.047/1.009
TARGET ABV: 5%

for aroma and remove from the heat. (Total boil time: 90 minutes.)

• Cool to at least 75°F and transfer to a sanitized primary fermentation bucket. Add the yeast starter and aerate the wort.

• Let ferment for at least **2 weeks or up to 4 weeks at 50°F**; then bring up to **60°F for 2 days**. Transfer to a sanitized jug or carboy for secondary fermentation. Continue to ferment for another **1 month or up to 3 months at 40°F**.

• Dissolve the sugar in ¼ (or 1) cup of boiling water and let cool. Mix with the beer, bottle, and store for **2 weeks or up to a year**. Refrigerate before drinking.

Spring Blossom Maibock

Where I live in California, the first days of spring are heralded with tiny white blossoms on all the orange trees. Their sweet floral perfume drifts through the open windows, making the whole house smell heavenly. In a burst of inspiration one spring, I added a few handfuls of orange blossoms to a maibock (*Mai* means "May" in German). The result was beyond my wildest expectations—a golden beer as light and sweet as sunshine infused with the delicate flavor and aroma of orange blossoms.

Brew Notes You'll need to make a yeast starter for this recipe to ensure good fermentation. You can use the blossoms from any flowering fruit tree or from edible flowers like elderflowers, lilacs, roses, or chamomile. Fresh petals can be frozen for 1 month. Also, I highly recommend investing in a lagering fridge and temperature controller (see page 206).

Make It Yours Try this style as a braggot and add some honey to the mix. You can also brew this without flowers for a more traditional maibock.

Beers to Try Dead Guy Ale (Rogue Ales), Mardi Gras Bok (Abita Brewing Company)

INGREDIENTS	1-GALLON	5-GALLON
White Labs German Bock Lager yeast, Wyeast Bohemian Lager yeast, or equivalent	½ package	1 package
Light dried malt extract	.90 oz (25 g or 2 heaping tbsps)	3.50 oz (100 g or ½ cup)
Pilsner malt (preferably German), milled	2 lbs (907 g)	10 lbs (4.54 kg)
Munich malt, milled	8 oz (227 g)	2½ lbs (1.13 kg)
Santiam pellet hops (6% AA), for bittering	.20 oz (5.50 g)	1 oz (28 g)
Hallertauer pellet hops (4.3% AA), for flavoring	.15 oz (4 g)	.75 oz (21 g)
Irish moss	¼ tsp	1 tsp
Fresh flower blossoms or petals, or half the amount in dried flowers	.50 to .75 oz (14 to 21 g or about 1 cup)	2.50 to 3.75 oz (70 to 105 g or about 5 cups)
Corn sugar, for bottling	.80 oz (22 g)	4 oz (113 g)

TARGET ORIGINAL/FINAL GRAVITY: 1.067/1.017
TARGET ABV: 6.6%

Follow the master method for brewing 1-gallon or 5-gallon all-grain batches as described on pages 54-59 (5-gallon measurements in parentheses).

• Using the yeast and malt extract, make a yeast starter 12 to 18 hours before you plan to brew, following the instructions in "How to Make a Yeast Starter," page 16.

• Heat **1 gallon (or 4 gallons) of water to 160°F**, then stir in the grains. Maintain a mash temperature of **148°F to 153°F** for 60 minutes. (Alternatively, do a 2-step infusion mash as described on page 206.) Raise the temperature of the mash to 170°F, then sparge using **1 gallon (or 2½ gallons)** of 170°F water to make 1½ (or 5½) gallons wort.

• Bring to a boil over high heat. Add the Santiam hops and boil vigorously for 40 minutes. Add the Hallertauer hops and the Irish moss and continue boiling for another 20 minutes. Remove from the heat. (Total boil time: 60 minutes.)

• Cool to at least 75°F and transfer to a sanitized primary fermentation bucket. Add the yeast starter and aerate the wort.

• Let ferment for at least **2 weeks or up to 4 weeks at 50°F**; then bring up to **60°F for 2 days**. Transfer to a sanitized jug or carboy for secondary fermentation. Continue to ferment for another **1 month or up to 3 months at 40°F**.

• A few days before you plan to bottle, place the flower blossoms in a sanitized mesh bag and add to the secondary. Taste daily and bottle when the beer tastes good to you. Do not let the beer sit for too long; the flavor will continue to become stronger and more vegetal the longer it sits.

• Dissolve the sugar in ¼ (or 1) cup of boiling water and let cool. Mix with the beer, bottle, and store for **2 weeks or up to a year**. Refrigerate before drinking.

McNally's Oktoberfest

I have to dedicate this beer to my dear friend Heather McNally who loves—and I mean *loves*—Oktoberfest. I'm talking both the beer and the fall festival that shares its name. No one can out-polka her on the dance floor or out-drink her at the bar, though she has the kind of infectious enthusiasm that makes you want to try. Like McNally herself, this smooth and malty Oktoberfest is a wholly happy-making brew that is capable of sending you out on the polka floor long after you swear your feet are too sore. *Prost!*

Brew Notes You'll need to make a yeast starter for this recipe to ensure good fermentation. Also, I highly recommend investing in a lagering fridge and temperature controller (see page 206).

Make It Yours Oktoberfests are a fairly standard formula of equal parts Munich, pilsner, and Vienna malts—keep this ratio and move up or down in quantity for more or less alcohol. If you're not bothered about keeping it true to style, try some woodsy West Coast hops.

Beers to Try Sam Adams Oktoberfest (Boston Beer Company), Ayinger Oktoberfest-Märzen (Brauerie Aying), Harpoon Octoberfest Beer (Harpoon Brewery)

INGREDIENTS	1-GALLON	5-GALLON
White Labs German Lager yeast, Wyeast Bohemian Lager yeast, or equivalent	½ package	1 package
Light dried malt extract	.90 oz (25 g or 2 heaping tbsps)	3.50 oz (100 g or 1½ cup)
Munich malt, milled	10 oz (283 g)	3⅛ lbs (1.42 kg)
German pilsner malt, milled	10 oz (283 g)	3⅛ lbs (1.42 kg)
Vienna malt, milled	10 oz (283 g)	3⅛ lbs (1.42 kg)
Crystal/Caramel 40 malt, milled	4 oz (113 g)	1¼ lbs (567 g)
Tettnanger pellet hops (3.7% AA), for bittering	.25 oz (7 g)	1.25 oz (35.50 g)
Saaz pellet hops (2.9% AA), for flavoring	.15 oz (4 g)	.75 oz (21 g)
Irish moss	¼ tsp	1 tsp
Corn sugar, for bottling	.80 oz (22 g)	4 oz (113 g)

TARGET ORIGINAL/FINAL GRAVITY: 1.056/1.013
TARGET ABV: 5.6%

Follow the master method for brewing 1-gallon or 5-gallon all-grain batches as described on pages 54-59 (5-gallon measurements in parentheses).

• Using the yeast and malt extract, make a yeast starter 12 to 18 hours before you plan to brew, following the instructions in "How to Make a Yeast Starter," page 16.

• Heat **1 gallon (or 3½ gallons) of water to 164°F**, then stir in the grains. Maintain a mash temperature of **154°F to 158°F** for 60 minutes. (Alternatively, do a 2-step infusion mash as described on page 206.) Raise the temperature of the mash to 170°F, then sparge using **1 gallon (or 3 gallons)** of 170°F water to make 1½ (or 5½) gallons wort.

• Bring to a boil over high heat. Add the Tettnanger hops and boil vigorously for 40 minutes. Add the Saaz hops and the Irish moss and continue boiling for another 20 minutes. Remove from the heat. (Total boil time: 60 minutes.)

• Cool to at least 75°F and transfer to a sanitized primary fermentation bucket. Add the yeast starter and aerate the wort.

• Let ferment for at least **2 weeks or up to 4 weeks at 50°F**, then bring up to **60°F for 2 days**. Transfer to a sanitized jug or carboy for secondary fermentation. Continue to ferment for another **month or up to 3 months at 40°F**.

• Dissolve the sugar in ¼ (or 1) cup of boiling water and let cool. Mix with the beer, bottle, and store for **2 weeks or up to a year**. Refrigerate before drinking.

Chocolate Doppelbock

The hallmark of a good doppelbock is a beer so rich and malty that you could drink a bottle and almost get away with calling it dinner. If you infuse it with bittersweet cacao nibs, you can also call it dessert. Either way, this is a true stick-to-your-ribs kind of beer, best saved for the deep days of winter when you don't have to be anywhere fast.

Brew Notes You'll need to make a yeast starter for this recipe to ensure good fermentation. The rich, sugary first runnings from the wort are boiled separately for this beer; read the directions carefully.

Make It Yours Swap the cacao nibs for freshly ground coffee beans—or use both! (See page 166.) If you want to brew this without add-ins, that's also a fine decision. Try experimenting with different malts, too.

Beer to Try Troegenator Double Bock (Troegs Craft Brewery)

INGREDIENTS	1-GALLON	5-GALLON
White Labs German Bock Lager yeast, Wyeast Bavarian Lager yeast, or equivalent	½ package	1 package
Light dried malt extract	.90 oz (25 g or 2 heaping tbsps)	3.50 oz (100 g or ½ cup)
Munich malt, milled	2¼ lbs (1.02 kg)	11¼ lbs (5.10 kg)
German pilsner malt, milled	8 oz (227 g)	2½ lbs (1.13 kg)
Crystal/Caramel 120 malt, milled	4 oz (113 g)	1¼ lbs (567 g)
Hallertauer pellet hops (4.3% AA), for bittering	.20 oz (5.50 g)	1 oz (28 g)
Hallertauer pellet hops (4.3% AA), for flavoring	.10 oz (3 g)	.50 oz (14 g)
Irish moss	¼ tsp	1 tsp
Roasted cacao nibs	2 oz (57 g or ½ cup)	10 oz (283 g or 2½ cups)
Corn sugar, for bottling	.70 oz (20 g)	3.50 oz (100 g)

TARGET ORIGINAL/FINAL GRAVITY: 1.079/1.024
TARGET ABV: 7.3%

Follow the master method for brewing 1-gallon or 5-gallon all-grain batches as described on pages 54-59 (5-gallon measurements in parentheses).

• Using the yeast and malt extract, make a yeast starter 12 to 18 hours before you plan to brew, following the instructions in "How to Make a Yeast Starter," page 16.

• Heat **1 gallon (or 4¼ gallons) of water to 164°F**, then stir in the grains. Maintain a mash temperature of **154°F to 158°F** for 60 minutes. Raise the temperature of the mash to 170°F. To collect the first runnings, drain ½ **(or 1) gallon** of liquid from the mash and set aside. Sparge as usual using **1 gallon (or 2½ gallons)** of 170°F water, to make 1 gallon (or 5 gallons) wort.

• Bring to a boil over high heat. Add the hops for bittering and boil vigorously for 40 minutes. Meanwhile, in a large saucepot bring the first runnings to a boil (be attentive for boil-overs!) and reduce by half. Add the first runnings, the hops for flavoring, and the Irish moss to the wort and continue boiling for another 20 minutes. Add the cacao nibs and remove from the heat. (Total boil time: 60 minutes.)

• Cool to at least 75°F and transfer to a sanitized primary fermentation bucket. Check the volume of your wort; add tap water as needed to make 1 gallon (or 5 gallons). Add the yeast starter and aerate the wort.

• Let ferment for at least **2 weeks or up to 4 weeks at 50°F**; then bring up to **60°F for 2 days**. Transfer to a sanitized jug or carboy for secondary fermentation, leaving behind the cacao nibs. Continue to ferment for another **month or up to 3 months at 40°F**.

• Taste the beer a few days before you plan to bottle. Add more cacao nibs if you wish. Taste daily and bottle when the beer tastes good to you. Dissolve the sugar in ¼ (or 1) cup of boiling water and let cool. Mix with the beer, bottle, and store for **2 weeks or up to a year**. Refrigerate before drinking.

Ode to San Francisco Steam Beer

I've been a wanderer much of my adult life—first to Oregon after college, then to Boston, then to Ohio. But when my husband and I arrived in the Bay Area, we knew this would be home. This beer, brewed in the steam beer style of San Francisco's first brewers, is an ode to my adopted city. It's made with a special strain of lager yeast that allows for slightly warmer fermentation temperatures. Around 65°F is perfect, which, not so coincidentally, is the average daytime temperature in San Francisco. The hops are a nod to the earthy, woodsy, minty eucalyptus you smell on a stroll through Golden Gate Park. High five, San Francisco! Thanks for giving me a place to call home.

Brew Notes You don't need a lagering fridge for this one, but pay careful attention to the daytime temperature when you make this beer; store your beer somewhere warmer or cooler if necessary.

Make It Yours A steam beer, also called a California Common, can be made with almost any lager style. Try any recipe in this chapter using the San Francisco Lager yeast and fermenting at 65°F. The beers will be different (less smooth and crisp, and perhaps with some fruity esters), but still worth the experiment.

Beer to Try Anchor Steam Beer (Anchor Brewing)

INGREDIENTS	1-GALLON	5-GALLON
White Labs San Francisco Lager yeast, Wyeast California Lager yeast, or equivalent	½ package	1 package
Pale ale malt, milled	1¼ lbs (567 g)	6¼ lbs (2.84 kg)
Honey malt, milled	8 oz (227 g)	2½ lbs (1.13 kg)
Crystal/Caramel 40 malt, milled	4 oz (113 g)	1¼ lbs (567 g)
Northern Brewer pellet hops (9.6% AA), for bittering	.10 oz (3 g)	.50 oz (14 g)
Northern Brewer pellet hops (9.6% AA), for flavoring	.10 oz (3 g)	.50 oz (14 g)
Perle pellet hops (8.9% AA), for flavoring	.05 oz (1.50 g)	.25 oz (7 g)
Irish moss	¼ tsp	1 tsp
Perle pellet hops (8.9% AA), for aroma	.15 oz (4 g)	.75 oz (21 g)
Corn sugar, for bottling	.80 oz (22 g)	4 oz (113 g)

TARGET ORIGINAL/FINAL GRAVITY: 1.052/1.016
TARGET ABV: 4.7%

Follow the master method for brewing 1-gallon or 5-gallon all-grain batches as described on pages 54–59 (5-gallon measurements in parentheses).

• Remove liquid yeast from the refrigerator and, if necessary, activate according to package instructions. Place on the counter to warm.

• Heat **1 gallon (or 3½ gallons) of water to 160°F**, then stir in the grains. Maintain a mash temperature of **148°F to 153°F** for 60 minutes. (Alternatively, do a 2-step infusion mash as described on page 206.) Raise the temperature of the mash to 170°F, then sparge using **1 gallon (or 3 gallons)** of 170°F water to make 1½ (or 5½) gallons wort.

• Bring to a boil over high heat. Add the Northern Brewer hops for bittering and boil vigorously for 40 minutes. Add the Northern Brewer and Perle hops for flavoring and the Irish moss and continue boiling for another 20 minutes. Add the Perle hops for aroma and remove from the heat. (Total boil time: 60 minutes.)

• Cool the wort to at least 75°F and transfer to the sanitized primary fermentation bucket. Add the yeast and aerate the wort.

• Let the wort ferment for at least **2 weeks or up to 4 weeks at 60°F to 65°F**, then transfer the beer to a sanitized jug or carboy for secondary fermentation. Continue to ferment and condition the beer for another **1 month or up to 3 months at 60°F to 65°F**.

• Dissolve the sugar in ¼ (or 1) cup of boiling water and let cool. Mix with the beer, bottle, and store for **2 weeks or up to a year**. Refrigerate before drinking.

COMMON PROBLEMS, EASY SOLUTIONS

This right here is your troubleshooting section. Brew enough beer and you'll run into a problem sooner or later. Hopefully, later. But whatever has you puzzled, look here for some answers.

BREWING PROBLEMS

My mash seems to drop below temperature, then shoot up after just a minute on the heat! I can't keep it steady. What can I do?

Keep your mash covered and don't stir too frequently; both can help reduce your heat loss. When you do stir the mash, stir it thoroughly since little pockets of hot or cool wort can throw off your temperature reading.

If it starts to drop below temperature, set the mash over high heat for 1 minute for a 1-gallon batch or 2 to 3 minutes for a 5-gallon batch. Turn off the heat, stir thoroughly, and check the temperature. Repeat in increments until you hit the middle of your temperature range.

While I was sparging my 5-gallon all-grain batch, the flow of wort slowed and then stopped altogether. What do I do?

My friend, I'm sorry to say that you've got what's called a "stuck mash"! First, make sure you have a few inches of wort floating over your grain bed; add more sparge water if you need to or scoop some away. Next, stick a long-handled spoon or paddle all the way through your mash to the bottom and give it a wiggle. Do this in a few spots to try to loosen up the grain bed. If possible, stir the grains a little. You will probably end up with a cloudier wort than usual, but at least you'll have wort!

Next time, make sure your grains are not ground too finely, your false bottom or mash screen is attached properly, you have 2 to 3 inches of wort over the grain bed at all times, and you don't try to sparge too quickly.

My wort boiled over the pot when I was starting the hop boil!

This happens at least once to every homebrewer. As the wort is coming to a boil, foam collects on the surface. Heat gets trapped underneath and can cause the wort to suddenly bubble up and boil over, especially if your pot is on the small side. If

you don't have a bigger pot, the best thing to do is keep a close eye on your wort as it comes to a boil. If it looks like your wort is in danger of boiling over at any point, quickly reduce the heat, stir the wort continuously, squirt water on the foam with a spray bottle, or remove the pot from the heat until it settles back down. Once the boiling wort has broken through the foam (called the "hot break"), it will settle down and there won't be as big a risk of boil-overs.

If your wort has boiled over, there's not much to do except clean it up and carry on. Your beer is fine, though you lost a little wort and may end up with a lower original gravity than expected.

I ended up with less than 1 gallon (or 5 gallons) of wort at the end of the boil.

Just top the wort off with tap water if needed to reach 1 gallon or 5 gallons. It's okay to use tap water because it is essentially sterile and carries very little risk of bacterial or wild yeast contamination. Alternatively, you can use leftover water from the sparging step or store-bought spring water.

I ended up with more than 1 gallon (or 5 gallons) of wort at the end of the boil.

Don't worry about it too much. Either you started the boil with a little too much liquid or your wort wasn't quite at a full, rolling boil the whole time. This batch will be a little more diluted than normal (and will wind up with a lower ABV), but it will still be tasty. Next time, keep an eye on your preboil volume and the strength of your boil. If you notice that you have too much wort before you start the boil, you can boil it for an extra 15 minutes or so before you start the hop additions to evaporate some of the excess.

I forgot to take my liquid yeast out of the fridge!

For best fermentation, the liquid yeast and the wort should be close to the same temperature when you combine them. If you take the yeast out of the fridge when you first start brewing, it should be warmed by the time you're ready to pitch it into the wort. If you forgot, place it in a bowl of warm water for half an hour to bring it up to temperature. (In the meantime, cover your wort with a lid to keep it protected while the yeast warms.)

How do I know if my beer is fermenting?

The best way to tell if your beer is fermenting is to look at the air lock. You should start seeing bubbles percolate through the air lock within about 24 hours of brewing. As long as you see bubbles, everything is fine.

Wait, was I supposed to put water in my air lock?

Yes! There should be a "fill line" on your air lock. Fill it with water to this mark. The water acts as a one-way gatekeeper, letting carbon dioxide out while preventing bugs, dust, or anything else from coming in. Water is fine, but you can also fill the air lock with sanitizer solution or vodka.

Okay, I forgot to put water in my air lock. Is my beer ruined?

There's a chance but probably not. There's a lot of activity in the first few days of fermentation, so hopefully, the force of carbon dioxide leaving the bucket will have prevented anything from getting in. Even so, keep an eye on your beer. If you start to notice weird, funky flavors or if the beer becomes syrupy or viscous, it's probably infected.

I used an air lock (properly!) but still don't see any bubbles.

If it's been 48 hours with nary a bubble, something is up. The most likely cause is that something was wrong with your yeast. Maybe it was old, or maybe you pitched it while the wort was still too hot, or maybe it wasn't stored properly before you pitched it. In any case, try pitching some fresh yeast. Whisk the wort vigorously after you add the yeast and wait another 24 hours. If you still don't see any bubbles, then something is wrong beyond my powers to anticipate here. Best to check with someone at your local homebrew store to figure it out.

However, if you weren't around in the first few days of fermentation, it might just be that the main fermentation has finished and you just didn't see it. Take a gravity reading; if it's less than it was on your brew day, then fermentation has occurred and you're good to go.

One more thought: If it's cold in your house (below 65°F), the yeast might just be sluggish. Try moving the beer somewhere warmer while it ferments.

Help! My beer stopped bubbling after a few days.

It's okay! The yeast is most active in the first few days of fermentation. Once it eats the most easily digested sugars, it slows down and gets to work on complex sugars and other compounds in the beer. You'll notice a significant drop-off in activity at this point. Let the beer sit for a few days so the sediment has time to settle, then transfer it to the secondary.

Help! My beer won't stop bubbling!

You'll still see the occasional bubble come through the air lock even after you transfer it to the secondary—that's fine. But if you see a lot of bubbles, like one every minute, something is wrong. The most likely explanation is that your beer has become infected and should be discarded. Pay more attention to the cleanliness of your equipment and sanitation next time around.

I opened my fermentation bucket to transfer the beer to the secondary and there's a layer of scum on the top of my beer or in a ring on the bucket. Is it ruined?

Probably not! There's a lot of activity in the first few days of fermentation that lifts a layer of yeast sediment, proteins, and hop resins (called "krausen") to the top of the beer and leaves a ring of gunk around the bucket. This layer usually falls to the bottom once the most vigorous stage of fermentation is done, but there may be some remaining. It's not harmful, so go ahead and transfer the beer to the secondary; any scummy stuff that gets transferred will settle on the bottom.

There's a thin layer of white stuff on the surface of my beer in the secondary. Is it ruined?

If the layer is very thin, you probably have a minor infection. Sometimes this happens and the beer tastes perfectly fine. An infection like this won't hurt you, so if the beer tastes okay, go ahead and bottle it as usual. If the flavor seems off or if the white layer starts to thicken or get really scuzzy, it's probably time to throw the batch out. It's a sad day, but lesson learned: pay more attention to cleanliness and sanitation next time.

I didn't hit my target original gravity or final ABV. Why?

First of all, don't worry too much. If you made any alcohol at all, you get a high five. The original gravity of the beer and finishing ABV are the result of lots of factors. As you get better at brewing, you'll get closer to your goal.

In the meantime, focus on keeping your mash temperature within the target range and keep a ratio of 1½ quarts of water per pound of grain. Also, check that your grains are being ground properly; it's more difficult to extract sugars from a very coarse grind with many unbroken grains (conversely, you get better extraction from finely ground grains, though they can be harder to sparge). The pH of your water can also affect sugar extraction; talk with someone at your local homebrewing store if you suspect this might be a factor.

FINISHED BEER PROBLEMS

Why did my beers gush when I opened them?

If the beer tastes okay, you most likely added too much corn sugar—maybe because your batch size was smaller than the recipe intended. Make sure the beers in this batch are completely chilled before you open them—that helps with the gushing. Read "How (and When) to Adjust the Amount of Priming Sugar," page 48, for details. If the beer tastes a little sour or off, they might have gushed because they had an infection. If only a few bottles gushed, the infection was probably because of dirty bottles. If all the bottles gushed, then the batch was infected sometime during brewing. The best help for that is to pay close attention to cleanliness and sanitation next time. (P.S. If the beer still tastes good to you, it's fine to drink.)

Why did my bottles explode?

See "Why did my beers gush?" above. Refrigerate any unexploded bottles immediately. They will likely gush when you open them, but once refrigerated, they shouldn't explode.

Why didn't my beer carbonate?

Did you remember to add the priming sugar? Did you wait 2 weeks before opening your beer? The beer needs this last little snack of sugar to produce enough carbon dioxide to carbonate the beer, and it needs about 2 weeks to fully carbonate the beers.

Were you storing your beer somewhere cold? Cold temperatures can make yeast slow to work. Move your beers somewhere warm, wait a week or two, and see if that helps.

Did you wait more than 3 months before bottling the beer? If so, the yeast has probably died or isn't active enough to fully carbonate your beer. Try uncapping the beers, adding a pinch of yeast, and recapping them. Next time, if you're bottling beer that's more than 3 months old, mix some fresh yeast into the beer before you bottle it.

Why does my beer look hazy?

Homebrews are unfiltered, so some of the haziness might be due to yeast sediment. When you pour, stop short of pouring the last half-inch; that should keep most of the sediment from going in your glass.

Your beer might also have chill haze. This is an aesthetic problem and not something wrong with your beer. It's caused by suspended proteins in the beer but won't affect its flavor or texture. You can reduce the likelihood of chill haze by keeping your wort at a full boil for the entire hop boil, adding Irish moss about 20 minutes before the end of the boil, and cooling the wort as quickly as possible before pitching the yeast.

Why is my beer syrupy/ropy/viscous?

Egads! You have an infection of a major order. If you drank some, don't worry; it won't harm you, though it's best to throw away the rest of the batch. This kind of infection is usually the result of poor sanitation, so pay more attention to this next time.

Why does my beer taste like . . . ?

Butterscotch or popcorn: This is from a buildup of diacetyl in your beer, usually a result of high fermentation temperatures. It's not harmful to drink and is a positive in some styles, like Scottish ales.

Canned corn or cooked vegetables: This is a mild infection from a kind of bacteria that can survive at low alcohol levels. You'll notice it in some low-alcohol beers or beers that had a slow start to fermentation.

Cardboard or sherry: This flavor is a sign of oxidization. It shows up sometimes in old, aged beers. If it's a young beer, there was too much exposure to oxygen during the brewing process or while transferring the beer.

Funky barnyards/old leather: Sounds like a wild yeast strain got into your beer. This is a positive flavor for sour beers. If you don't want it showing up in your everyday ales, pay very close attention to sanitation.

Green apples/unripe fruit: If the beer is young, let it sit another week or two; the yeast in the bottle should break down the compounds responsible for this flavor. If the beer tastes more like tart green apples, it might have a minor lactobacillus or other bacterial infection. This is actually a positive flavor in some beers, especially sour ales. Even if this was an accident, if you like the flavor, keep drinking it!

Hard alcohols/fusel alcohol/nail polish remover: High-alcohol beers sometimes smell and taste like, yes, alcohol! If it's not a high-ABV beer, the aroma might come from stressed yeast during a warm fermentation.

Rotten eggs: This could be an infection but more likely is a by-product of fermentation (especially with lagers). Make sure your beer is somewhere cool and let it sit for another few weeks to give the yeast time to break down the sulfur compounds.

Skunks: This is caused by light hitting the beer. It can happen at any stage of brewing, so be sure to keep buckets and jugs of fermenting beer away from direct sunlight, and bottle your beer in brown bottles.

Sour apples/vinegar/tart candy: This is a sign of a lactobacillus infection. It's a good thing when added intentionally to sour ales, but you might not like it showing up in your pale ale. Better sanitation next time, amigo!

Tannins/black tea: Astringent flavors like sucking on a tea bag or eating an unripe pear can result from accidentally heating your mash above 170°F or from pressing on the grains as you sparged; both can extract tannins from the grains.

Is my beer still safe to drink if it smells or tastes like any of these things?

As long as there is some alcohol in your beer, nothing can survive that will actually harm you. If your beer has an infection but is still pretty tasty, then sure, you can drink it! But don't force yourself to drink something you don't like. It's much better—and more fun—to brew a new batch and drink some craft brew while you wait.

GLOSSARY: HOMEBREWER'S LINGO

ABBEY ALE: Belgian ale brewed with medium-roasted malts and Belgian yeast. Light gold to reddish color with moderate malt flavor and spicy and/or fruity flavors. Little to no hop aroma and flavor. Typically 5% to 7% ABV.

ALCOHOL BY VOLUME (ABV): This is a measure of the alcohol content of the beer. We can determine the alcohol content in homebrews by calculating the difference between the original gravity and the final gravity; this indicates how much sugar was converted into alcohol during fermentation.

AMBER ALE: An ale brewed with medium roasted malts. Light amber to copper brown color with moderate to strong malt flavor. Hop aroma and flavor varies. Typically 4% to 6% ABV.

AROMA HOPS: Any variety of hops added to the wort at the end of the hop boil to give the beer hop aromas.

ATTENUATION: The amount of sugar consumed by the yeast. Attenuation of 100% would mean that all the sugars in the beer have been consumed. Brewers typically get 65% to 85% attenuation in their brews.

BARLEYWINE: An ale brewed with medium to dark roasted malts. Deep gold to brown in color with strong malt flavor. Hop aroma and flavor varies, higher in American than British versions. Typically 8% to 12% ABV.

BASE MALTS: Lightly toasted malted grains that add a lot of sugar to beer but not a lot of flavor. They make up the majority of the grain bill in most beers.

BERLINER WEISSE: German wheat ale with lightly toasted malts and soured with a sour mash or with wild yeast (Brettanomyces) and bacteria. Light yellow to gold color with light malt flavor and a tart sour flavor. Little to no hop aroma and flavor. Typically 3% to 4% ABV.

BLACK IPA: An IPA brewed with a small amount of very dark roasted malts. Dark brown to black color with light malt and some roasty flavor. Moderate to high hop aroma and flavor. Typically 6% to 7% ABV.

BITTERING HOPS: Any variety of hops added to the wort at the beginning of the hop boil to add bitter flavors to the brew.

BOCK: German lager brewed with medium toasted malts and German lager yeast. Amber to brown color with strong malt flavor. Little to no hop aroma and flavor. Typically 6% to 7% ABV.

BOTTLE SHOCK: A period of time right after beer is bottled when you may notice harshness or other off flavors. This disappears after 2 weeks or so.

BOTTLING BUCKET: The bucket in which you mix beer with the priming sugar and transfer the beer into bottles. Your primary fermentation bucket, stockpot, or other container large enough to hold your beer can be used as the bottling bucket.

BREW DAY: The day on which you make the wort, boil it, and pitch the yeast.

BRITISH BITTER: British ale brewed with lightly toasted malts and British hops. Yellow to dark gold color with moderate malt flavor. Moderate hop aroma and flavor. Typically 3% to 4% ABV.

BROWN ALE: An ale brewed with a mix of medium and dark roasted malts. Brown in color with strong malt flavor. Moderate to high hop aroma and flavor. Typically 4% to 6% ABV.

CALIFORNIA COMMON: American lager brewed with medium toasted malts, American hops, and lager yeast at warmer temperatures than typical for lagers. Amber to light brown color with moderate malt flavor. Moderate to high hop aroma and flavor. Typically 4% to 6% ABV.

DIACETYL: A compound created during fermentation that can give beers a buttery or butterscotch-like flavor. These compounds are usually broken down by the yeast by the time the beer is bottled.

DOPPELBOCK: German lager brewed with medium to dark toasted malts and German lager yeast. Dark amber to dark brown color with strong malt flavor. Little to no hop aroma and flavor. Typically 7% to 10% ABV.

DOUBLE BEER: See Imperial Beer.

DRY HOPPING: Adding hops directly to the beer in the secondary to give beer aroma but no bitterness.

DUBBEL: Belgian ale brewed with medium to dark roasted malts and Belgian yeast. Dark amber to brown color with moderate to high malt flavor and spicy and/or fruity flavors. Little to no hop aroma and flavor. Typically 6% to 8% ABV.

ESTERS: Chemical compounds created by yeast that add fruity aromas and flavors to beer.

EXTRA SPECIAL BITTER (ESB): British ale brewed with lightly toasted malts and British hops. Light gold to copper color with moderate malt flavor. Moderate hop aroma and flavor. Typically 5% to 6% ABV.

FERMENTABLE SUGARS: Simple sugars that the yeast can easily consume.

FINAL GRAVITY (FG): The specific gravity of beer once it has finished fermenting. By comparing the original gravity to the final gravity, we can determine how much sugar was converted into alcohol during fermentation and the alcohol by volume (ABV) of the finished beer.

FLAVORING HOPS: Any variety of hops added to the wort midway through the hop boil, giving the beer a mix of bitter flavors and hop flavors.

GOSE: German wheat ale brewed with lightly toasted malts and salt, and soured with a sour mash or with wild yeast (Brettanomyces) and bacteria. Light yellow to gold color with light malt flavor and a soft sour flavor. Little to no hop aroma and flavor. Typically 3% to 4% ABV.

GRAIN BILL: All the grains in a beer recipe.

GUEUZE: Belgian beer brewed with light toasted malts, Belgian yeast, and wild (Brettanomyces) yeast and bacteria. Light yellow color with light malt flavor and tart, sour flavors from the wild yeast and bacteria. Aged batches are often blended with young batches. Typically 5% to 8% ABV.

HEFEWEIZEN: German wheat ale brewed with lightly toasted malts, wheat malts, and German yeast. Pale yellow to gold color with light malt flavor and banana and clove flavors. Little to no hop aroma and flavor. Typically 4% to 6% ABV.

HOP BOIL: Also just called "the boil," this is the step in the brewing process where the wort is boiled and hops are added.

HOT BREAK: The moment at the beginning of the hop boil when the boiling wort starts to break through the layer of foam that has collected at the top, indicating that it's time to start adding hops.

IBUS (INTERNATIONAL BITTERING UNITS): A standard unit of measurement used in the brewing industry for the level of bitterness in a beer.

IMPERIAL BEERS (ALSO DOUBLE BEERS): Any style of ale or lager brewed with more malts and hops than typical. The ABV is also usually several points higher.

INDIA PALE ALE (IPA): An ale brewed with lightly to medium toasted malts. Pale gold to deep copper color with low to medium malt flavor. Moderate to high hop aroma and flavor, higher in American than British versions. Typically 6% to 7% ABV.

IRISH ALE: An ale brewed with medium roasted malts, Reddish to brown in color with a moderate caramelized malt flavor. Little to no hop aroma and flavor. Typically 4% to 6% ABV.

KRAUSEN: The thick, foamy layer of yeast sediment, proteins, and hop resins that is lifted to the top of the beer during the first few days of fermentation. It typically collapses and settles to the bottom of the beer once active fermentation slows.

LAMBIC: Belgian beer brewed with light toasted malts, fruit, Belgian yeast, and wild (brettanomyces) yeast and bacteria. Color varies based on the fruit used, light malt flavor, strong fruit flavors, tart or sour flavors from the wild yeast and bacteria. Little to no hop aroma and flavor. Typically 5% to 7% ABV.

MAIBOCK: German lager brewed with medium toasted malts and German lager yeast. Light gold to amber color with strong malt flavor. Little to no hop aroma and flavor. Typically 6% to 7% ABV.

MARZEN (ALSO OKTOBERFEST): German lager brewed with medium toasted malts and German lager yeast. Gold to copper color with moderate to strong malt flavor. Little to no hop aroma and flavor. Typically 5% to 6% ABV.

MASH: The step in the brewing process where malted grains are mixed with water in order to extract their sugars.

NONFERMENTABLE SUGARS: Sugars that the yeast can't eat, like dextrins. They remain in the beer after fermentation, adding sweetness and body.

OKTOBERFEST: See Marzen.

ORIGINAL GRAVITY (OG): The specific gravity of beer before it starts fermenting and is rich with sugar. By comparing the original gravity to the final gravity, we can determine how much sugar was converted into alcohol during fermentation and the alcohol by volume (ABV) of the finished beer.

PALE ALE: An ale brewed with lightly toasted malts. Light gold to light amber color and moderate malt flavor. Moderate hop aroma and flavor, higher in American than British versions. Typically 5% to 6% ABV.

PHENOLS: Compounds created by the yeast that can add a range of flavors and aromas to beer, from spicy and clove-like flavors to medicinal and plastic-like flavors.

PILSNER: German lager brewed with very lightly toasted malts and German lager yeast. Pale straw to gold color with moderate malt flavor. Low to moderate hop aroma and flavor. Typically 4% to 5% ABV.

PITCH: To add yeast to the beer.

PITCH RATE: The exact number of yeast cells added to any given batch of beer. At a beginner brewing level, 1 package of yeast per 5-gallon batch or ½ package of yeast per 1-gallon batch is fine.

PORTER: An ale brewed with dark roasted malts. Medium to very dark brown color and strong malt flavor with a roasted quality. Moderate to high hop aroma and flavor. Typically 5% to 7% ABV.

PRIMARY FERMENTATION: The first stage of beer fermentation when the yeast is most active. This typically lasts 5 to 7 days.

PRIMARY FERMENTER (ALSO, "THE PRIMARY"): The container in which primary fermentation happens, usually a bucket slightly larger than the volume of the beer.

PRIMING: Adding a dose of sugar to beer just before it's bottled in order to carbonate.

PRIMING SUGAR: The sugar added to beer in order to carbonate. Usually this is corn sugar, but it can also be table sugar, honey, maple syrup, or any other fermentable sugar.

RACK (RACKING): Transferring beer from one container to another.

ROGGENBIER: German ale brewed with medium toasted malts, rye malts, and German yeast. Light amber to reddish brown color with moderate malt flavor and some spiciness. Low hop aroma and flavor. Typically 4% to 6% ABV.

QUADRUPEL: Belgian ale brewed with medium to dark roasted malts and Belgian yeast. Light to deep brown color with moderate to high malt flavor and spicy and/or fruity flavors. Little to no hop aroma and flavor. Typically 8% to 11% ABV.

SAISON: Belgian ale brewed with light to medium toasted malts and Belgian yeast. Pale yellow to gold color with light malt flavor and spicy and/or fruity flavors. Low hop aroma and flavor. Typically 5% to 7% ABV.

SCOTCH ALE (ALSO WEE HEAVY): An ale brewed with medium roasted malts and sometimes smoked malts. Reddish to brown in color with a very strong caramelized malt flavor. Little to no hop aroma and flavor. Typically 6% to 10% ABV.

SCOTTISH ALE: An ale brewed with medium roasted malts. Reddish to brown in color with a strong caramelized malt flavor. Little to no hop aroma and flavor. Typically 3% to 5% ABV.

SECONDARY FERMENTATION: The second, slower stage of beer fermentation wherein complex sugars and other compounds are eaten by the yeast and sediment drops to the bottom of the beer, clarifying it.

SECONDARY FERMENTER (ALSO, "THE SECONDARY"): The container in which the secondary fermentation happens, usually a jug or carboy.

SESSION BEER (SESSIONABLE BEERS): Any style of beer with less than 5% ABV.

SPARGE: The process of separating the wort from the mashed grains and rinsing any remaining sugars off the grains.

SPECIALTY MALTS: Specially roasted malted grains that add flavor and color to beers but not much sugar. They are used to supplement the base malts.

SPECIFIC GRAVITY (SG): This is a measure of the density of the beer as compared to water. Sugar increases density, so a high specific gravity indicates a lot of sugars and a low specific gravity indicates fewer sugars. As beer ferments and sugars are converted into alcohol and carbon dioxide, both the density and the specific gravity of the beer decrease. By taking a specific gravity reading before fermentation begins (original gravity) and another reading at the end (final gravity), we can determine how much sugar was converted into alcohol during fermentation and the alcohol by volume (ABV) of the finished beer.

STEAM BEER: See California Common.

STOUT: An ale brewed with dark roasted malts. Opaque black color and strong malt flavor with a roasted quality. Hop aroma and flavor can vary. Typically 5% to 8% ABV.

STRIKE TEMPERATURE: The temperature of the water before the grains are added.

STRIKE WATER: The water mixed with the grains to make the mash.

STUCK FERMENTATION: When a beer stops fermenting earlier than expected and still contains a fair amount of fermentable sugars.

STUCK MASH: When grains become so compacted during sparging that wort can no longer drain through them.

TRIPEL: Belgian ale brewed with light roasted malts and Belgian yeast. Light gold to dark orange color with moderate to high malt flavor and spicy and/or fruity flavors. Little to no hop aroma and flavor. Typically 7% to 10% ABV.

WEE HEAVY: See Scotch Ale.

WHEAT BEER: An ale brewed with more than 25% wheat in the grain bill. Pale yellow to gold color with low to moderate malt sweetness and some graininess from the wheat. Hop aroma and flavor varies, higher in American ales than other versions. Typically 4% to 6% ABV.

WITBIER: Belgian wheat ale brewed with light malts, wheat malts, and Belgian yeast. White to pale yellow color with light malt flavor, grainy sweetness from the wheat, and some spicy flavor. Low hop aroma and flavor. Typically 4% to 6% ABV.

WORT: Unfermented beer.

YEAST STARTER: A mini mash made with water, malt extract, and yeast, prepared 12 to 18 hours ahead of brewing to build a healthy, strong population of yeast. Used mostly for high-alcohol beers and lagers but can also be used to refresh expired yeast.

RECOMMENDED RESOURCES

BOOKS ON BREWING

At one point or another, I consulted all of these books in my beer-brewing research. They run the gamut from fun weekend reads to super-technical brew geek manuals. All together, they make a very valuable and comprehensive homebrewing library.

Beer Craft: Six-Packs from Scratch, a Simple Guide to Making Great Beer by William Bostwick and Jessi Rymill

Brew Like a Monk: Culture and Craftsmanship in the Belgian Tradition by Stan Hieronymus

Brewed Awakening: Behind the Beers and Brewers Leading the World's Craft Brewing Revolution by Joshua M. Bernstein

Brewing Classic Styles: 80 Winning Recipes Anyone Can Brew by Jamil Zainasheff and John J. Palmer

The Brooklyn Brewshop's Beer Making Book: 52 Seasonal Recipes for Small Batches by Erica Shea and Stephen Valand

The Complete Beer Course: Boot Camp for Beer Geeks, from Novice to Expert in Twelve Tasting Classes by Joshua M. Bernstein

The Complete Joy of Homebrewing, 4th edition, by Charlie Papazian

The Craft of Stone Brewing Co.: Liquid Lore, Epic Recipes, and Unabashed Arrogance by Greg Koch and Steve Wagner with Randy Clemens

Designing Great Beers: The Ultimate Guide to Brewing Classic Beer Styles by Ray Daniels

Homebrew Beyond the Basics: All-Grain Brewing and Other Next Steps by Mike Karnowski

The Homebrew Handbook: 75 Recipes for the Aspiring Backyard Brewery by Dave Law and Beshlie Grimes

The Homebrewer's Answer Book: Solutions to Every Problem, Answers to Every Question by Ashton Lewis

The Homebrewer's Companion: With Recipes, Techniques and Equipment Information for the Advanced Homebrewer, 2nd Edition, by Charlie Papazian

How to Brew: Everything You Need to Know to Brew Beer by John Palmer

Make Some Beer: Small-Batch Recipes from Brooklyn to Bamberg by Erica Shea and Stephen Valand

The Naked Brewer: Fearless Homebrewing Tips, Tricks & Rule-Breaking Recipes by Christina Perozzi and Hallie Beaune

Principles of Brewing Science: A Study of Serious Brewing Issues by George Fix

Sacred and Herbal Healing Beers: The Secrets of Ancient Fermentation by Stephen Harrod Buhner

A Year of Beer: 260 Seasonal Homebrew Recipes compiled by Amahl Tuczyn

BREWING SUPPLIES

MoreBeer
http://morebeer.com (with retail locations in California)—for beer brewing ingredients, supplies, and equipment

Northern Brewer
www.northernbrewer.com (with retail locations in Minnesota)—for brewing ingredients, supplies, and equipment

Penzeys Spices
www.penzeys.com (with retail locations in the United States)—for spices, herbs, and other flavorings

Mountain Rose Herbs
www.mountainroseherbs.com—for spices, herbs, and other flavorings

BeerSmith Home Brewing Software
http://beersmith.com—beer design software for homebrewers from Bradley Smith

ACKNOWLEDGMENTS

To my husband, Scott: Words really cannot express how grateful I am to have you in my life and by my side. Your support through this project and beyond mean everything to me. Thank you for drinking even the not-so-good beer experiments. I love you.

To my family—Joyce, Dean, Andrew, Darci, Jensen, Evelyn, Jesse, Bonnie, Russ, Ingrid, and Jacqui: Thank you for loving me and encouraging me, for all the beer-related newspaper clippings, and for being generally stellar people. I am lucky to have you for my family.

To my agents, Jennifer Griffin and Angela Miller: I'm so grateful to have you both in my corner. Thank you for your unflagging support and for always taking the time to explain even the nittiest of the gritty details.

To my editor, Lisa Westmoreland: I've absolutely loved working with you on this project. It has felt truly collaborative, and this book is better, stronger, and awesomer for it. High five!

To my Ten Speed design team—Katy Brown and Tatiana Pavlova: Once again, you have taken what felt like an awkward, pimple-faced idea of a book and made it into something pretty and polished. Thank you.

To my photographer, Katie Newburn, and beer stylist, Jaimi Holker, and their incredible assistants: I can't stop looking at the beautiful photos you guys created. Thank you so much for bringing these beers to life and making them look so glamorous.

To Duke Geren: Thank you for stepping in to give this book a much-needed technical eye and helping to smooth out the wrinkles. I owe you several beers.

To my incredible team of recipe testers—Eva and Alex Howe, Paul Marcos, Sheri Codiana, Courtney Wilburn, Bob Kunz, Jeni Bannoura, Leigh McBain, Maggie Smith, Kat Goodale, Ariel Knutson, Chris DeNoia, Jon Spee, Brant Butler, Charles Thresher, Dewayne Browning,

Jeff DeWeese, Gilbert Seward: I wish we all lived closer together so we could share a round of beers! Your help, advice, and feedback over the course of this project have been invaluable. Thank you from the bottom of my pint glass.

To my friends and cohorts at The Kitchn—Faith, Sara Kate, Cambria, Ariel, Christine, Anjali, Kelli, and all our contributors and readers: I love that I get to spend my days with all of you. Thank you for weathering my many space-cadet moments as I've put this book together. Next round is on me, for sure.

To the fellows at MoreBeer—Gary, Keith, Joe, Sean, and all you handsome lads: Thank you times infinity for sharing your brewing know-how with me over the past few years and for making the MoreBeer Los Altos store feel like a second home. And also for finding me a ladder for the grain mill.

To the lovely ladies of the South Bay Salon—Danielle, Sheri, Cheryl, Coco, and Michelle: What can I say? You share my deep love of waffles, you inspire me to push beyond my own limits, you tell me I'm pretty even when my shirt is on backward, and most of all, you are my friends. For all that, I thank you.

To Jana and Troy: Thank you for my first taste of homebrew. I was hooked from first sip.

All the recipes in this book were developed, tweaked, and perfected using the BeerSmith homebrewing software. A ginormous thanks to Bradley Smith for engineering this program and making it available to the humble home-brewing masses.

ABOUT THE AUTHOR

EMMA CHRISTENSEN is the recipe editor for the popular homecooking website The Kitchn (www.TheKitchn.com), and a graduate of the Cambridge School for Culinary Arts in Cambridge, Massachusetts. A former beer reviewer for the *Columbus Dispatch*, she is a dedicated homebrewer always eager for the chance to nerd out about fermentation. Emma lives in the San Francisco Bay Area. To learn more, visit www.emmaelizabethchristensen.blogspot.com.

DANIELLE TSI

INDEX

A

Abbey Ale, A Very Good, 133
Affogato Milk Stout, 113
Air lock, 28, 219
Alcohol content
  calculating, 44
  factors for, 194, 220
  mash temperature and, 102
Ale family, 19, 20. *See also*
  individual styles
All-Day Dry Irish Stout, 112
All-Extract Amber Ale, 49
All-extract brewing method,
  40–47
All-Grain Amber Ale, 62
All-grain brewing method, 54–61
Alpha acid, 10–11, 154
Amarillo SMASH Pale Ale, 77
Amber ales
  All-Extract Amber Ale, 49
  All-Grain Amber Ale, 62
  Partial-Extract Amber Ale, 53
Ambient temperature, 128–29,
  154
American ales
  American Summer Wheat
    Ale, 162
  characteristics of, 20
  Two-Left-Feet American
    Barleywine, 87
  A Very Good American Brown
    Ale, 95
  A Very Good American Pale
    Ale, 71
  A Very Good IPA, 83
Autosiphons, 29

B

Baking ingredients, 167–68
Barleywines
  Figgy Pudding British
    Barleywine, 127
  Two-Left-Feet American
    Barleywine, 87
Batch size, 1-gallon vs. 5-gallon,
  54, 64–66

Beer
  alcohol content of, 44, 102
  ale family, 19, 20
  aroma of, 91
  body of, 194
  clarity of, 90
  color of, 90, 194
  definition of, 19
  designing your own, 192–94
  gravity of, 43, 78
  hazy, 220
  lager family, 19, 21
  off flavors in, 221
  pouring, 90
  serving, 47, 52, 59
  siphoning, 45–46
  styles, 19
  tasting, 91, 154, 180, 221
  See also Bottling;
    Homebrewing; *individual*
    styles and recipes
Beer log, keeping, 155
Belgian ales
  Bitter Monk Belgian-Style Pale
    Ale, 73
  characteristics of, 20, 130
  Fuzzy Nose Sour Ale, 137
  Lavender-Orange Witbier, 165
  Maple Cider Dubbel, 134
  Peach Melba Sour Lambic, 139
  Tropical Island Tripel, 136
  A Very Good Abbey Ale, 133
  See also Saisons
Berliner Weisse, Sweet-Tart, 160
Bitter Brit English-Style Pale
  Ale, 72
Bitter Monk Belgian-Style Pale
  Ale, 73
Bocks
  characteristics of, 21
  Chocolate Doppelbock, 215
  Spring Blossom Maibock, 212
Books, 180–81
Boss-Level Barrel-Aged Imperial
  Stout, 114
Bottle caps, 31

Bottles
  brown glass, 31
  buying new, 31
  exploding, 220
  gushing, 220
  labeling and dating, 155
  reusing, 31
Bottling
  equipment, 29, 31
  process, 47, 52, 59
  timing of, 79
Braggot, Brown Bear Seeks
  Honey, 98
Brett, 140
Brewing equipment, 27–28
Brewing methods
  all-extract, 40–47
  all-grain, 54–61
  overview of, 38–39
  partial-extract, 50–52
Brewing software, 193
British ales
  Bitter Brit English-Style Pale
    Ale, 72
  characteristics of, 20, 118
  Figgy Pudding British
    Barleywine, 127
  High Seas British IPA, 124
  Sugar and Spice Strong Ale,
    125
  A Very Good British Mild, 121
  See also Porters; Stouts
Brown ales
  Brown Bear Seeks Honey
    Braggot, 98
  Chai-Spiced Winter Warmer,
    101
  characteristics of, 92
  The Great Pumpkin Ale, 99
  Pecan Pie Brown Ale, 96
  A Very Good American Brown
    Ale, 95

C

Cacao nibs
    Caramel-Coconut Wee
        Heavy, 151
    Chocolate Doppelbock, 215
    Gluten-Free Chocolate
        Porter, 202
California commons. *See* Steam
    beers
Campari IPA, 89
Caramel-Coconut Wee Heavy,
    151
Carbonation, lack of, 220
Carboys, 29
Centennial Dry-Hopped
    Double IPA, 84
Chai-Spiced Winter
    Warmer, 101
Chicory Rye Porter, Red Eye, 179
Chill haze, 220
Chipotle Porter, Smoky, 111
Chocolate. *See* Cacao nibs
Cider
    Happy Hard Cider, 205
    Maple Cider Dubbel, 134
Coconut
    Caramel-Coconut Wee Heavy,
        151
    Tropical Island Tripel, 136
Colanders, 27
Cold weather, brewing in, 129
Continuous hopping, 116

D

Dark Pumpernickel Roggenbier,
    174
Day Hiker Irish Red, 148
Decoction mash, 206
Dextrins, 102
Diacetyl, 207, 221
Doppelbock, Chocolate, 215
Double-Take Black IPA, 86
Dry hopping, 116

E

Equipment
    bottling, 29, 31
    brewing, 27–28
    buying, 22, 34, 78
    checklists, 33
    fermenting, 28–29
    general, 24
    importance of, 78
    for lagers, 206, 208
    for 1-gallon vs. 5-gallon
        batch, 54, 64
    sanitizing, 41, 78, 154
    setting out, 154
    for sour beers, 140

F

Farmers' Market Gruit, 191
Fermentation
    bucket, 28
    one-stage, 59
    primary, 38, 44, 52, 58, 79
    secondary, 39, 45, 47, 52, 59,
        79
    temperatures for, 128–29,
        192, 194
    zero signs of, 79, 219
Fermenting equipment, 28–29
Figgy Pudding British
        Barleywine, 127
Final gravity, 43, 44
Finnish Juniper Rye Sahti
        Ale, 177
First runnings, boiling, 103
Foaminess, 194
Fruits, 16, 166–67, 192. *See also*
        individual fruits
Fuzzy Nose Sour Ale, 137

G

German ales
    characteristics of, 20
    Dark Pumpernickel
        Roggenbier, 174
    Salty Dog Gose, 161
    Sweet-Tart Berliner Weisse,
        160
    A Very Good Wheat Beer
        (Hefeweizen), 159

Gluten-free beers
    characteristics of, 196
    Gluten-Free Chocolate Porter,
        202
    Gluten-Free Saison, 200
    Happy Hard Cider, 205
    Jasmine Honey Sparkler, 203
    A Very Good Gluten-Free Pale
        Ale, 199
Gose, Salty Dog, 161
Grain bags, 27
Grains
    adjunct, 6, 7
    chewing, 180
    common, 7
    mashing process for, 54–56
    milling, 50, 54
    sparging, 56–57
    steeping, 50
    storing, 35
    See also Malts
Grapefruit
    Salty Dog Gose, 161
Gravity, 43, 44
The Great Pumpkin Ale, 99
Gruit, Farmers' Market, 191

H

Happy Hard Cider, 205
Haziness, 220
Head retention, 194
Hefeweizen, 159
Herbs, 16, 167
    Farmers' Market Gruit, 191
High Seas British IPA, 124
Homebrewing
    books, 180–81
    clubs, 180
    habits for, 154–55
    legality of, 3
    rewards of, 1
    safety of, 3
    space for, 2
    starting, 2
    troubleshooting, 218–21
    See also Brewing methods;
        Equipment
Homebrew stores, 34–35

Honey
    Brown Bear Seeks Honey
        Braggot, 98
    Gluten-Free Saison, 200
    Jasmine Honey Sparkler, 203
Hop boil, 38, 41, 218
Hops
    adding, 13, 41, 51, 116, 194
    adjusting, 117
    alpha acid of, 10–11, 154
    bittering, 116, 117, 194
    changing, 192
    forms of, 13
    noble, 11
    storing, 13, 35
    tasting, 180
    uses for, 12–13
    varieties of, 12, 117
Hot break, 40
Hydrometers, 28, 44
Hydrometer tubes, 28

I
India pale ales (IPAs)
    Campari IPA, 89
    Centennial Dry-Hopped
        Double IPA, 84
    characteristics of, 80
    Double-Take Black IPA, 86
    High Seas British IPA, 124
    Two-Left-Feet American
        Barleywine, 87
    A Very Good IPA, 83
Infections, signs of, 219, 220–21
Infusion mash, 2-step, 206–7
Ingredients
    adding other, 16, 166–68
    measuring, 24
    setting out, 154
    See also Hops; Malts;
        Water; Yeast
Irish moss, 16
Irish red ales
    characteristics of, 20, 142
    Day Hiker Irish Red, 148
    A Very Good Irish Red Ale, 147
Irish Stout, All-Day Dry, 112

J
Jasmine Honey Sparkler, 203
Jugs, 29
Juniper Rye Sahti Ale,
    Finnish, 177

K
Kombucha, 141
Krausen, 219

L
Lactobacillus, 140
Lagers
    characteristics of, 208
    Chocolate Doppelbock, 215
    definition of, 21
    making, 206–7, 208
    McNally's Oktoberfest, 214
    Ode to San Francisco Steam
        Beer, 217
    Spring Blossom Maibock, 212
    styles of, 19, 21
    A Very Good Pilsner, 211
Lambic, Peach Melba Sour, 139
Lavender-Orange Witbier, 165
Legal issues, 3
Lemons
    American Summer Wheat
        Ale, 162
    Lemonade Stand Shandy, 189

M
Maibock, Spring Blossom, 212
Malts
    base, 6, 7
    changing, 192
    common, 7
    extracts, 9–10
    making, 6
    role of, 6
    specialty, 6, 7
    whole grain, 6, 9
    See also Grains
Mangoes
    Tropical Island Tripel, 136
Maple Cider Dubbel, 134
Marzens. See Oktoberfests

Mash
    decoction, 206
    enzymatic reactions in, 102
    sour, 141
    stuck, 218
    temperature of, 78, 102, 103,
        192, 194, 218
    2-step infusion, 206–7
Mashing process, 54–56
Mash out, 56
McNally's Oktoberfest, 214
Measuring, 24
Mesh hop bags, 29
Mistakes, 3, 79

N
No Apologies Imperial
    Rye Ale, 178
Notes, taking, 155
Nuts, 168
    Pecan Pie Brown
        Ale, 96

O
Oak cubes and chips, 168
Ode to San Francisco
    Steam Beer, 217
Oktoberfests
    characteristics of, 21
    McNally's Oktoberfest, 214
Oranges
    Lavender-Orange Witbier, 165
Original gravity, 43, 44, 78, 220

P
Paddles, long-handled, 27
Pale ales
    Amarillo SMASH Pale Ale, 77
    Bitter Brit English-Style Pale
        Ale, 72
    Bitter Monk Belgian-Style
        Pale Ale, 73
    characteristics of, 68
    Pine Woods Pale Ale, 74
    Riding Lawn Mower Pale
        Ale, 186
    A Very Good American Pale
        Ale, 71
    A Very Good Gluten-Free Pale
        Ale, 199
    A Very Good Rye Pale Ale, 173

Partial-Extract Amber Ale, 53
Partial-extract brewing method, 50–52
Peach Melba Sour Lambic, 139
Pecan Pie Brown Ale, 96
Pediococcus, 140
Pilsners
    characteristics of, 21
    A Very Good Pilsner, 211
Pine Woods Pale Ale, 74
Pitch rate, 79
Porters
    characteristics of, 104
    Gluten-Free Chocolate Porter, 202
    Red Eye Chicory Rye Porter, 179
    Smoky Chipotle Porter, 111
    stouts vs., 104
    A Very Good Porter, 107
Pouring, 90
Priming sugar, 39, 47, 48
Pumpernickel Roggenbier, Dark, 174
Pumpkin Ale, The Great, 99

R
Racing canes, 29
Raspberries
    Peach Melba Sour Lambic, 139
Red Eye Chicory Rye Porter, 179
Riding Lawn Mower Pale Ale, 186
Roggenbier, Dark Pumpernickel, 174
Rye ales
    characteristics of, 170
    Dark Pumpernickel Roggenbier, 174
    Finnish Juniper Rye Sahti Ale, 177
    No Apologies Imperial Rye Ale, 178
    Red Eye Chicory Rye Porter, 179
    A Very Good Rye Pale Ale, 173

S
Safety issues, 3
Sahti Ale, Finnish Juniper Rye, 177
Saisons
    Gluten-Free Saison, 200
    Watermelon Saison, 188
Salty Dog Gose, 161
Sanitation, 41, 78, 154
Scales, electronic kitchen, 24
Scotch ales and wee heavies
    Caramel-Coconut Wee Heavy, 151
    characteristics of, 20, 142
    Smoke and Scotch Ale, 152
Scottish ales
    boiling first runnings for, 103
    characteristics of, 20, 142
    A Very Good Scottish Ale, 145
    See also Scotch ales and wee heavies
Session ales
    All-Day Dry Irish Stout, 112
    characteristics of, 182
    Farmers' Market Gruit, 191
    Lemonade Stand Shandy, 189
    Riding Lawn Mower Pale Ale, 186
    A Very Good British Mild, 121
    A Very Good Session Ale, 185
    Watermelon Saison, 188
Shandy, Lemonade Stand, 189
Siphoning, 45–46
Smoke and Scotch Ale, 152
Smoky Chipotle Porter, 111
Software, 193
Sorghum, 196, 199
Sour beers
    base for, 140
    definition of, 140
    equipment for, 140
    experimental, 141
    Fuzzy Nose Sour Ale, 137
    Peach Melba Sour Lambic, 139
    with sour mash, 141
    yeast and bacteria for, 140–41

Sparging, 56–57, 218
Sparkler, Jasmine Honey, 203
Specific gravity, 43, 44
Spices, 16, 166, 167, 192
Spoons, long-handled, 27
Spring Blossom Maibock, 212
Steam beers
    characteristics of, 21
    Ode to San Francisco Steam Beer, 217
Stockpots, 27
Stouts
    Affogato Milk Stout, 113
    All-Day Dry Irish Stout, 112
    Boss-Level Barrel-Aged Imperial Stout, 114
    characteristics of, 104
    porters vs., 104
    A Very Good Stout, 109
Stovetops, 24
Strainers, 27
Strike temperature, 103
Substitutions, 155, 192
Sugar, 16, 39, 47, 48
Sugar and Spice Strong Ale, 125
Sweet-Tart Berliner Weisse, 160

T
Tasting, 91, 154, 180, 221
Tea, 168
    Jasmine Honey Sparkler, 203
    Tea Time Extra-Special Bitter (ESB), 122
Thermometers
    instant-read, 24
    oven, 28
Timers, 24, 154
Tropical Island Tripel, 136
Troubleshooting, 218–21
Tubing, plastic, 29
Two-Left-Feet American Barleywine, 87

V

Vegetables, 167

A Very Good Abbey Ale, 133

A Very Good American Brown
 Ale, 95

A Very Good American Pale
 Ale, 71

A Very Good British Mild, 121

A Very Good Gluten-Free Pale
 Ale, 199

A Very Good IPA, 83

A Very Good Irish Red Ale, 147

A Very Good Pilsner, 211

A Very Good Porter, 107

A Very Good Rye Pale Ale, 173

A Very Good Scottish Ale, 145

A Very Good Session Ale, 185

A Very Good Wheat Beer
 (Hefeweizen), 159

W

Warm weather, brewing in,
 128–29

Water, 10

Watermelon Saison, 188

Wheat beers
 American Summer Wheat
  Ale, 162
 characteristics of, 156
 Lavender-Orange Witbier,
  165
 Salty Dog Gose, 161
 Sweet-Tart Berliner Weisse,
  160
 A Very Good Wheat Beer
  (Hefeweizen), 159

Wine thief, 29

Witbier, Lavender-Orange, 165

Wort
 aerating, 43, 51, 58
 boiling, 38, 40, 51, 58, 218
 cooling, 38, 41–43, 51, 58, 78
 definition of, 38
 making, 38, 40
 original gravity of, 43
 separating, from grains,
  56–57
 transferring, to fermentation
  bucket, 43, 51, 58

Wort chiller, 28, 42

Y

Yeast
 adding, 43, 51, 58, 78–79
 changing, 192
 forms of, 14, 15
 function of, 14
 for sour beers, 140–41
 starters, 15, 16
 storing, 14, 35
 temperatures for, 14, 42, 128,
  218
 varieties of, 14, 15

All rights reserved.
Published in the United States by Ten Speed Press, an imprint of the
Crown Publishing Group, a division of Random House LLC,
a Penguin Random House Company, New York.
www.crownpublishing.com
www.tenspeed.com

Ten Speed Press and the Ten Speed Press colophon are registered trademarks of Random House LLC.

Library of Congress Cataloging-in-Publication Data
Christensen, Emma, author.
 Brew better beer : learn (and break) the rules for making IPAs, sours,
 Belgian beers, porters, barleywines, lagers, ancient ales, and
 gluten-free beers / Emma Christensen.
    pages cm
1. Brewing--Amateurs' manuals. I. Title.
 TP570. C557 2015
 663'.3--dc23
                            2014031950

Hardcover ISBN: 978-1-60774-631-7
eBook ISBN: 978-1-60774-632-4

Printed in China

Design by Tatiana Pavlova and Katy Brown

10 9 8 7 6 5 4 3 2 1

First Edition